13.99

New Casebooks

THE TEMPEST

New Casebooks

Further titles are in preparation

New Casebooks Series
Series Standing Order
ISBN 0–333–71702–3 hardcover
ISBN 0–333–69345–0 paperback
(outside North America only)

You can receive future titles in this series as they are published by placing a standing order. Please contact your bookseller or, in case of difficulty, write to us at the address below with your name and address, the title of the series and the ISBN quoted above.

Customer Services Department, Macmillan Distribution Ltd
Houndmills, Basingstoke, Hampshire RG21 6XS, England

New Casebooks

THE TEMPEST

WILLIAM SHAKESPEARE

EDITED BY R. S. WHITE

First published 1999 by
MACMILLAN PRESS LTD
Houndmills, Basingstoke, Hampshire RG21 6XS
and London
Companies and representatives throughout the world

ISBN 0-333-64441-7 hardcover
ISBN 0-333-64442-5 paperback

A catalogue record for this book is available from the British Library.

This book is printed on paper suitable for recycling and made from
fully managed and sustained forest sources.

10   9   8   7   6   5   4   3   2   1
08 07 06 05 04 03 02 01 00 99

Printed in Hong Kong

Typeset by EXPO Holdings, Malaysia

Published in the United States of America 1999 by
ST. MARTIN'S PRESS, INC.,
Scholarly and Reference Division,
175 Fifth Avenue, New York, N.Y. 10010

ISBN 0-312-22031-6

Contents

v

Acknowledgements

The editor and publishers wish to thank the following for permission to use copyright material:

Francis Barker and Peter Hulme, for 'Nymphs and reapers heavily vanish: the discursive con-texts of *The Tempest*' from *Alternative Shakespeares*, ed. John Drakakis (1985), pp. 191–205, Methuen & Co, by permission of Routledge; John Gillies, for material from *Shakespeare and the Georgaphy of Difference* (1994), pp. 140–55, by permission of Cambridge University Press; Stephen Greenblatt, for material from *Shakespearean Negotiations: The Circulation of Social Energy in Renaissance England* (1988), Clarendon Press, pp. 142–63. Copyright © 1988 the Regents of the University of California, by permission of Oxford University Press and University of California Press; Terence Hawkes, for material from *That Shakespeharian Rag: Essays on a Critical Process* (1986), Methuen & Co, pp. 1–26, by permission of Routledge; Ania Loomba, for material from *Gender, Race, Renaissance Drama* (1989), Oxford University Press, Delhi, pp. 142–58, by permission of the author; Ruth Nevo, for material from *Shakespeare's Other Language* (1987), Methuen & Co, pp. 130–60, by permission of Routledge; David Norbrook, for '"What cares these roarers for the name of king?": Language and Utopia in *The Tempest*' from *The Politics of Tragicomedy: Shakespeare and After*, ed. Gordon McMullan and Jonathan Hope (1992), Methuen & Co, pp. 21–54, by permission of Routledge; Stephen Orgel, for 'Prospero's Wife', *Representations*, 8, Fall (1984), 1–13. Copyright © 1984 by the Regents of the University of California, by permission of University of California Press; Annabel Patterson, for material from *Shakespeare and the Popular Voice* (1989), pp. 154–62, by permission of Blackwell Publishers; Ann Thompson, for '"Miranda, Where's Your Sister?":

Reading Shakespeare's *The Tempest*' from *Feminist Criticism: Theory and Practice*, ed. Susan Sellers (1991), Harvester, by permission of Prentice-Hall Europe, pp. 45–55.

Every effort has been made to trace the copyright holders but if any have been inadvertently overlooked the publishers will be pleased to make the necessary arrangement at the first opportunity.

General Editors' Preface

The purpose of this series of New Casebooks is to reveal some of the ways in which contemporary criticism has changed our understanding of commonly studied texts and writers and, indeed, of the nature of criticism itself. Central to the series is a concern with modern critical theory and its effect on current approaches to the study of literature. Each New Casebook editor has been asked to select a sequence of essays which will introduce the reader to the new critical approaches to the text or texts being discussed in the volume and also illuminate the rich interchange between critical theory and critical practice that characterises so much current writing about literature.

In this focus on modern critical thinking and practice New Casebooks aim not only to inform but also to stimulate, with volumes seeking to reflect both the controversy and the excitement of current criticism. Because much of this criticism is difficult and often employs an unfamiliar critical language, editors have been asked to give the reader as much help as they feel is appropriate, but without simplifying the essays or the issues they raise. Again, editors have been asked to supply a list of further reading which will enable readers to follow up issues raised by the essays in the volume.

The project of New Casebooks, then, is to bring together in an illuminating way those critics who best illustrate the ways in which contemporary criticism has established new methods of analysing texts and who have reinvigorated the important debate about how we 'read' literature. The hope is, of course, that New Casebooks will not only open up this debate to a wider audience, but will also encourage students to extend their own ideas, and think afresh about their responses to the texts they are studying.

John Peck and Martin Coyle
University of Wales, Cardiff

Introduction: Prospero 2000

R. S. WHITE

Shakespeare's plays may no longer be regarded as 'universal' in the old sense of the word, but they can apparently be infinitely re-contextualised and adapted for different cultures and for successive generations. Even the text or texts of particular plays which have been transmitted by successive publishers since Shakespeare's days are seen more as versions of what Shakespeare himself wrote, and we will never have a single, sacred and original witness to the author's 'last word'. *The Tempest* exists in only one version from close to his own time, that in the First Folio, but even so this was published seven years after Shakespeare's death, and has some internal evidence of re-vision by the dramatist, perhaps in response to problems his acting company found in staging the play, or perhaps evidencing a rewriting for a specific occasion or stage.[1] In addition, Shakespeare may not have claimed inspired originality for his works. His age favoured 'imi-tation' or adaptation of some respected source, and all but three of his plays are based quite closely on former works by other writers. *The Tempest* is one of the three exceptions, and yet, although we have found no dominant source for it, there are many secondary sources and analogues ranging from Ovid to travel documents and even to Shakespeare's own earlier plays. In an interesting book by Donna B. Hamilton,[2] the argument is mounted that the play itself is a creative, Jacobean 'imitation' of earlier sources, primarily Virgil's *Aeneid*, adapted for contemporary, political purposes. The genre of tragi-comedy based on romance sources was fashionable, and Shakespeare as a professional man of the theatre had to take heed of fashion and give audiences what they wanted. We shall also never know the responses of Shakespeare's audiences to the play; whether they saw it, as Jonathan Bate suggests, as a humanist education,[3] or, as recent critics have argued, as a comment on the causes and effects of the English empire and colonialism in general.

What we have, then, under the title of William Shakespeare's *The Tempest*, is not an authoritative text against which all subsequent performances can be judged as authentic or inauthentic, but rather a pretext for an unending series of imitations and adaptations – and even the non-existent, originary work by Shakespeare was merely a pretext to adapt the works of others to the stage. This Introduction will examine the process of continuing revision of *The Tempest* to suit new cultural contexts down the centuries. It is a peculiarity of this play that it has inspired more creative adaptations than probably any other text ever written.

I

The habit started in the century in which it was first performed (1611), when William Davenant in 1667 revised the play (with John Dryden adding some passages), calling it *The Tempest, or The Enchanted Island*. Only one third of Shakespeare's text survived, and the changes are considerable. Davenant's intentions were different from those of modern adapters, since he saw himself as 'purifying' Shakespeare's rather rough dramaturgy and poetry, bringing it into line with neoclassical norms about art. Nonetheless, his version appropriates the play just as firmly as later ones, since he tones down the content relating to politics and sexuality, and highlights comedy and farce. His own conservative age seemed to 'need' such changes. In 1674, Thomas Shadwell used Davenant's and Dryden's text as the basis for an opera, subsuming yet further thematic content beneath spectacle and theatricalism. This held the stage right through to the 1740s. Even when, in 1746, a performance in Drury Lane claimed to present the play 'As written by Shakespeare, never acted there before', it could be seen as simply a version, still incorporating some of Shadwell's material.

The subsequent stage history of *The Tempest*, and particularly the portrayals of Caliban in different political and colonial contexts, is traced by Trevor R. Griffiths in the article '"This Island's mine": Caliban and Colonialism'.[4] Griffiths concludes that theatrical responses are a barometer of changing attitudes to colonialism, race and empire. A whole book has been devoted to the mutations of Caliban alone: *Shakespeare's Caliban: A Cultural History* by Alden T. Vaughan and Virginia Mason Vaughan,[5] noting the various representations of this character ranging from monstrous savage to colonial victim. (It is an ironic rejoinder to those who claim Shakespeare as tory and monarchist that his two great rebels, Falstaff and Caliban, have attracted far more lengthy and sympathetic attention than their respective 'masters', Hal/Henry V and Prospero.) Griffiths argues that the Dryden–Davenant adaptations show Caliban as a 'comic wodwo' whose rebelliousness gives an opportunity for the adapters to reveal their 'anti-democratic sentiments'; late nineteenth-century Social Darwinists saw him as a 'missing link' in evolution from beast to man, while other Victorians saw Caliban as evoking pity for the degraded slave. Caliban was also portrayed as a republican, in William and Robert Broughs' *The Enchanted Isle* (1848), paving the way for more modern anti-Imperial and postcolonial approaches which have become almost obligatory in late twentieth-century productions.

It is in the twentieth century that imaginative rewriting of *The Tempest* has become something of an art form in itself. Most of these versions are not intended to improve or refine Shakespeare's text, but unashamedly to use it for some ulterior and contemporary application. In appropriating it for some cause, these adaptations can be said to restore attention to the serious, political potential in the play, to a degree which makes the works entirely new creations, often in quite different genres. Resistance to power and arbitrary authority are common stances. W. H. Auden in the 1930s, during the build-up to World War Two, rewrote the play as a poem, *The Mirror and the Sea*. It is not difficult to locate in his adaptation the concern he shared with many socialists in Britain about the advent of fascism, as he depicts the fragile communitarianism of characters who help and love each other, pitted against the dangerous and chilling individualism of Antonio:

> *Your all is partial, Prospero;*
> *My will is all my own;*
> *Your need to love shall never know*
> *Me: I am I, Antonio,*
> *By choice myself alone.*

The distinction had run through the debate about 'will to power' and the individualistic 'superman' from the time of Nietzsche onwards, culminating in the emergence of fascism and communism which Auden is implicitly portraying.

In other versions it is Prospero who is the object of attack and resistance. New World (postcolonial) rewritings, in particular, have come thick and fast: George Lamming's *Water with Berries* (1973) is a Caribbean novel written on the 'old Prospero–Caliban theme'. Aimé Césaire in the 1930s dramatised the play as *Une Tempête*, dealing with the fate of uprooted and insurgent African slaves, from Caliban's point of view. As Chantal Zabus traces, *The Tempest* was used in many English-Canadian novels between 1847 and 1974,[6] sometimes, paradoxically, as a myth of imperialism and sometimes as a 'manifesto of decolonisation'. Generally speaking, novels from the 'new world' like Canada pursued the latter path, alongside republican, anti-imperial political movements. Unexpectedly, we find that one of Miranda's modern descendants is Walt Disney's Pocahontas. The mid-nineteenth-century American play by Charlotte Barnes, *The Forest Princess; or, Two Centuries Ago* (played in Liverpool in 1844 and in Philadelphia in 1848) is a revision of *The Tempest* written, as Mary Loeffelholz explains, at a time when Shakespeare 'was undergoing a complex conversion in the United States – from pre-Revolutionary Tory to something like an American national romantic'.[7] Pocahontas the native American is conceived as a Miranda, 'a good-will ambassadress from the new nation to the old kingdom', and as a new and subsequently influential model of American womanhood. Thomas Cartelli's 'Prospero in Africa: *The Tempest* as colonialist text and pretext'[8] examines the influence of the play on writers like the Kenyan Ngugi Wa Thiongo and the West Indian George Lamming. He looks at 'the repeated use of *The Tempest* as a site on which the age-old conflicts between coloniser and colonised continue to be played out and rehearsed'.[9] In the postcolonial approach used by Cartelli and Loomba (essay 7), formerly canonical works of English literature such as Conrad's *Heart of Darkness* and *The Tempest*, can be viewed as part of the colonising process, erasing cultures just as effectively as colonialism erased customs. We see *The Tempest* as a play which has been culpably complicit in the brutal history of the British empire, and as 'responsible' (Cartelli's word) for the ways in which it has been read to vindicate this history. Another widely cited work in the same vein is Paul Brown's '"This thing of darkness I acknowledge mine": *The Tempest* and the discourse of colonialism'.[10] A useful counterweight to both essays (and other postcolonial accounts) is by Deborah Willis, 'Shakespeare's *The Tempest* and the Discourse of Colonialism'.[11] Willis vigorously contests at least Brown's essay as anachronistic and as falling into the trap to which Barker and Hulme (essay 2) alert us: reading the play as if it uncritically endorses Prospero's position, and in addition oversimplifying that position. Willis goes on to pick up Auden's hint that the truly threatening 'other' to Prospero is not Caliban but Antonio, who is seen as a figure demonstrating 'aggression unmodulated by a sense of familial or communal bonds'.[12]

Very diverse film adaptations have been made. *Forbidden Planet* (1956) was, for its time, an expensive and interesting science fiction film, where the setting is a technologically advanced human society in the year 2257 imposing itself on an alien planet. Robby the Robot is a guileless equivalent of Ariel in his most helpful guise, even able to simulate a perfect bourbon. Caliban becomes a Freudian projection of Prospero's (Dr Morbius's) own unconscious mind, a thing of darkness which the *magus* must acknowledge as his own in the deepest sense. Produced at a time when questions were being raised about the ethical responsibilities of scientists towards the utilisation of technological inventions such as the atom bomb (Robby, although programmed to be completely obedient, is also programmed never to take human life), and at a time of Cold War between capitalist and soviet systems, the film becomes Hollywood's comment on the dominant debates of the 1950s. The film's existence reminds us that Shakespeare's play is the mother of all sci-fi, and its premonitions of multi-media must have been evident in the technicalities of the Jacobean marriage masque which was one of the most technologically sophisticated demonstrations of theatrical pyrotechnics seen on stage up to its time. Derek Jarman's low budget and gentle *The Tempest* (1980) was seen as nostalgic of flower-power escapism, its Prospero being a young but prematurely experienced figure. The line 'Our revels now are ended' in retrospect has the prophetic quality of 'the carnival is over', since Margaret Thatcher became British Prime Minister in 1979, and the 1980s can be seen as a grim decade when unemployment was used as a weapon against the youth culture which dominated in the 1960s and 1970s. Set in a decaying Victorian mansion, the version has recently been analysed from the point of view of gay politics.[13] Miranda was played by Toyah Wilcox, a popular punk rock singer of the time, and the marriage masque is a zany and unexpectedly touching scene in which Elisabeth Welch sings 'Stormy Weather', preceded by dozens of sailors dancing to the hornpipe, and accompanied by autumn leaves falling, and followed by black and white silence and melancholy. Peter Greenaway's *Prospero's Books* (1991) is postmodern in flavour, drawing eclectically from computer technology, Renaissance painting, and postcolonial theory, among other cultural sources. John Gielgud's is the only voice we hear until the last section, as he not only 'plays' Prospero, but also evokes an older, thespian tradition, existing alongside other, more recent filmic references. That the age of Prospero is genuinely indeterminate seems to be established by the fact that Gielgud, who made the role uniquely his own, first played it when he was 26 in 1930, then several times through to 1973 when he was 69, and he appears as a sprightly, naked Prospero filmed at the age of 86 in Greenaway's film. Greenaway centrally pays homage to the power of the written word, speculating on the actual books owned by Prospero, 24 of them, ranging from *The Book of Water*, through books on geometry, the physiology of childbirth, the dead, languages, to *The Book of Games*, the final one being the complete works of Shakespeare snatched from the water at the last minute by Caliban. The power of the written word is sanctified, as it is in Umberto Eco's *The Name of the Rose*. Greenaway has also provided another kind of adaptation by writing a novel, *Prospero's Creatures*, imagining the voyage back to Naples after the play is over.

What in the play lends itself to such extraordinary and diverse appropriations? One could say that *The Tempest* illustrates to an extreme degree two tenets of recent literary theory: that all culture is intertextual, and that literature is not an absolute 'given' but something constructed and reconstructed by readers, and other creative writers. Different thematic aspects can very clearly be identified as ones that have transcultural relevance, such as the art of ruling, authority, justice and revenge, forgiveness, slavery, the politics of subjugation and its psychological equivalent of the nature of repression, colonialism, patriarchy and the 'dutiful' daughter, and so on. The critics represented in this volume analyse such themes.

There may, though, be other reasons for the creative potential of *The Tempest*. The story is as tight and straightforward as one can imagine, like a fable by Æsop without the moral, without any of the complexities of a romantic comedy with a disguised heroine, or the mysteries of a *Hamlet*, or the narrative sprawl of a history play or *King Lear*; and its time sequence is limited, unlike, say, that of *Antony and Cleopatra*. Shakespeare rehearses 'the story so far' to the audience by allowing Prospero to peer into 'the dark backward and abysm of time' as he explains to Miranda what happened in a time before she can remember. (Memory itself is a thematic concern of the play, since Prospero and Caliban, at least, spend much of their time recalling the past.) More simply, *The Tempest* obeys the literary rules set down by Aristotle, since it is unified in time, place and action.

The action itself is dominated by Prospero. He is clearly obsessed with controlling those around him, partly out of necessity and partly out of choice, but some things, like the young lovers' imputed sexual impulses, elude total coercion. He is a man of moods, swinging between triumphant vindication, anger, and despair. Self-control seems to be something that is harder than control of events, and his most hard-won gesture is the altruism of turning vindictiveness towards his foes into forgiveness of them. All these facets can lead to two different ways of acting, or 'reading' Prospero in the play. Older critics gave him almost god-like status, and they certainly saw his power as benevolent and justifiable.[14] More recently he has been seen as murky and problematical in his motivations.[15] Which reading we adopt depends on how strongly we identify with Caliban. Sympathy with Caliban is a Romantic creation of Schlegel, Coleridge and Hazlitt, and it has proved tenacious.[16] The Prospero–Caliban relationship, like the Prospero–Ariel one, seems to raise questions about the creative process itself, about the interplay between Prospero's knowledge and Caliban's world of nature.

II

The bare bones of Shakespeare's plot allow a rewriter to make it illustrate a series of themes, or dwell on particular issues. Some that are related and seem dominant are power, authority and usurpation. Prospero is a ruler, once and future duke of Milan, and the present ruler of the island. The story can easily be interpreted as being 'about' ruling, about good and bad government. Even in the turbulent storm scene, debate rages over who has authority on a ship rather than on land. Prospero had originally been a 'bad' ruler because he neglected the worldly affairs of state; then he learns the art of ruling in the simple, experimental environment of the island, and prepares himself to be a 'good' ruler of Milan. We are also given other models of government: Alonso may not be a bad ruler, but he is one whose claim to authority is suspect and flawed, which makes his reign almost necessarily a brief one. Gonzalo provides a cameo picture of an anarchist or prototype communist state:

> I' th' commonwealth I would by contraries
> Execute all things, for no kind of traffic
> Would I admit; no man of magistrate;
> Letters [learning] should not be known; riches, poverty,
> And use of service, none; contract, succession,
> Bourn, bound of land, tilth, vineyard, none;
> No use of metal, corn, or wine, or oil;
> No occupation, all men idle, all,
> And women too, but innocent and pure;
> No sovereignty –
>
> (II.i.145–54)

The sardonic, less than 'pure and innocent' Sebastian dryly points out the contradiction in Gonzalo's scheme to turn the island into an enlightened state: 'Yet he would be king on't'. David Norbrook (essay 9) traces the links between *The Tempest*, especially Gonzalo's programme, and Thomas More's vision of political organisation in *Utopia* (1516).

Another aspect of the play's political theme which most writers in this book take up, is usurpation. Prospero's brother usurped the dukedom, Prospero annexed the island from its native inhabitants. This alone has enough topical relevance to explain the play's current revival: as empires rise and fall, countries which were once autonomous become subject colonial nations and later independent states indelibly marked by the coloniser's assumptions and world view – postcolonial, in short. Some day it may come to be widely accepted that in the second half of the twentieth century even the richer, developed countries have been subjected to the cultural imprint of the United States, through Coca Cola, Walt Disney, and the Internet, and the process is analogous to Prospero teaching Caliban not just any language but one in particular. There are, moreover, local applications around the world: the subjugation of the native Americans, the occupation of Northern Ireland, Russian annexation of eastern Europe, French colonial rule in Africa and the Pacific, and so on. The Mabo legislation in Australia raises exactly the questions raised by Caliban – who owns the island, the native or the usurper. As the writers of *The Empire Writes Back* summarise: '*The Tempest* has been perhaps the most important text used to establish a paradigm for postcolonial readings of canonical works.'[17]

(I don't think it has yet been done, but there may be room for a study of *The Tempest* as an observation of the dynamics of tourism which is so much a twentieth-century phenomenon.)

The particular fertility of readings and adaptations which dwell on power relations stems from the play's neat splicing of three different narratives of power, each of which can be manipulated depending on where one wishes to invest one's sympathies: Prospero gaining revenge over his usurping brother, and finally grudgingly forgiving him and his cohort when they are defeated; Prospero's control of the island's 'natives', Sycorax, Caliban and Ariel (and the prior narrative of Ariel's imprisonment by Sycorax); and the romance plot between Miranda and Ferdinand, which is rather recalcitrant in resisting Prospero's full control. The first narrative turns on politics, the second on colonialism, the third on gender, and each raises open questions of the exercise of power.

Power over people is politics, power over objects is technological control, which this Prospero has in abundance. He demonstrates it from the first scene in which he raises a storm, right through to the masque. This aspect might open up another appropriation: our envisagement of the postmodern Prospero, Prospero 2000. The present analogy for his 'most potent art' is one that has surfaced several times already in this introduction: the computer. The storm raised at the beginning by Ariel under Prospero's command is an anticipation of 'virtual reality'. The clothes of those shipwrecked are left clean and dry, just as one can control and tidy a messy screen or document with a touch of the 'Clean Up Desktop' key. The island itself can be configured apparently at will, as to some it is fertile and to others barren, just as the Internet can be informative for those who know how to use it and meaningless to those who don't. The jargon of the world wide web – surfing, navigating, cruising – points to the implicit analogy of a vast sea of information washing around the island of the isolated but 'in touch' expert with state-of-art computing facilities. Prospero manipulates his little world with the expertise of somebody playing a series of interactive media games, and it seems he has been playing these games of virtual reality for the duration of his stay on the island.

> I have bedimmed
> The noontide sun, called forth the mutinous winds,
> And 'twixt the green sea and the azured vault
> Set roaring war; to the dread rattling thunder
> Have I given fire, and rifted Jove's stout oak

> With his own bolt; the strong-based promontory
> Have I made shake, and by the spurs plucked up
> The pine and cedar. Graves at my command
> Have waked their sleepers, oped, and let 'em forth
> By my so potent art.
>
> (V.i.41–7)

But Prospero finally vows to abjure this rough magic, and in a gesture like one of destroying his computer, to break his staff and to drown his book 'deeper than did ever plummet sound'. Why? One answer is that the technology has done its work, allowing him to while away the time and learn the arts of manipulation well enough to allow him to return to a life of civic duty. But another answer operates more psychologically. Living in a world of self-created *virtual* reality seems to have left Prospero inhuman, lacking in curiosity, indifferent to novelty and surprise. He needs to be told by a spirit who is 'but air' that his feelings should be moved ('Mine would, sir, were I human' [V.i.19]), and his response to his daughter's 'O brave new world that hath such creatures in't' is a jaded ''Tis new to thee'. He seems radically sceptical of all reality as if it is merely virtual and without substance:

> These our actors,
> As I foretold you, were all spirits and
> Are melted into air, into thin air,
> And, like the baseless fabric of this vision,
> The cloud-capped towers, the gorgeous palaces,
> The solemn temples, the great globe itself,
> Yea, all which it inherit, shall dissolve,
> And like this insubstantial pageant faded,
> Leave not a rack behind. We are such stuff
> As dreams are made on, and our little life
> Is rounded with a sleep.
>
> (IV.i.148–58)

The impact of this speech has always seemed to be the personal statement of a dramatist in the seventeenth century 'vexed' that his plays seem to have been so evanescent and impermanent. In it we detect a note of frustration and premonitions of an ending in 'despair' (V.i.331) unless set free from the enthralment of a knowledge, even an addiction which has usurped the world of living, loving, feeling human beings where even a Caliban can feel wonder and delight at the jay's nest and nimble marmoset. The audience's applause is all that is needed for the actor playing Prospero to be liberated from his role, and for the play to end. For our hypothetical Prospero 2000, the computer must be switched off, with the mixed feelings of reluctance and relief as power and control are relinquished.

After political power and technological control, other aspects of *The Tempest* lend themselves to thematisation if an adapter should choose. One is essentially of psychological interest – the nature of the unexpected changes wrought in Prospero. Although the play looks unpromising for feminist analysis, it can, and has, yielded insights into the nature of patriarchal society, just as it can point also to the nature of class structure along the lines provided by Marxist analysis. At the centre of the play is a Book, and the play is as focused on the power of words as is Umberto Eco's *The Name of the Rose*. Prospero's is a book of magic, but what it suggests is how powerful in effecting purposes and changing reality language might be.

III

As well as lending itself to endless adaptations, then, *The Tempest* provides a testing ground for virtually all the new literary theories that can be devised. The rest of this volume is devoted to providing some examples. The roll-call of approaches sounds like Polonius's parody of Elizabethan dramatic genres: new historicism, historico-political, postcolonial, feminism, Marxism, cultural materialism, psychoanalysis, and so on. The play has, in fact, received more attention from new theorists than perhaps any other by Shakespeare – certainly than any other comedy or romance. This may be because *The Tempest* raises social and political issues that have a contemporary currency, and theory is far better in addressing issues than it is in dealing with, for example, language or theatrical effectiveness. We find reflections of such issues as power and authority, political government, the nature and psychology of colonialism, racial difference and racism, the position of women in patriarchy, the self-reflexiveness of literary art with its magus-like creator. All but the last of these are brought to the fore in essays here, and the artist's self-construction through his artefact is a central issue in the film versions by Jarman and Greenaway, in very different ways.

The issues concerned with art and creativity – the relationships between the artist and his work, the work and its readers and audiences, *The Tempest* and its antecedents by Shakespeare, its running discussion about the power of language to control thought – are the ones least adequately addressed by the essays in this volume. This in itself may reveal a blind spot in issues-based, theoretically inclined criticism, which at times runs the risk of creating a new version of the confusion between art of the seventeenth century and 'life' of the twentieth. Prospero, like his creator, is nothing if not a supreme artist, controlling and constructing the island, not only through his unexplained but potent magical 'art', but also through his necromantic 'book'. This book may be as humble as a dictionary (not available in its modern form to Shakespeare and his contemporaries), since language itself is power, and it is through words that the essential power is exercised, the magic exerted. Caliban is one to recognise this, when he acknowledges that Prospero (or Miranda) has taught him language with which to curse. Prospero himself seems to locate his source of power in language in his famous speeches in Act IV. Ariel can be read as embodying variously the agency of imagination which can turn words and things into poetry and art, since the haunting song 'Full fathom five thy father lies ...' (I.i.397–405) seems to describe the process by which living people and experiences are transformed into 'something rich and strange' through the gradual workings of memory and the shaping quality of art, both associated with the sea's motions in this play. Or the 'art' may be nothing but theatrical in this most meta-dramatic of plays, reflecting the playwright's conscientious anxieties about bringing the dead to life (Julius Caesar, Macbeth, Hamlet) and killing them off again day after day for the spectacle of several thousands of people in the playhouse's audience.[18]

Running alongside the numerous adaptations and rewritings of *The Tempest*, we find a set of critical interpretations which, taken as a group, demonstrate, once again, the play's centrality and ripeness for appropriation. Over the last twenty years or so, during the great upheavals in literary studies caused by a new emphasis on theory, this play has time and again been used as a test and yardstick for the effectiveness of each new approach as it has appeared. You will find in the endnotes to each essay a brief description of where each lies on the map of literary criticism, and the section on Further Reading supplies more references for those who wish to explore particular approaches. Cultural materialism, new historicism, feminism, deconstructionism, postcolonialism and other -isms will be encountered as the new tools available, not to analyse or explicate the play, but to construct it, often in the likeness of the critic. Underneath the process of appropriation may run an intriguing link drawn by Stephen Orgel (essay 1), Ruth Nevo (essay 4) and Ann Thompson (essay 8) between the play and psychiatry, a symbiosis between a written work, designed for stage performance, which manages to capture something of the infinite potential and provisionality of the human mind itself, in its processes of moving between conscious and unconscious fields, making sense of the world, and charting the selectiveness of memory, in endlessly reshapable ways. As a fable, parable or myth (a story that both explains and changes the way we see the world), *The Tempest* has been as potent and suggestive as the myths of Pygmalion and Orpheus have been for centuries, *The Heart of Darkness* and *Wuthering Heights* for our own century. Together with *Hamlet* it may be Shakespeare's most applicable paradigm for the contemporary world.

NOTES

[All quotations from *The Tempest* are taken from the single volume edition of The Oxford Shakespeare, *The Tempest*, ed. Stephen Orgel (Oxford, 1987)].

1. For a theorised account of the bibliographical problems of the text of *The Tempest*, see Leah S. Marcus, 'Introduction: The blue-eyed witch', in *Unediting the Renaissance: Shakespeare, Marlowe, Milton* (London and New York, 1996), pp. 1–37.

2. Donna B. Hamilton, *Virgil and 'The Tempest': The Politics of Imitation* (Columbus, OH, 1990).

3. Jonathan Bate, 'The Humanist *Tempest*', *Shakespeare: La Tempête: Études Critiques* (Actes du Colloque de Besançon, Université de Franche-Comté, 1993), pp. 5–20.

4. Trevor R. Griffiths, '"This Island's mine": Caliban and Colonialism', *Yearbook of English Studies*, 13 (1983), 159–80.

5. Cambridge (1991).

6. Chantal Zabus, 'A Calibanic Tempest in Anglophone and Francophone New World Writing', *Canadian Literature, Littératur Canadienne*, 104 (1985), 35–51.

7. Mary Loeffelholz, 'Miranda in the New World: *The Tempest* and Charlotte Barnes's *The Forest Princess*', in *Women's Re-Visions of Shakespeare: On the Responses of Dickinson, Woolf, Rich, H. D.,*

George Eliot, and Others (Urbana and Chicago, 1990), pp. 58–75. The generalisation draws upon work by Page Smith, *The Nation Comes of Age* (New York, 1981), p. 177; and Esther Cloudman Dunn, *Shakespeare in America* (New York and London, 1939, repr. 1968).

8. Thomas Cartelli, in *Shakespeare Reproduced*, ed. Jean F. Howard and Marion F. O'Connor (New York and London, 1987), pp. 99–115.

9. Ibid., p. 101.

10. Paul Brown, in *Political Shakespeare: New Essays in Cultural Materialism*, ed. Jonathan Dollimore and Alan Sinfield (Ithaca, NY, 1985), pp. 48–71.

11. Deborah Willis, *Studies in English Literature*, 29 (1989), 277–89.

12. Ibid., 286.

13. Kate Chedgzoy, *Shakespeare's Queer Children: Sexual Politics and Contemporary Culture* (Manchester, 1995).

14. See, for example, G. Wilson Knight, *The Crown of Life* (London, 1948), R. G. Hunter, *Shakespeare and the Comedy of Forgiveness* (New York, 1965), and the film *Forbidden Planet*.

15. See, for example, R. S. White, '*Let Wonder Seem Familiar': Endings in Shakespeare's Romance Vision* (London, 1985), p. 168, and many of the critics in this volume.

16. See *Hazlitt's Criticism of Shakespeare: A Selection*, ed. R. S. White (Lampeter, 1996), p. 125.

17. Bill Ashcroft, Gareth Griffiths and Helen Tiffin, *The Empire Writes Back: Theory and Practice in Post-Colonial Literatures* (London, 1989), p. 190.

18. For a meta-dramatic analysis, see Anne Righter, *Shakespeare and the Idea of the Play* (Harmondsworth, 1969), and the Introduction to Anne Righter's (Barton's) edition of *The Tempest* (Harmondsworth, 1968).

1

Prospero's Wife

STEPHEN ORGEL

This essay is not a reading of *The Tempest*. It is a consideration of
five related moments and issues. I have called it *Prospero's Wife*
because some of it centres on her, but as a figure conspicuous by her
absence from the play, I take her as a figure of my larger subject: the
absent, the unspoken, that seems to me the most powerful and problematic presence in *The Tempest*. In its outlines, the play seems a
story of privatives: withdrawal, usurpation, banishment, becoming
lost, shipwreck. As an antithesis, a principle of control, preservation, re-creation, the play offers only magic, embodied in a single
figure, the extraordinary power of Prospero.

FAMILY HISTORY

Prospero's wife is alluded to only once in the play, in Prospero's
reply to Miranda's question, 'Sir, are you not my father?'

> Thy mother was a piece of virtue, and
> She said thou wast my daughter; and thy father
> Was Duke of Milan; and his only heir
> And princess: no worse issued.
>
> (I.ii.55–9)[1]

Prospero's wife is identified as Miranda's mother, in a context implying that although she was virtuous, women as a class are not, and
that were it not for her word, Miranda's legitimacy would be in
doubt. The legitimacy of Prospero's heir, that is, derives from her
mother's word. But that word is all that is required of her in the

15

play; once he is assured of it, Prospero turns his attention to himself and his succession, and he characterises Miranda in a clause that grows increasingly ambivalent: 'his only heir / And princess: no worse issued.'

Except for this moment, Prospero's wife is absent from his memory. She is wholly absent from her daughter's memory: Miranda can recall several women who attended her in childhood, but no mother. The attitudes implied toward wives and mothers here are confirmed shortly afterward when Prospero, recounting his brother Antonio's crimes, demands that Miranda 'tell me / If this might be a brother', and Miranda takes the question to be a charge of adultery against Prospero's mother:

> I should sin
> To think but nobly of my grandmother:
> Good wombs have borne bad sons.
> (I.ii.118–20)

She immediately translates Prospero's attack on his brother into an attack on his mother (and the best she can produce in her grand-mother's defence is a 'not proved'); and whether or not she has cor-rectly divined her father's intentions, Prospero makes no objection.

The absent presence of the wife and mother in the play consti-tutes a space that is filled by Prospero's creation of surrogates and a ghostly family: the witch Sycorax and her monster child Caliban (himself, as becomes apparent, a surrogate for the other wicked child, the usurping younger brother), the good child/wife Miranda, the obedient Ariel, the violently libidinised adolescent Ferdinand. The space is filled, too, by a whole structure of wifely allusion and reference: widow Dido, model at once of heroic fidelity to a mur-dered husband and the destructive potential of erotic passion; the witch Medea, murderess and filicide; three exemplary goddesses, the bereft Ceres, nurturing Juno, and licentious Venus; and Alonso's daughter Claribel, unwillingly married off to the ruler of the modern Carthage and thereby lost to her father forever.

Described in this way, the play has an obvious psychoanalytic shape. I have learned a great deal from Freudian treatments of it, most recently from essays by David Sundelson, Coppélia Kahn, and Joel Fineman in the volume called *Representing Shakespeare*.[2] It is almost irresistible to look at the play as a case history – *whose* case history is a rather more problematic question and one that criticism has not, on the whole, dealt with satisfactorily: not, obviously, that of the characters. I want to pause first over what it means to consider the play as a case history.

In older psychoanalytic paradigms (say Ernest Jones's), the critic is the analyst, Shakespeare the patient, the plays his fantasies. The trouble with this paradigm is that it misrepresents the analytic situation in a fundamental way. The interpretation of analytical material is done in conjunction with, and in large measure by, the patient, not the analyst; what the analyst does is to *enable* the patient, to free the patient to interpret. An analysis done without the patient, like Freud's of Leonardo, will be revealing only about the analyst. A more recent paradigm, in which the audience's response is the principal analytic material, seems to me based on even more fundamental misconceptions, first because it treats an audience as an entity, a unit, and moreover a constant one; and more problematically, because it conceives of the play as an objective event, so that the critical question becomes, 'This is what happened: how do we respond to it?'

To take the psychoanalytic paradigm seriously, however, and treat the plays as case histories, is surely to treat them *not* as objective events but as collaborative fantasies and to acknowledge thereby that we, as analysts, are implicated in the fantasy. It is not only the patients who create the shape of their histories, and when Bruno Bettelheim observes that Freud's case histories 'read as well as the best novels',[2] he is probably telling more of the truth than he intends.[3] Moreover, the crucial recent advances in our understanding of Freud and psychoanalysis have been precisely critical acts of close and inventive reading – there are, in this respect, no limits to the collaboration. But if we accept this as our paradigm and think of ourselves as Freud's or Shakespeare's collaborators, we must also acknowledge that our reading of the case will be revealing, again, chiefly about ourselves. This is why every generation, and perhaps every reading, produces a different analysis of its Shakespearean texts. In the same way, recent psychoanalytic theory has replaced Freud's central Oedipal myth with a drama in which the loss of the seducing mother is the crucial infant trauma. As men, we used to want assurance that we could successfully compete with or replace or supersede our fathers; now we want to know that our lost mothers will return. Both of these no doubt involve real perceptions, but they also undeniably serve particular cultural needs.

Shakespeare plays, like case histories, derive from the observation of human behaviour, and both plays and case histories are imaginative constructs. Whether or not either is taken to be an objective report of behaviour has more to do with the reader than the reporter, but it has to be said that Shakespearean critics have more often than not treated the plays as objective accounts. Without such an assumption, a book with the title *The Girlhood of Shakespeare's Heroines* would be incomprehensible. We feel very far from this famous and popular Victorian work now, but we still worry about consistency and motivation in Shakespearean texts, and much of the commentary in an edition like the Arden Shakespeare is designed to explain why the characters say what they say – that is, to reconcile what they say with what, on the basis of their previous behaviour, we feel they ought to be saying. The critic who worries about this kind of consistency in a Shakespeare text is thinking of it as an objective report.

But all readings of Shakespeare, from the earliest seventeenth-century adaptations through eighteenth-century attempts to produce 'authentic' or 'accurate' texts to the liberal fantasy of the old Variorum Shakespeare, have been aware of deep ambiguities and ambivalences in the texts. The eighteenth century described these as Shakespeare's errors and generally revised them through plausible emendation or outright rewriting. The argument was that Shakespeare wrote in haste and would have written more perfect plays had he taken time to revise; the corollary to this was, of course, that what we want are the perfect plays Shakespeare did not write rather than the imperfect ones that he did. A little later the errors became not Shakespeare's but those of the printing house, the scribe, the memory of the reporter or the defective hearing of the transcriber; but the assumption has always been that it is possible to produce a 'perfect' text: that beyond or behind the ambiguous, puzzling, inconsistent text is a clear and consistent one.

Plays, moreover, are not only – and one might argue, not primarily – texts. They are performances, too, originally designed to be read only in order to be acted out, and the gap between the text and its performance has always been, and remains, a radical one. There always has been an imagination intervening between the texts and their audiences, initially the imagination of producer, director, or actor (roles that Shakespeare played himself), and since that time the imagination of editors and commentators as well. These are texts that have always had to be realised. Initially unstable, they have remained so despite all attempts to fix them. All attempts to produce an authentic, correct, that is, stable text have resulted only in an extraordinary variety of versions. Their differences can be described as minor only if one believes that the real play is a Platonic idea, never realised but only approached and approximately represented by its text.

This is our myth: the myth of a stable, accurate, authentic, legitimate text, a text that we can think of as Shakespeare's legitimate heir. It is, in its way, a family myth, and it operates with peculiar force in our readings of *The Tempest*, a play that has been, for the last hundred and fifty years, taken as a representation of Shakespeare himself bidding farewell to his art, as Shakespeare's legacy.

THE MISSING WIFE

She is missing as a character, but Prospero, several times explicitly, presents himself as incorporating the wife, acting as both father and mother to Miranda, and, in one extraordinary passage, describes the voyage to the island as a birth fantasy:

> When I have decked the sea with drops full salt,
> Under my burden groaned, which raised in me
> An undergoing stomach, to bear up
> Against what should ensue.
> (I.ii.155–8)

To come to the island is to start life over again – both his own and Miranda's – with himself as sole parent, but also with himself as favourite child: he has been banished by his wicked, usurping, possibly illegitimate younger brother Antonio. This too has the shape of a Freudian fantasy: the younger child is indeed the usurper in the family, and the kingdom he usurps is the mother. On the island, Prospero undoes the usurpation, recreating kingdom and family with himself in sole command.

But not quite, because the island is not his alone – or if it is, then he has repeopled it with all parts of his fantasy, the distressing as well as the gratifying. When he arrives he finds Caliban, child of the witch Sycorax, herself a victim of banishment. The island provided a new life for her too, as it did literally for her son, with whom she was pregnant when she arrived. Sycorax died some time before

Prospero came to the island; Prospero never saw her, and everything he knows about her he has learned from Ariel. Nevertheless, she is insistently present in his memory – far more present than his own wife – and she embodies to an extreme degree all the negative assumptions about women that he and Miranda have exchanged.

It is important, therefore, that Caliban derives his claim to the island from his mother: 'This island's mine, by Sycorax my mother' (I.ii.333). This has interesting implications to which I shall return, but here I want to point out that he need not make the claim this way. He could derive it from mere prior possession: he was there first. This, after all, would have been the sole basis of Sycorax's claim to the island, but it is an argument that Caliban never makes. And in deriving his authority from his mother, he delivers himself into Prospero's hands: Prospero declares him a bastard, 'got by the devil himself / Upon thy wicked dam' (I.ii.321–2), thereby both disallowing any claim from inheritance and justifying his loathing for Caliban.

But is it true that Caliban is Sycorax's bastard by Satan? How does Prospero know this? Not from Sycorax: Prospero never saw her. Not from Caliban: Sycorax died before she could even teach her son to speak. Everything Prospero knows about the witch he knows from Ariel – her appearance, the story of her banishment, the fact that her pregnancy saved her from execution. Did Sycorax also tell Ariel that her baby was the illegitimate son of the devil? Or is this Prospero's contribution to the story, an especially creative piece of invective and an extreme instance of his characteristic assumptions about women? Nothing in the text will answer this question for us; and it is worth pausing to observe first that Caliban's claim seems to have been designed so that Prospero can disallow it, and second that we have no way of distinguishing the facts about Caliban and Sycorax from Prospero's invective about them.

Can Prospero imagine no good mothers, then? The play, after all, moves toward a wedding, and the most palpable example we see of the magician's powers is a betrothal masque. The masque is presided over by two exemplary mothers, Ceres and Juno; and the libidinous Venus with her destructive son Cupid has been banished from the scene. But the performance is also preceded by the most awful warnings against sexuality, male sexuality this time: all the libido is presumed to be Ferdinand's while Miranda remains Prospero's innocent child. Ferdinand's reassuring reply, as David Sundelson persuasively argues,[4] includes submerged fantasies of rape and more than a hint that when the lust of the wedding night cools, so will his marital devotion:

> the murkiest den,
> The most opportune place, the strong'st suggestion
> Our worser genius can, shall never melt
> Mine honor into lust, to take away
> The edge of that day's celebration ...
> (IV.i.25–9)

This is the other side of the assumption that all women at heart are whores: all men at heart are rapists – Caliban, Ferdinand, and of course that means Prospero too.

THE MARRIAGE CONTRACT

The play moves toward marriage, certainly, and yet the relations it postulates between men and women are ignorant at best, characteristically tense, and potentially tragic. There is a familiar Shakespearean paradigm here: relationships between men and women interest Shakespeare intensely, but not, on the whole, as husbands and wives. The wooing process tends to be what it is here: not so much a prelude to marriage and a family as a process of self-definition – an increasingly unsatisfactory process, if we look at the progression of plays from *As You Like It, Much Ado about Nothing, Twelfth Night* through *All's Well that Ends Well, Measure for Measure, Troilus and Cressida* to *Antony and Cleopatra* and *Cymbeline*. If we want to argue that marriage is actually the point of the comic wooing process for Shakespeare, then we surely ought to be looking at how he depicts marriages; and here Petruchio and Kate, Capulet and Lady Capulet, Claudius and Gertrude, Othello and Desdemona, Macbeth and Lady Macbeth, Cymbeline and his queen, Leontes and Hermione will not persuade us that comedies ending in marriages have ended happily – or if they have, it is only because they have ended there, stopped at the wedding day.

What happens after marriage? Families in Shakespeare tend not to consist of husbands and wives and their offspring but of a parent and a child, usually in a chiastic relationship – father and daughter, mother and son. When there are two children, they tend to be presented as alternatives or rivals: the twins of *The Comedy of Errors*, Sebastian and Viola, infinitely substitutable for each other; or the good son–bad son complex of Orlando and Oliver, Edgar and Edmund. We know that Shakespeare himself had a son and two daughters, but that family configuration never appears in the plays. Lear's three daughters are quite exceptional in Shakespeare, and even they are dichotomised into bad and good. We may also recall Titus Andronicus's four sons and a daughter and Tamora's three sons, hardly instances to demonstrate Shakespeare's convictions about the comforts of family life.

The family paradigm that emerges from Shakespeare's imagination is a distinctly unstable one. Here is what we know of Shakespeare's own family: he had three brothers and three sisters who survived beyond infancy, and his parents lived into old age. At eighteen he married a woman of twenty-four by whom he had a daughter within six months, and a twin son and daughter a year and a half later. Within six more years he had moved permanently to London, and for the next twenty years – all but the last three years of his life – he lived apart from his wife and family. Nor should we stop here: we do not in the least know that Susanna, Hamnet, and Judith were his only children. He lived in a society without contraceptives, and unless we want to believe that he was either exclusively homosexual or celibate, we must assume a high degree of probability that there were other children. That they are not mentioned in his will may mean that they did not survive, but it also might mean that he made separate, non-testamentary provision for them. Certainly the plays reveal a strong interest in the subject of illegitimacy.

Until quite late in his career, he seems to have expressed his strongest familial feelings not toward children or wives but toward parents and siblings. His father dies in 1601, the year of *Hamlet*, his mother in 1608, the year of *Coriolanus*. And if we are thinking about usurping bastard younger brothers, it cannot be coincidental that the younger brother who followed him into the acting profession was named Edmund. There are no dramatic correlatives comparable to these for the death of his son Hamnet in 1596. If we take the plays to express what Shakespeare thought about himself (an assumption that strikes me as by no means axiomatic) then we will say that he was apparently free to think of himself as a father – to his two surviving daughters – only after the death of both his parents: 1608 is the date of *Pericles* as well as *Coriolanus*.

One final biographical observation: Shakespearean heroines marry very young, in their teens. Miranda is fifteen. We are always told that Juliet's marriage at fourteen is not unusual in the period, but in fact it is unusual in all but upper-class families. In Shakespeare's own family, his wife married at twenty-four and his daughters at twenty-four and thirty-one. It was Shakespeare himself who married at eighteen. The women of Shakespeare's plays, of course, are adolescent boys. Perhaps we should see as much of Shakespeare in Miranda and Ariel as in Prospero.

POWER AND AUTHORITY

The psychoanalytic and biographical questions raised by *The Tempest* are irresistible, but they can supply at best partial clues to its nature. I have described the plays as collaborative fantasies, and it is not only critics and readers who are involved in the collaboration. It is performers and audiences, too, and I take these terms in their largest senses, to apply not merely to stage productions but also to the theatrical dimension of the society that contains and is mirrored by the theatre. Cultural concerns, political and social issues, speak through *The Tempest* – sometimes explicitly, as in the open-ended discussion of political economy between Gonzalo, Antonio, and Sebastian in Act II. But in a broader sense, family structures and sexual relations become political structures in the play, and these are relevant to the political structures of Jacobean England.

What is the nature of Prospero's authority and the source of his power? Why is he Duke of Milan and the legitimate ruler of the island? Power, as Prospero presents it in the play, is not inherited but self-created: it is magic, or 'art', an extension of mental power and self-knowledge, and the authority that legitimises it derives from heaven – *Fortune* and *Destiny* are the terms used in the play. It is Caliban who derives his claim to the island from inheritance, from his mother.

In the England of 1610, both these positions represent available, and indeed normative, ways of conceiving of royal authority. James I's authority derived, he said, both from his mother and from God. But deriving one's legitimacy from Mary Queen of Scots was ambiguous at best, and James always felt exceedingly insecure about it. Elizabeth had had similar problems with the sources of her authority, and they centred precisely on the question of her legitimacy. To those who believed that her father's divorce from

Katherine of Aragon was invalid (that is, to Roman Catholics), Elizabeth had no hereditary claim; and she had, moreover, been declared legally illegitimate after the execution of her mother for adultery and incest. Henry VIII maintained Elizabeth's bastardy to the end; her claim to the throne derived exclusively from her designation in the line of succession, next after Edward and Mary, in her father's will. This ambiguous legacy was the sole source of her authority. Prospero at last acknowledging the bastard Caliban as his own is also expressing the double edge of kingship throughout Shakespeare's lifetime (the ambivalence will not surprise us if we consider the way kings are represented in the history plays). Historically speaking, Caliban's claim to the island is a good one.

Royal power, the play seems to say, is good when it is self-created, bad when it is usurped or inherited from an evil mother. But of course the least problematic case of royal descent is one that is not represented in these paradigms at all; it is one that derives not from the mother but in the male line from the father: the case of Ferdinand and Alonso, in which the wife and mother is totally absent. If we are thinking about the *derivation* of royal authority, then, the absence of a father from Prospero's memory is a great deal more significant than the disappearance of a wife. Some have dealt with this in a psychoanalytic framework, whereby Antonio becomes a stand-in for the father, the real usurper of the mother's kingdom.[5] Here again, however, the realities of contemporary kingship seem more enlightening, if not inescapable. James in fact had a double claim to the English throne, and the one through his father, the Earl of Darnley, was in the strictly lineal respects somewhat stronger than that of his mother. Both Darnley and Mary were direct descendants of Henry VII, but under Henry VIII's will, which established the line of succession, descendants who were not English-born were specifically excluded. Darnley was born in England, Mary was not. Indeed, Darnley's mother went from Scotland to have her baby in England precisely in order to preserve the claim to the throne.

King James rarely mentioned this side of his heritage, for perfectly understandable reasons. His father was even more disreputable than his mother; and given what was at least the public perception of both their characters, it was all too easy to speculate about whether Darnley was even in fact his father.[6] For James, as for Elizabeth, the derivation of authority through paternity was extremely problematic. Practically, James's claim to the English throne depended on Elizabeth's naming him her heir (we recall Miranda's legitimacy depending on her mother's word), and James correctly saw this as a continuation of the protracted negotiations between Elizabeth and his mother. His legitimacy, in both senses, thus derived from two mothers, the chaste Elizabeth and the sensual Mary, whom popular imagery represented respectively as a virgin goddess ('a piece of virtue') and a lustful and diabolical witch. James's sense of his own place in the kingdom is that of Prospero, rigidly paternalistic but incorporating the maternal as well: the king describes himself in *Basilicon Doron* as 'a loving nourish father' providing the commonwealth with 'their own nourishmilk'.[7] The very etymology of the word *authority* confirms the metaphor: *augeo*, increase, nourish, cause to grow. At moments in his public utterances, James sounds like a gloss on Prospero: 'I am the husband, and the whole island is my lawful wife; I am the head, and it is my body.'[8] Here the incorporation of the wife has become literal and explicit. James conceives himself as the head of a single-parent family. In the world of *The Tempest*, there are no two-parent families. All the dangers of promiscuity and bastardy are resolved in such a conception – unless, of course, the parent is a woman.

My point here is not that Shakespeare is representing King James as Prospero or Caliban or both, but that these figures embody the predominant modes of conceiving of royal authority in the period. They are Elizabeth's and James's modes, too.

THE RENUNCIATION OF MAGIC

Prospero's magic power is exemplified, on the whole, as power over children: his daughter Miranda, the bad child Caliban, the obedient but impatient Ariel, the adolescent Ferdinand, the wicked younger brother Antonio, and indeed, the shipwreck victims as a whole, who are treated like a group of bad children. Many critics talk about Prospero as a Renaissance scientist and see alchemical metaphors in the grand design of the play. No doubt there is something in this; but what the play's action presents is not experiments and empiric studies but a fantasy about controlling other people's minds. Does the magic work? We are given a good deal of evidence of it: the masque, the banquet, the harpies, the tempest itself. But the great scheme is not to produce illusions and good weather: it is to bring about reconciliation, and here we would have to say that it works only indifferently well. 'They being penitent', says Prospero to Ariel,

'The sole drift of my purpose doth extend / Not a frown further' (V.i.28–30). The assertion opens with a conditional clause whose conditions are not met: Alonso is penitent, but the chief villain, the usurping younger brother Antonio, remains obdurate. Nothing, not all Prospero's magic, can redeem Antonio from his essential badness. Since Shakespeare was free to have Antonio repent if that is what he had in mind – half a line would have done for critics craving a reconciliation – we ought to take seriously the possibility that repentance is not what he had in mind. Perhaps, too, penitence is not what Prospero's magic is designed to elicit from his brother.

Why is Prospero's power conceived as magic? Why, in returning to Milan, does he renounce it? Most commentators say that he gives up his magic when he no longer needs it. This is an obvious answer, but it strikes me as too easy, a comfortable assumption cognate with the view that the play concludes with reconciliation, repentance, and restored harmony. To say that Prospero no longer needs his magic is to beg all the most important questions. What does it mean to say that he needs it? Did he ever need it, and if so, why? And does he in fact give it up?

Did he ever need magic? Prospero's devotion to his secret studies is what caused all the trouble in the first place – this is not an interpretation of mine; it is how Prospero presents the matter. If he has now learned to be a good ruler through the exercise of his art, that is also what taught him to be a bad one. So the question of his need for magic goes to the heart of how we interpret and judge his character: is the magic a strength or a weakness? To say that he no longer needs it is to say that his character changes in some way for the better; that by renouncing his special powers he becomes fully human. This is an important claim. Let us test it by looking at Prospero's renunciation.

What does it mean for Prospero to give up his power? Letting Miranda marry and leaving the island are the obvious answers, but they can hardly be right. Miranda's marriage is *brought about* by the magic; it is part of Prospero's plan. It pleases Miranda, certainly, but it is designed by Prospero as a way of satisfying himself. Claribel's marriage to the King of Tunis looks less sinister in this light: daughters' marriages, in royal families at least, are designed primarily to please their fathers. And leaving the island, reassuming the dukedom, is part of the plan, too. Both of these are presented as acts of renunciation, but they are in fact what the exercise of Prospero's magic is intended to effect, and they represent his triumph.

Prospero renounces his art in the great monologue at the beginning of Act V, 'Ye elves of hills, brooks, standing lakes and groves', and for all its valedictory quality, it is the most powerful assertion of his magic that the play gives us. It is also a powerful literary allusion, a close translation of a speech of Medea in Ovid,[9] and it makes at least one claim for Prospero that is made nowhere else in the play, that he can raise the dead. For Shakespeare to present this as a *renunciation* speech is upping Prospero's ante, to say the least.

In giving up his magic, Prospero speaks as Medea. He has incorporated Ovid's witch, prototype of the wicked mother Sycorax, in the most literal way – verbatim, so to speak – and his 'most potent art' is now revealed as translation and impersonation. In this context, the distinction between black magic and white magic, Sycorax and Prospero, has disappeared. Two hundred lines later, Caliban too is revealed as an aspect of Prospero: 'This thing of darkness I acknowledge mine.'

But Caliban is an aspect of Antonio, the evil child, the usurping brother. Where is the *real* villain in relation to Prospero now? Initially Antonio had been characterised, like Caliban and Sycorax, as embodying everything that is antithetical to Prospero; but in recounting his history to Miranda, Prospero also presents himself as deeply implicated in the usurpation, with Antonio even seeming at times to be acting as Prospero's agent: 'The government I cast upon my brother'; '[I] to him put the manage of my state'; 'my trust ... did beget of him / A falsehood', and so forth. If Prospero is accepting the blame for what happened, there is a degree to which he is also taking the credit. Antonio's is another of the play's identities that Prospero has incorporated into his own; and in that case, what is there to forgive?

Let us look, then, at Prospero forgiving his brother in Act V. The pardon is enunciated – 'You, brother mine, that entertain ambition ... I do forgive thee' (ll.75–8)[10] – and qualified at once ('unnatural though thou art'), reconsidered as more crimes are remembered, some to be held in reserve ('at this time I will tell no tales' [ll.128–9]), all but withdrawn ('most wicked sir, whom to call brother / Would even infect my mouth' [ll.130–1]), and only then confirmed through forcing Antonio to relinquish the dukedom, an act that is presented as something he does unwillingly. The point is not only that Antonio does not repent here but also that he is not allowed to repent. Even his renunciation of the crown is Prospero's act: 'I do ... require / My dukedom of thee, which perforce, I know, / Thou must restore' (ll.1131–4). In Prospero's drama, there is no room for Antonio to act of his own free will.

The crime that Prospero holds in reserve for later use against his brother is the attempted assassination of Alonso. Here is what happened: Prospero sends Ariel to put all the shipwreck victims to sleep except Antonio and Sebastian. Antonio then persuades Sebastian to murder Alonso – his brother – and thereby become king of Naples. Sebastian agrees, on the condition that Antonio kill Gonzalo. At the moment of the murders, Ariel reappears and wakes Gonzalo:

> My master through his art foresees the danger
> That you his friend are in; and sends me forth –
> For else his project dies – to keep them living.
> (II.i.293–5)

This situation has been created by Prospero, and the conspiracy is certainly part of his project – this is why Sebastian and Antonio are not put to sleep. If Antonio is not forced by Prospero to propose the murder, he is certainly acting as Prospero expects him to do and as Ariel says Prospero 'through his art foresees' that he will. What is clearly taking place is Prospero restaging his usurpation and maintaining his control over it this time. Gonzalo is waked rather than Alonso so that the old courtier can replay his role in aborting the assassination.

So at the play's end, Prospero still has usurpation and attempted murder to hold against his brother, things that still disqualify Antonio from his place in the family. Obviously there is more to Prospero's plans than reconciliation and harmony – even, I would think, in the forthcoming happy marriage of Ferdinand and Miranda. If we look at that marriage as a political act (the participants are, after all, the children of monarchs) we will observe that in order to prevent the succession of his brother, Prospero is marrying his daughter to the son of his enemy. This has the effect of excluding Antonio from any future claim on the ducal throne, but it also effectively disposes of the realm as a political entity: if Miranda is the heir to the dukedom, Milan through the marriage becomes part of the kingdom of Naples, not the other way round. Prospero recoups his throne from his brother only to deliver it over, upon his death, to the King of Naples once again. The usurping Antonio stands condemned, but the effects of the usurpation, the link with Alonso and the reduction of Milan to a Neapolitan fiefdom are, through Miranda's wedding, confirmed and legitimised. Prospero has not regained his lost dukedom; he has usurped his brother's. In this context, Prospero's puzzling assertion that 'every third thought shall be my grave' can be seen as a final assertion of authority and control: he has now arranged matters so that his death will remove Antonio's last link with the ducal power. His grave is the ultimate triumph over his brother. If we look at the marriage in this way, giving away Miranda is a means of preserving his authority, not of relinquishing it.

A BIBLIOGRAPHICAL CODA

The significant absence of crucial wives from the play is curiously emphasised by a famous textual crux. In Act IV Ferdinand, overwhelmed by the beauty of the masque being presented by Prospero, interrupts the performance to say,

> Let me live here ever.
> So rare a wondered father and a wise
> Makes this place Paradise.
> (ll.122–4)

Critics since the eighteenth century have expressed a nagging worry about Ferdinand's celebrating his betrothal by including Prospero but not Miranda in his paradise. In fact, what Ferdinand said, as Jeanne Addison Roberts demonstrated only in 1978, reads in the earliest copies of the folio, 'So rare a wondered father and a *wife*', but the crossbar of the *f* broke early in the print run, turning it to a long *s* and thereby eliminating Miranda from Ferdinand's thoughts of wonder.[11] The odd thing about this is that Rowe and Malone in their eighteenth-century editions emended *wise* to *wife* on logical grounds, the Cambridge Shakespeare of 1863 lists *wife* as a variant reading of the folio, and Furnivall's 1895 photographic facsimile was made from a copy that reads *wife*, and the reading is preserved in Furnivall's parallel text. Nevertheless, after 1895 the wife became invisible: bibliographers lost the variant, and textual critics consistently denied its existence until Roberts pointed it out. Even Charlton Hinman with his collating machines claimed that there were no variants whatever in this entire forme of the folio. And yet when Jeanne Roberts examined the Folger Library's copies of the book, including those that Hinman had collated, she found

that two of them have the reading *wife*, and two more clearly show
the crossbar of the *f* in the process of breaking. We find only what
we are looking for or are willing to see. Obviously *wife* is a reading
whose time has come.

From *Representations*, 8 (1984), 1–13.

NOTES

[Stephen Orgel's 'Prospero's Wife' is in a sense 'pre-theory', in that it draws
its central perspective from the tradition of psychoanalytical theory, and it
is unashamedly fragmentary (examining 'five related moments and issues')
rather than a discursive 'reading'. However, it has been taken as seminal by
later critics, mainly because it builds analysis upon 'the absent, the unspoken', rather than what is fully explicated in the plays. (This approach has an
important textual parallel, in seeing the text itself as unstable, unfixed, and
resisting final, 'authoritative' definition.) These absences lead us to thematic
presences such as 'privatives' like 'withdrawal, usurpation, becoming lost,
shipwreck'. Absent wives and mothers raise the issues of *lacunae* (gaps in
the text) and suppressed patterns, which in turn have become important to
poststructuralist and feminist critics alike. Prospero's magic is seen at base
as control over children, an authority and power which, like King Lear, he
ostensibly renounces while in fact preserving. After all, Prospero does not
'retire' into passivity but returns to Milan to take back his position of
power. Quotations are from *The Tempest*, ed. Frank Kermode (Arden
edition, London, 1954). Ed.]

1. In this instance, I have restored the folio punctuation of line 59.

2. Murray M. Schwartz and Coppélia Kahn (eds), *Representing
   Shakespeare* (Baltimore, 1980).

3. Bruno Bettelheim, *The New Yorker*, 1 March 1982, p. 53.

4. David Sundelson, 'So Rare a Wonder'd Father: Prospero's *Tempest*', in
   Representing Shakespeare, p. 48.

5. Coppélia Kahn makes this point, following a suggestion of Harry Berger,
   Jr, in 'The Providential Tempest and the Shakespearean Family', in
   Representing Shakespeare, p. 238. For an alternative view, see the excep-
   tionally interesting discussion by Joel Fineman, 'Fratricide and
   Cuckoldry: Shakespeare's Doubles', in *Representing Shakespeare*, p. 104.

6. The charge that he was David Rizzio's child was current in England in
   the 1580s, spread by rebellious Scottish Presbyterian ministers. James
   expressed fears that it would injure his chance of succeeding to the
   English throne, and he never felt entirely free of it.

7. C. H. McIlwain, *Political Works of James I* (Cambridge, MA, 1918), p. 24.

8. From the 1603 speech to parliament; McIlwain, *Political Works*, p. 272.

9. *Metamorphoses*, 7:197–209, apparently at least partly refracted through Golding's English version.

10. Kermode and most editors read 'entertained', but I have restored the folio reading, which seems to me unexceptionable.

11. '"Wife" or "Wise" – *The Tempest 1. 1786*', *University of Virginia Studies in Bibliography*, 31 (1978).

2

Nymphs and Reapers Heavily Vanish: the Discursive Con-texts of *The Tempest*

FRANCIS BARKER AND PETER HULME

I

No one who has witnessed the phenomenon of midsummer tourism at Stratford-upon-Avon can fail to be aware of the way in which 'Shakespeare' functions today in the construction of an English past: a past which is picturesque, familiar and untroubled. Modern scholarly editions of Shakespeare, amongst which the Arden is probably the most influential, have seemed to take their distance from such mythologising by carefully locating the plays against their historical background. Unfortunately such a move always serves, paradoxically, only to highlight in the foregrounded text preoccupations and values which turn out to be not historical at all, but eternal. History is thus recognised and abolished at one and the same time. One of the aims of this essay is to give a closer account of this mystificatory negotiation of 'history', along with an examination of the ways in which the relationship between text and historical context can be more adequately formulated. Particular reference will be made to the way in which, in recent years, traditional notions of the historical sources of the text have been challenged by newer analyses which employ such terms as 'intertextuality' and 'discourse'. To illustrate these, a brief exemplary reading will be offered of *The Tempest*. But to begin with, the new analyses themselves need setting in context.

II

The dominant approach within literary study has conceived of the text as autotelic, 'an entity which always remains the same from one moment to the next';[1] in other words a text that is fixed in history and, at the same time, curiously free of historical limitation. The text is acknowledged as having been produced at a certain moment in history; but that history itself is reduced to being no more than a background from which the single and irreducible meaning of the text is isolated. The text is designated as the legitimate object of literary criticism, *over against* its contexts, whether they be arrived at through the literary-historical account of the development of particular traditions and genres or, as more frequently happens with Shakespeare's plays, the study of 'sources'. In either case the text has been separated from a surrounding ambit of other texts over which it is given a special pre-eminence.

In recent years, however, an alternative criticism, often referred to as 'structuralist' and 'poststructuralist', has sought to displace radically the primacy of the autotelic text by arguing that a text indeed 'cannot be limited by or to ... the originating moment of its production, anchored in the intentionality of its author'.[2] For these kinds of criticism exclusive study of the moment of production is defined as narrowly 'historicist' and replaced by attention to successive *inscriptions* of a text during the course of its history.[3] And the contextual background – which previously had served merely to highlight the profile of the individual text – gives way to the notion of *intertextuality*, according to which, in keeping with the Saussurean model of language, no text is intelligible except in its differential relations with other texts.[4]

The break with the moment of textual production can easily be presented as liberatory; certainly much work of importance has stemmed from the study of inscription. It has shown for example that texts can never simply be *encountered* but are, on the contrary, repeatedly constructed under definite conditions: *The Tempest* read by Sir Walter Raleigh in 1914 as the work of England's national poet is very different from *The Tempest* constructed with full textual apparatus by an editor/critic such as Frank Kermode, and from the 'same' text inscribed institutionally in that major formation of 'English Literature' which is the school or university syllabus and its supporting practices of teaching and examination.[5]

If the study of the inscription and reinscription of texts has led to important work of historical description, it has also led to the formulation of a political strategy in respect of literary texts, expressed here by Tony Bennett when he calls for texts to be 'articulated with new texts, socially and politically mobilised in different ways within different class practices'.[6] This strategy also depends, therefore, on a form of intertextuality which identifies in all texts a potential for new linkages to be made and thus for new political meanings to be constructed. Rather than attempting to derive the text's significance from the moment of its production, this politicised intertextuality emphasises the present use to which texts can now be put. This approach undercuts itself, however, when, in the passage from historical description to contemporary rearticulation, it claims for itself a radicalism which it cannot then deliver. Despite speaking of texts as always being 'installed in a field of struggle',[7] it denies to itself the very possibility of combating the dominant orthodoxies. For if, as the logic of Bennett's argument implies, 'the text' were wholly dissolved into an indeterminate miscellany of inscriptions, then how could any confrontation between different but contemporaneous inscriptions take place: what would be the ground of such a contestation?[8] While a genuine difficulty in theorising 'the text' does exist, this should not lead inescapably to the point where the only option becomes the voluntaristic ascription to the text of meanings and articulations derived simply from one's own ideological preferences. This is a procedure only too vulnerable to pluralistic incorporation, a recipe for peaceful co-existence with the dominant readings, not for a contestation of those readings themselves. Struggle can only occur if two positions attempt to occupy the same space, to appropriate the 'same' text; 'alternative' readings condemn themselves to mere irrelevance.

Our criticism of this politicised intertextuality does not however seek to reinstate the autotelic text with its single fixed meaning. Texts are certainly not available for innocent, unhistorical readings. Any reading must be made *from* a particular position, but is not *reducible* to that position (not least because texts are not infinitely malleable or interpretable, but offer certain constraints and resistances to readings made of them). Rather, different readings struggle with each other on the site of the text, and all that can count, however provisionally, as knowledge of a text, is achieved through this discursive conflict. In other words, the onus on new readings, especially radical readings aware of their own theoretical and political positioning, should be to proceed by means of a *critique* of the dominant readings of a text.

We say critique rather than simply criticism, in reference to a powerful radical tradition which aims not merely to disagree with its rivals but to *read their readings*: that is, to identify their inadequacies and to explain why such readings come about and what ideological role they play.[9] Critique operates in a number of ways, adopting various strategies and lines of attack as it engages with the current ideological formations, but one aspect of its campaign is likely to have to remain constant. Capitalist societies have always presupposed the naturalness and universality of their own structures and modes of perception, so, at least for the foreseeable future, critiques will need to include an *historical* moment, countering capitalism's self-universalisation by reasserting the rootedness of texts in the contingency of history. It is this particular ground that what we have been referring to as alternative criticism runs the risk of surrendering unnecessarily. As we emphasised earlier, the study of successive textual inscriptions continues to be genuinely important, but it must be recognised that attention to such inscriptions is not logically dependent on the frequent presupposition that *all* accounts of the moment of production are either crudely historicist or have recourse to claims concerning authorial intentionality. A *properly* political intertextuality would attend to successive inscriptions without abandoning that no longer privileged but still crucially important *first* inscription of the text. After all, only by maintaining our right to make statements that we can call 'historical' can we avoid handing over the very notion of history to those people who are only too willing to tell us 'what really happened'.

III

In order to speak of the Shakespearean text as an historical utterance, it is necessary to read it with and within series of *con-texts*.[10] These con-texts are the precondition of the plays' historical and political signification, although literary criticism has operated systematically to close down that signification by a continual process of

occlusion. This may seem a strange thing to say about the most notoriously bloated of all critical enterprises, but in fact 'Shakespeare'
has been force-fed behind a high wall called Literature, built out of
the dismantled pieces of other seventeenth-century discourses. Two
particular examples of the occlusive process might be noted here.
First, the process of occlusion is accomplished in the production of
critical meaning, as is well illustrated by the case of Caliban. The occlusion of his political claims – one of the subjects of the present
essay – is achieved by installing him at the very centre of the play,
but only as the ground of a nature/art confrontation, itself of un-
doubted importance for the Renaissance, but here, in Kermode's
account, totally without the historical contextualisation that would
locate it among the early universalising forms of incipient bourgeois
hegemony.[11] Secondly, source criticism, which might *seem* to
militate against autotelic unity by relating the text in question to
other texts, in fact only obscures such relationships. Kermode's
paragraphs on 'The New World' embody the hesitancy with
which Shakespearean scholarship has approached the problem.
Resemblances between the *language* of the Bermuda pamphlets
and that of *The Tempest* are brought forward as evidence that
Shakespeare 'has these documents in mind' but, since this must
remain 'inference' rather than 'fact', it can only have subsidiary importance, 'of the greatest interest and usefulness', while clearly not
'fundamental to [the play's] structure of ideas'. Such 'sources' are
then reprinted in an appendix so 'the reader may judge of the verbal
parallels for himself', and the matter closed.[12]

And yet such closure proves premature since, strangely, source
criticism comes to play an interestingly crucial role in Kermode's
production of a site for *The Tempest's* meaning. In general, the full-
ness of the play's unity needs protecting from con-textual contamination, so 'sources' are kept at bay except for the odd verbal
parallel. But occasionally, and on a strictly *singular* basis, that unity
can only be protected by recourse to a notion of source as explanatory of a feature otherwise aberrant to that posited unity. One
example of this would be Prospero's well-known irascibility, pecu-
liarly at odds with Kermode's picture of a self-disciplined, reconciliatory white magician, and therefore to be 'in the last analysis,
explained by the fact that [he] descend[s] from a bad-tempered
giant-magician'.[13] Another would be Prospero's strange perturbation
which brings the celebratory masque of Act IV to such an abrupt
conclusion, in one reading (as we will demonstrate shortly) the most

important scene in the play, but here explained as 'a point at which an oddly pedantic concern for classical structure causes it to force its way through the surface of the play'.[14] In other words the play's unity is constructed only by shearing off some of its 'surface' complexities and explaining them away as irrelevant survivals or unfortunate academicisms.

Intertextuality, or con-textualisation, differs most importantly from source criticism when it establishes the necessity of reading *The Tempest* alongside congruent texts, irrespective of Shakespeare's putative knowledge of them, and when it holds that such congruency will become apparent from the constitution of discursive networks to be traced independently of authorial 'intentionality'.

IV

Essential to the historico-political critique which we are proposing here are the analytic strategies made possible by the concept of *discourse*. Intertextuality has usefully directed attention to the relationship *between* texts: discourse moves us towards a clarification of just what kinds of relationship are involved.[15]

Traditionally *The Tempest* has been related to other texts by reference to a variety of notions: *source*, as we have seen, holds that Shakespeare was influenced by his reading of the Bermuda pamphlets. But the play is also described as belonging to the *genre* of pastoral romance and is seen as occupying a particular place in the *canon* of Shakespeare's works. Intertextuality has sought to displace work done within this earlier paradigm, but has itself been unable to break out of the practice of connecting text with text, of assuming that single texts are the ultimate objects of study and the principal units of meaning.[16] Discourse, on the other hand, refers to the *field* in and through which texts are produced. As a concept wider than 'text' but narrower than language itself (Saussure's *langue*), it operates at the level of the enablement of texts. It is thus not an easy concept to grasp because discourses are never simply observable but only approachable through their effects just as, in a similar way, grammar can be said to be *at work* in particular sentences (even those that are ungrammatical), governing their construction but never fully present 'in' them. The operation of discourse is implicit in the regulation of what statements can and cannot be made and the forms that they can legitimately take. Attention to discourse therefore moves the focus from the interpretative problem of meaning to questions of instrumentality and function. Instead of *having* meaning, statements should be seen as *performative of* meaning; not as possessing some portable and 'universal' content but, rather, as instrumental in the organisation and legitimation of power-relations – which of course involves, as one of its components, control over the constitution of meaning. As the author of one of the first modern grammars said, appropriately enough in 1492, 'language is the perfect instrument of empire'.[17] Yet, unlike grammar, discourse functions effectively precisely because the question of codifying its rules and protocols can never arise: the utterances it silently governs speak what appears to be the 'natural language of the age'. Therefore, from within a given discursive formation no general rules for its operation will be drawn up except against the ideological grain; so the constitution of the discursive fields of the past will, to some degree, need comprehending through the excavatory work of historical study.

To initiate such excavation is of course to confront massive problems. According to what we have said above, each individual text, rather than a meaningful unit in itself, lies at the intersection of different discourses which are related to each other in a complex but ultimately hierarchical way. Strictly speaking, then, it would be meaningless to talk about the unity of any given text – supposedly the intrinsic quality of all 'works of art'. And yet, because literary texts *are* presented to us as characterised precisely by their unity, the text must still be taken as a point of purchase on the discursive field – but in order to demonstrate that, athwart its alleged unity, the text is in fact marked and fissured by the interplay of the discourses that constitute it.

V

The ensemble of fictional and lived practices, which for convenience we will simply refer to here as 'English colonialism', provides *The Tempest's* dominant discursive con-texts.[18] We have chosen here to concentrate specifically on the figure of usurpation as the nodal point of the play's imbrication into this discourse of colonialism. We shall look at the variety of forms under which usurpation appears in the text, and indicate briefly how it is active in organising the text's actual diversity.[19]

Of course conventional criticism has no difficulty in recognising the importance of the themes of legitimacy and usurpation for *The Tempest*. Indeed, during the storm-scene with which the play opens, the issue of legitimate authority is brought immediately to the fore. The boatswain's peremptory dismissal of the nobles to their cabins, while not, according to the custom of the sea, strictly a mutinous act, none the less represents a disturbance in the normal hierarchy of power relations. The play then proceeds to recount or display a series of actual or attempted usurpations of authority: from Antonio's successful palace revolution against his brother, Prospero, and Caliban's attempted violation of the honour of Prospero's daughter – accounts of which we hear retrospectively; to the conspiracy of Antonio and Sebastian against the life of Alonso and, finally, Caliban's insurrection, with Stephano and Trinculo, against Prospero's domination of the island. In fact it could be argued that this series *is* the play, in so far as *The Tempest* is a dramatic action at all. However, these rebellions, treacheries, mutinies and conspiracies, referred to here collectively as usurpation, are not *simply* present in the text as extractable 'Themes of the Play'.[20] Rather, they are differentially embedded there, figural traces of the text's anxiety concerning the very matters of domination and resistance.

Take for example the play's famous *protasis*, Prospero's long exposition to Miranda of the significant events that predate the play. For Prospero, the real beginning of the story is his usurpation twelve years previously by Antonio, the opening scene of a drama which Prospero intends to play out during *The Tempest* as a comedy of restoration. Prospero's exposition seems unproblematically to take its place as the indispensable prologue to an understanding of the present moment of Act I, no more than a device for conveying essential information. But to see it simply as a neutral account of the play's prehistory would be to occlude the contestation that follows insistently throughout the rest of the first act, of Prospero's version of true beginnings. In this narration the crucial early days of the relationship between the Europeans and the island's inhabitants are covered by Prospero's laconic 'Here in this island we arriv'd' (I.ii.171). And this is all we would have were it not for Ariel and Caliban. First Prospero is goaded by Ariel's demands for freedom into recounting at some length how his servitude began, when, at their first contact, Prospero freed him from the cloven pine in which he had earlier been confined by Sycorax. Caliban then offers his compelling and defiant counter to Prospero's single sentence when, in a powerful speech, he recalls the initial mutual trust which was broken by Prospero's assumption of the political control made possible by the power of his magic. Caliban, 'Which first was mine own King', now protests that 'here you sty me / In this hard rock, whiles you do keep from me / The rest o'th' island' (I.ii.344–6).

It is remarkable that these contestations of 'true beginnings' have been so commonly occluded by an uncritical willingness to identify Prospero's voice as direct and reliable authorial statement, and therefore to ignore the lengths to which the play goes to dramatise its problems with the proper beginning of its own story. Such identification hears, as it were, only Prospero's play, follows only his stage directions, not noticing that Prospero's play and *The Tempest* are not necessarily the same thing.[21]

But although different beginnings are offered by different voices in the play, Prospero has the effective power to impose his construction of events on the others. While Ariel gets a threatening but nevertheless expansive answer, Caliban provokes an entirely different reaction. Prospero's words refuse engagement with Caliban's claim to original sovereignty ('This island's mine, by Sycorax my mother, / Which thou tak'st from me', I.ii.333–4). Yet Prospero is clearly disconcerted. His sole – somewhat hysterical – response consists of an indirect denial ('Thou most lying slave', I.ii.346) and a counter accusation of attempted rape ('thou didst seek to violate / The honour of my child', I.ii.349–50), which together foreclose the exchange and serve in practice as Prospero's only justification for the arbitrary rule he exercises over the island and its inhabitants. At a stroke he erases from what we have called Prospero's play all trace of the moment of his reduction of Caliban to slavery and appropriation of his island. For, indeed, it could be argued that the series of usurpations listed earlier as constituting the dramatic action all belong to that play alone, which is systematically silent about Prospero's own act of usurpation: a silence which is curious, given his otherwise voluble preoccupation with the theme of legitimacy. But, despite his evasiveness, this moment ought to be of decisive *narrative* importance since it marks Prospero's self-installation as ruler, and his acquisition, through Caliban's enslavement, of the means of supplying the food and labour on which he and Miranda are completely dependent: 'We cannot miss him: he does make our fire, / Fetch in our wood, and serves in offices / That profit us' (I.ii.313–15). Through its very occlusion of Caliban's version of proper beginnings, Prospero's disavowal is itself performative of the discourse of colonialism, since this particular reticulation of denial of dispossession with retrospective justification for it, is the characteristic trope by which European colonial regimes articulated their authority over land to which they could have no conceivable legitimate claim.[22]

The success of this trope is, as so often in these cases, proved by its subsequent invisibility. Caliban's 'I'll show thee every fertile inch o'th' island' (II.ii.148) is for example glossed by Kermode with 'The colonists were frequently received with this kindness, though treachery might follow', as if this were simply a 'fact' whose relevance to *The Tempest* we might want to consider, without seeing that to speak of 'treachery' is already to interpret, from the position of colonising power, through a purported 'description'. A discursive analysis would indeed be alive to the use of the word 'treachery' in a colonial context in the early seventeenth century, but would be aware of how it functioned for the English to explain to themselves the *change* in native behaviour (from friendliness to hostility) that was in fact a *reaction* to their increasingly disruptive presence. That this was an explanatory trope rather than a description of behaviour is nicely caught in Gabriel Archer's slightly bemused comment: 'They are naturally given to trechery, howbeit we could not finde it in our travell up the river, but rather a most kind and loving people'.[23] Kermode's use of the word is of course by no means obviously contentious: its power to shape readings of the play stems from its continuity with the grain of unspoken colonialist assumptions.

So it is not just a matter of the occlusion of the play's initial colonial moment. Colonialist legitimation has always had then to go on to tell its own story, inevitably one of native violence: Prospero's play performs this task within *The Tempest*. The burden of Prospero's play is already deeply concerned with producing legitimacy. The purpose of Prospero's main plot is to secure recognition of his claim to the usurped duchy of Milan, a recognition sealed in the blessing given by Alonso to the prospective marriage of his own son to Prospero's daughter. As part of this, Prospero reduces Caliban to a role in the supporting sub-plot, as instigator of a mutiny that is programmed to fail, thereby forging an equivalence between Antonio's initial *putsch* and Caliban's revolt. This allows Prospero to annul the memory of his failure to prevent his expulsion from the dukedom, by repeating it as a mutiny that he will, this time, forestall. But, in addition, the playing out of the colonialist narrative is thereby completed: Caliban's attempt – tarred with the brush of Antonio's supposedly self-evident viciousness – is produced as final and irrevocable confirmation of the natural treachery of savages.

Prospero can plausibly be seen as a playwright only because of the control over the other characters given him by his magic. He can freeze Ferdinand in mid-thrust, immobilise the court party at will, and conjure a pack of hounds to chase the conspirators. Through this physical control he seeks with considerable success to manipulate the mind of Alonso. Curiously though, while the main part of Prospero's play runs according to plan, the sub-plot provides the only real moment of drama when Prospero calls a sudden halt to the celebratory masque, explaining, aside:

> I had forgot that foul conspiracy
> Of the beast Caliban and his confederates
> Against my life: the minute of their plot
> Is almost come.
>   (IV.i.139–42)

So while, on the face of it, Prospero has no difficulty in dealing with the various threats to his domination, Caliban's revolt proves uniquely disturbing to the smooth unfolding of Prospero's plot. The text is strangely emphatic about this moment of disturbance, insisting not only on Prospero's sudden vexation, but also on the 'strange hollow, and confused noise' with which the Nymphs and Reapers – two lines earlier gracefully dancing – now 'heavily vanish'; and the apprehension voiced by Ferdinand and Miranda:

> **Ferdinand**   This is strange: your father's in some passion
>   That works him strongly.
> **Miranda**   Never till this day
>   Saw I him touch'd with anger, so distemper'd.
>   (IV.i.143–5)

For the first and last time Ferdinand and Miranda speak at a distance from Prospero and from his play. Although this disturbance is immediately glossed over, the hesitation, occasioned by the sudden remembering of Caliban's conspiracy, remains available as a site of potential fracture.

The interrupted masque has certainly troubled scholarship, introducing a jarring note into the harmony of this supposedly most highly structured of Shakespeare's late plays. Kermode speaks of the 'apparently inadequate motivation' for Prospero's perturbation,[24] since there is no obvious reason why he should so excite himself over an easily controllable insurrection.

What then is the meaning of this textual excess, this disproportion between apparent cause and effect? There are several possible answers, located at different levels of analysis. The excess obviously marks the recurrent difficulty that Caliban causes Prospero – a difficulty we have been concerned to trace in some detail. So, at the level of character, a psychoanalytic reading would want to suggest that Prospero's excessive reaction represents his disquiet at the irruption into consciousness of an unconscious anxiety concerning the grounding of his legitimacy, both as producer of his play and, *a fortiori*, as governor of the island. The by now urgent need for action forces upon Prospero the hitherto repressed contradiction between his dual roles as usurped and usurper. Of course the emergency is soon contained and the colonialist narrative quickly completed. But, none the less, if only for a moment, the effort invested in holding Prospero's play together as a unity is laid bare.

So, at the formal level, Prospero's difficulties in staging his play are themselves 'staged' by the play that we are watching, this moment presenting for the first time the possibility of distinguishing between Prospero's play and *The Tempest* itself.

Perhaps it could be said that what is staged here in *The Tempest* is Prospero's anxious determination to keep the sub-plot of his play in its place. One way of distinguishing Prospero's play from *The Tempest* might be to claim that Prospero's carefully established relationship between main and sub-plot is reversed in *The Tempest*, whose *main* plot concerns Prospero's anxiety over his *sub*-plot. A formal analysis would seem to bear this out. The climax of Prospero's play is his revelation to Alonso of Miranda and Ferdinand playing chess. This is certainly a true *anagnorisis* for Alonso, but for us a merely theatrical rather than truly dramatic moment. *The Tempest's* dramatic climax, in a way its only dramatic moment at all, is, after all, this sudden and strange disturbance of Prospero.

But to speak of Prospero's anxiety being staged by *The Tempest* would be, on its own, a recuperative move, preserving the text's unity by the familiar strategy of introducing an ironic distance between author and protagonist. After all, although Prospero's anxiety over his sub-plot may point up the *crucial* nature of that 'sub' plot, a generic analysis would have no difficulty in showing that *The Tempest* is ultimately complicit with Prospero's play in treating Caliban's conspiracy in the fully comic mode. Even before it begins, Caliban's attempt to put his political claims into practice is arrested by its implication in the convention of clownish vulgarity represented by the 'low-life' characters of Stephano and Trinculo, his conspiracy framed in a grotesquerie that ends with the dubiously amusing sight of the conspirators being hunted by dogs, a fate, incidentally, not unknown to natives of the New World. The shakiness of Prospero's position is indeed staged, but in the end his version of history remains *authoritative*, the larger play acceding as it were to the containment of the conspirators in the safely comic mode, Caliban allowed only his poignant and ultimately vain protests against the venality of his co-conspirators.

That this comic closure is necessary to enable the European 're-conciliation' which follows hard on its heels – the patching up of a minor dynastic dispute within the Italian nobility – is, however, itself symptomatic of the text's own anxiety about the threat posed to its decorum by its New World materials. The lengths to which the play has to go to achieve a legitimate ending may then be read as the quelling of a fundamental disquiet concerning its own functions within the projects of colonialist discourse.

No adequate reading of the play could afford not to comprehend *both* the anxiety and the drive to closure it necessitates. Yet these aspects of the play's 'rich complexity' have been signally ignored by European and North American critics, who have tended to listen exclusively to Prospero's voice: after all, he speaks their language. It has been left to those who have suffered colonial usurpation to discover and map the traces of that complexity by reading in full measure Caliban's refractory place in both Prospero's play and *The Tempest*.[25]

VI

We have tried to show, within the limits of a brief textual analysis, how an approach via a theory of discourse can recognise *The Tempest* as, in a significant sense, a play imbricated within the discourse of colonialism; and can, at the same time, offer an explanation of features of the play either ignored or occluded by critical practices that have often been complicit, whether consciously or not, with a colonialist ideology.

Three points remain to be clarified. To identify dominant discursive networks and their mode of operation within particular texts should by no means be seen as the end of the story. A more exhaustive analysis would go on to establish the precise articulation of discourses within texts: we have argued for the discourse of colonialism as the articulatory *principle* of *The Tempest's* diversity but have touched only briefly on what other discourses are articulated and where such linkages can be seen at work in the play.

Then again, each text is more than simply an *instance* of the operation of a discursive network. We have tried to show how much of *The Tempest's* complexity comes from its *staging* of the distinctive moves and figures of colonialist discourse. Discourse is always performative, active rather than ever merely contemplative; and, of course, the mode of the theatre will also inflect it in particular ways, tending, for example, through the inevitable (because structural) absence of any direct authorial comment, to create an effect of distantiation, which exists in a complex relationship with the countervailing (and equally structural) tendency for audiences to identify with characters presented – through the language and conventions of theatre – as heroes and heroines. Much work remains to be done on the articulation between discursive performance and mode of presentation.

Finally, we have been concerned to show how *The Tempest* has been severed from its discursive con-texts through being produced by criticism as an autotelic unity, and we have tried therefore to exemplify an approach that would engage with the fully dialectical relationship between the detail of the text and the larger discursive formations. But nor can theory and criticism be exempt from such relationships. Our essay too must engage in the discursive struggle that determines the history within which the Shakespearean texts will be located and read: it matters what kind of history that is.

From *Alternative Shakespeares*, ed. John Drakakis (London, 1985), pp. 191–205.

NOTES

[Francis Barker and Peter Hulme use *The Tempest* to illustrate the terms and concepts which underpin poststructuralist criticism. New theory is crucial in allowing us to see 'that Prospero's play and *The Tempest* are not necessarily the same thing', since traditional criticism has tended to accept the ruling-class attitude of Prospero as the one that dominates and determines our responses. They see the action of the play in terms of a series of usurpations, and they raise the issue of 'anxiety' which is central to Greenblatt's essay (5). Quotations from *The Tempest*, ed. Frank Kermode (Arden edition, London, 1954). Ed.]

1. E. D. Hirsch, *Validity in Interpretation* (New Haven, CT, 1967), p. 46.

2. T. Bennett, 'Test and History' in Peter Widdowson (ed.), *Re-Reading English* (London, 1982), pp. 223–36, p. 227; drawing on the argument of Jacques Derrida, 'Signature, event context', *Glyph*, 1 (1977), 172–98.

3. For the theory behind the concept of inscription see Renée Balibar, *Les Français fictifs: le raport des styles littéraires au français national* (Paris, 1974) and 'National language, education, literature', in F. Barker et al. (eds), *The Politics of Theory* (Colchester, 1983), pp. 79–99; P. Macherey and R. Balibar, 'On literature as an ideological form: Some Marxist hypotheses', *Oxford Literary Review*, 3 (1978), 43–58; and Tony Davies, 'Education, ideology and literature', *Red Letters*, 7 (1978), 4–15. For an accessible collection of essays which put this theory to work on the corpus of English literature, see Widdowson, *Re-Reading English*.

4. Intertexuality is a term coined by Julia Kristeva in 1970, from her reading of the seminal work of Mikhail Bakhtin.

5. For Raleigh's *Tempest* see Terence Hawkes, 'Swisser-Swatter: Making a Man of English Letters', in *Alternative Shakespeares*, ed. John Drakakis (London, 1985), pp. 226–46; Kermode is editor of the Arden edition of *The Tempest* (1964); on the formation of 'English' see Davies, 'Education, ideology and literature'.

6. Bennett, 'Text and History', p. 224.

7. Ibid., p. 229.

8. Stanley Fish, *Is There a Text in this Class? The Authority of Interpretive Communities* (Cambridge, MA, 1980), p. 165, whose general argument is similar to Bennett's, admits that in the last analysis he is unable to answer the question: what are his interpretative acts interpretations *of*?

9. Marx's work was developed out of his critique of the concepts of classical political economy that had dominated economic thought in the middle of the nineteenth century. We choose here to offer a critique of Kermode's introduction to the Arden because of the *strengths* of his highly regarded and influential work.

10. Con-texts with a hyphen, to signify a break from the inequality of the usual text/context relationship. Con-texts are themselves *texts* and must be *read with*: they do not simply make up a background.

11. Kermode, Arden edition, p. lxiii.

12. Ibid., p. xxviii.

13. Ibid., p. lxiii.

14. Ibid., p. lxxv.

15. Colin MacCabe, 'On Discourse', *Economy and Society*, 8 (1979), 279–307 offers a helpful guide through some of discourse's many usages. The concept of discourse at work in the present essay draws on Michel Foucault's investigation of the discursive realm. A useful introduction to his theorisation of discourse is provided by Foucault's essays. His most extended theoretical text is *The Archaeology of Knowledge* (London, 1972). However, a less formal and in many ways more suggestive treatment of discourse is practised and, to a certain extent theorised, in his early works on 'madness' and in more recent studies of the prison and of sexuality, where discourse is linked with both the institutional locations in which it circulates and the power functions it performs. For a cognate approach to discourse see the theory of 'utterance' developed by Valentin Volosinov, *Marxism and the Philosophy of Language* (New York, 1973).

16. On the weakness of Kristeva's own work in this respect see J. Culler 'Jacques Derrida', in J. Sturrock (ed.), *Structuralism and Since* (London, 1981), pp. 105–7.

17. Antonio de Nebrija, quoted in Lewis Hanke, *Aristotle and the American Indians* (Bloomington, IN, 1959), p. 8.

18. In other words we would shift the emphasis from the futile search for the texts Shakespeare 'had in mind' to the establishment of significant patterns within the larger discursive networks of the period. The notion of 'English colonialism' can itself be focused in different ways. The widest focus would include present con-texts, the narrowest would concentrate on the con-texts associated with the initial period of English colonisation of Virginia, say 1585 to 1622. In the first instance many of the relevant texts would be found in the contemporary collections of Hakluyt (1903–5) and Purchas (1905–7). For congruent approaches see James Smith, '*The Tempest*', in *Shakespearian and Other Essays* (Cambridge, 1974), pp. 159–261; Charles Frey, '*The Tempest* and the New World', *Shakespeare Quarterly*, 30 (1979), pp. 29–41; Stephen Greenblatt, *Renaissance Self-Fashioning: From More to Shakespeare* (Chicago, 1980), ch. 4; and Peter Hulme, 'Hurricanes in the Caribbees: The constitution of the discourse of English colonialism', in Francis Barker et al. (eds), *1642; Literature and Power in the Seventeenth Century* (Colchester, 1981), pp. 55–83.

19. See Macherey, 'On literature as an ideological form'. Macherey characterises the literary text not as unified but as plural and diverse. Usurpation should then be regarded not as the centre of a unity but as the principle of a diversity.

20. Kermode's second heading (Arden edition, p. xxiv).

21. This is a weak form of the critical fallacy that, more chronically, reads Prospero as an autobiographical surrogate for Shakespeare himself.

22. This trope is studied in more detail in Peter Hulme '*Of the caniballes*': *the Discourse of European Colonialism* (forthcoming) chs 3 and 4. See also Francis Jennings, *The Invasion of America: Indians, Colonialism and the Cant of Conquest* (New York, 1976).

23. Gabriel Archer, 'The Description of the now discovered river and county of Virginia ...' (1607), in D. Quinn et al. (eds), *New American World*, vol. 5 (London, 1979).

24. Kermode, Arden edition, p. lxxv.

25. See for example George Lamming, *The Pleasures of Exile* (1960, New York, 1984). Aimé Césaire's rewriting of the play, *Une Tempête: D'Après 'la Tempête' de Shakespeare – Adaptation pour un théâtre nègre* (Paris, 1969), has Caliban as explicit hero. For an account of how Caliban remains refractory for contemporary productions of *The Tempest* see Trevor R. Griffiths, '"This Island's Mine": Caliban and Colonialism', *Yearbook of English Studies*, 13 (1983), 159–80.

3

Playhouse – Workhouse

TERENCE HAWKES

TEMPEST AND CHIPS

I am eating fish and chips in Stratford-upon-Avon. To be precise, I am doing so while leaning on a lock-gate at the point where the Stratford canal flows into the river Avon. Slightly to my left is the Royal Shakespeare Theatre where I have just attended a performance of *The Tempest*. Slightly to my right is a fish-and-chip shop.

A major concern of this essay lies in the encounter of Nature and Culture. Stratford, both a natural and cultural centre of England, seems to offer a particularly fruitful location in this respect. Here a river (Nature) joins a canal (Culture) in a setting where one kind of Englishness (the Royal Shakespeare Theatre) confronts another (a fish-and-chip shop) in the sale of quintessentially English goods. Here, certainly, one Stratford appears to engage with its opposite. My capacity to ingest both fails to allay a sense of broad and potent distinctions.

One of them, suitably transmuted, lies close to the heart of *The Tempest*, that late play traditionally supposed to have been written here in Stratford. We can begin to discern it in the opposition of Prospero to Caliban. Some of the detailed symbolic freight of that confrontation will be further unpacked at subsequent points in this essay, but we can start by sketching some of its general implications.

MASTER OF ARTS

Most critics would recognise in *The Tempest* the lineaments of the 'pastoral drama' described by Frank Kermode.[1] Focusing on the opposition of Nature and Culture, pitting their representatives, Caliban and Prospero, firmly against each other, this seems to be the play's organising principle. And in the context of contemporary Elizabethan and Jacobean concerns with the reinforcement and development of the settlements in the North American New World, the conflict takes on, as Kermode and others have argued, a 'colonial' dimension.[2]

Elizabethan expansion to the West readily prompted metaphors of the 'planting' and 'cultivation' of new growths, whether of tobacco and other crops, or of new forms of social life itself. The 'plantations' of Ulster and of Virginia and the stratagems and concepts these provoked for dealing with an indigenous population generate a discourse which propels a good deal of the imaginative writing of the time and occasionally pushes it to the limits of sense:

> *Guiana*, whose rich feet are mines of golde,
> Whose forehead knockes against the roofe of Starres,
> Stands on her tip-toes at faire *England* looking,
> Kissing her hand, bowing her mightie breast,
> And euery signe of all submission making,
> To be her sister, and the daughter both
> Of our most sacred Maide: whose barrennesse
> Is the true fruite of vertue, rhat may get,
> Beare and bring foorth anew in all perfection,
> What heretofore sauage corruption held
> In barbarous *Chaos*; and in this affaire
> Become her father, mother, and her heire.[3]

The colliding figures of fruitful kinship reeling through such verses nevertheless suggest a complex context in which the trope of Prospero as Planter, with the aboriginal Caliban as unnourishable growth or Slave seems reasonably straightforward and unexceptionable.

However, the matter has dimensions which perhaps derive from a rather more deeply rooted experience than the relatively immediate one of the colonial enterprise. Of course, the texts relating to that enterprise inhabit the same discursive field as *The Tempest*, deploy the same presuppositions, and accept the same map of the conceptual terrain. The story of the wreck and subsequent miraculous preservation of Sir Thomas Gates, Sir George Summers and the company of the *Sea Adventure* in the Bermudas in 1609 was widely known. William Strachey's *A True Reportory of the Wrack and Redemption of Sir Thomas Gates* may in any case have been seen in manuscript form by Shakespeare, and further details could easily be found in Silvester Jourdain's *A Discovery of the Barmudas, Otherwise called the Ile of Divels* (1610).

But the complex relationship between Prospero and Caliban hardly springs from these 'sources'.[4] Its basis lies in the operations of a discourse which precedes and generates all of them: one whose systematic disposition of categories developed nearer home, rooted in and geared to long-embedded political notions familiar enough to all British citizens, including those who had never travelled further west than Stratford itself. If the colonisers brought a ready-made framework of ideas with them and if, like most travellers, they never ventured beyond its horizons – indeed, imposed these on whatever novelties confronted them – then it seems reasonable to suggest that the roots of the Prospero–Caliban relationship extend beyond that of Planter to Slave to find their true nourishment in the ancient home-grown European relationships of master and servant, landlord and tenant.

Thus the tropical 'paradise' described by Gonzalo (II.i.138ff.) turns, for definition, on legal notions with whose precepts and consequences most of the audience would be familiar, since they touched their daily lives: 'contract, succession, / Bourn, bound of land, tilth'. And those issues probed at the centre of the play involve moral concepts long invested in the mundane business of the diurnal round. As a number of critics have noticed, the task of carrying logs, an appropriate and familiar emblem for the brute manual work, the 'wooden slavery' as Ferdinand punningly calls it, that was a standard feature of quotidian British life, clearly functions as a symbolic means of contrasting Ferdinand with Caliban. Thus it lends the 'captive log-bearing Prince' motif recognised by Kermode the additional dimension of more imme-diate social commentary. Ferdinand acknowledges the moral – not to say social – profit which accrues to his labour, and in con-sequence bears his burden willingly:

> I must remove
> Some thousands of these logs, and pile them up,
> Upon a sore injunction: my sweet mistress
> Weeps when she sees me work, and says, such baseness
> Had never like executor. I forget:
> But these sweet thoughts do even refresh my labours,
> Most busiest when I do it.
>
> (III.i.9–15)

Although Miranda readily offers to share his task (III.i.23–4), Ferdinand manages to reconcile himself to it in the name of love:

> for your sake
> Am I this patient log-man.
>   (III.i.66–7)

Caliban, by contrast, bears logs only unwillingly. The play clearly nominates his work as straightforward slavery from the beginning, and our initial encounter with his disembodied voice takes place in that confirming context:

> **Prospero**   ... What, ho! slave! Caliban!
>   Thou earth, thou! speak.
> **Caliban** (within)   There's wood enough within.
>   (I.ii.315–16)

Repeatedly urged to 'Fetch us in fuel; and be quick' (I.ii.368), Caliban bears his 'burthen of wood' (II.ii.s.d.) with an appropriately ill grace, reinforced by curses against his masters and his wretched fate.

In Ferdinand's case, then, work seems to be a burden which, nobly borne, offers plentiful compensation. His attitude thus accords well with a range of moral doctrines that colonisation claimed to substantiate, and confirms an overall position succinctly expressed in the disgust with which Strachey cites the reports of some of the colonists:

> An incredible example of their idlenesse, is the report of Sir Thomas Gates, who affirmeth, that after his first comming thither, he hath seene some of them eat their fish raw, rather then they would goe a stones cast to fetch wood and dresse it.
>   (cit. Kermode, p. 140)

But the moral drawn by the reports resolves into an apothegm which doubtless would have sprung no less readily to the lips of many a contemporary Elizabethan employer on his native soil: '*Dei laboribus omnia vendunt*, God sels us all things for our labour' (ibid.). Caliban's complete refusal of this principle finds an appropriately revolutionary mode of expression when he turns the log-bearing exercise neatly against Prospero, advising his fellow conspirators on the efficacy of a 'log' to 'batter his skull' (III.ii.87–8).

Clearly a major contradiction stares at us here, threatening to dislocate the bars of the discourse which cage it in the play. It centres on the familiar paradox of work. From one point of view, work traditionally represents a punishment inflicted on human beings as a penalty for Adam's sin. And the play seems to endorse this, to the extent that Ferdinand's patience with respect to his work will be rewarded by the ultimate removal of its burden. Indeed, he is a clear candidate, on the island, for membership of that perfect world outlined by Gonzalo, in which work would be proscribed altogether:

> All things in common Nature should produce
> Without sweat or endeavour
> (II.i.155–6)

However, Antonio's comment that the result of such idleness would be a society of 'whores and knaves' (l.162) rests on a wholly opposed view: that work is good: it restrains carnal appetite and channels human energy to useful, moral and socially supportive ends. A related paradox obviously operates in respect of work's opposite. The absence of work, conceived as leisure or play, can only rank as good. But the same condition can also result from indolence, and that makes it the breeding ground of turpitude. If Gonzalo's vision of perfection attempts to straddle the contradiction –

> no kind of traffic
> Would I admit ...
> No occupation; all men idle, all;
> And women too, but innocent and pure
> (II.i.144–51)

– its unavoidable chasms yawn in the punctuating, deflating commentary supplied by Sebastian and Antonio, and they gape wider and wider in the opposition drawn between the attitude to work of Ferdinand and Caliban.

The play clearly uses that opposition as the focus through which it presents the relationship of each to Prospero. And this relationship involves power. In effect, Prospero deploys manual work as the negotiable instrument by whose means his power can be ratified and reinforced. Ferdinand's acceptance of work's moral, restraining function and the commitment to harmonious social order which that signifies is both rewarded and symbolised by his winning of Miranda's hand. But Caliban's rejection of work and thus of the subservience to which the relationship with Prospero condemns him smoulders throughout as a disturbing threat until it irrupts into actuality at a crucial moment in the play.

In effect, his master-murdering projects draw him into the referential field of a specific Elizabethan and Jacobean bugbear, the 'masterless man' who haunted the margins of that society and (supposedly) the suburbs of its cities. Ungoverned, unrestrained, challenging from the periphery the central ligature on which social order rested, such a figure offered fertile ground for the seeds of moral panic. The very label 'masterless', clearly signalling a refusal of a power-relationship based on servitude and work, served to define and intensify the role of masters and even to establish a sense of corporate identity among them.[5]

The play carefully sets Caliban in, or places him against a landscape whose pastoral mode conflicts with and offers to comment on his own unmitigated and potentially unmastered savagery. The graceful dancing of idealised Reapers, the 'sunburn'd sicklemen' with their 'rye-straw hats' and their 'country footing' conjured up by the goddesses Juno, Ceres and Iris, takes place in a kind of idealised Warwickshire landscape from which the overt signs of manual work have been decorously drained:

> thy rich leas
> Of wheat, rye, barley, vetches, oats and pease;
> Thy turfy mountains, where live nibbling sheep,
> And flat meads thatch'd with stover, them to keep;
> Thy banks with pioned and twilled brims,
> Which spongy April at thy hest betrims
> (IV.i.60–5)

Nobody seems to toil in this agrarian paradise of bursting plenitude:

> Earth's increase, foison plenty,
> Barns and garners never empty;
> Vines with clust'ring bunches growing;
> Plants with goodly burthen bowing
> (IV.i.110–13)

And yet, clearly, this pastoral pageant (produced and directed by Prospero) serves to support an established and work-dominated social order, to which it might be said to bring spectacular reinforcement. As Louis Adrian Montrose points out, the pastoral mode in the Elizabethan and Jacobean period had a central political function in its 'symbolic mediation of social relationships', relationships which were 'intrinsically relationships of power'.[6] It is appropriate, then, that Prospero the master, the power-broker, is also here the play-maker, the pastoral-monger. If playing, and the use of drama and spectacle, performed a sustaining ideological role in this society, it clearly also sustained the currency of work in which the society dealt. By means of such 'playing', for instance involving the spectacular trappings of the legal system and its recourse to ostentatious, publicly displayed punishment, masters established a work-enforcing magistracy over their servants. In this sense, play meant work: or rather, play enabled work to mean – to signify the extent and purpose of its economic, political and social office.

When thoughts of the revolution planned by 'the beast Caliban' begin to impinge upon Prospero's pastoral play-world, its 'majestic vision', as Ferdinand calls it, disintegrates, the revels end, their fabric dissolves, and nymphs, reapers and sicklemen vanish 'heavily'. As if in sympathy with that disruption we also hear what the stage direction terms 'a strange, hollow and confused noise'. To twentieth-century ears, it might for all the world be a shop steward's whistle or a police siren.

PURSUED BY A BEARE

It is a noise which draws us irresistibly to the Midlands. Indeed, in so far as *The Tempest* has been thought to have been written in Shakespeare's retirement in Stratford, with the Bard himself cast as the retiring magus, those 'turfy mountains where live nibbling sheep' have been assigned a local habitation, with their hint of a characteristically English pastoral scene, fondly drawn from the memory and experience of the Warwickshire playwright.

And yet if we follow that process through, forgetting for the moment the New World exotica, something rather disturbing begins to happen to the sheep. They undergo a bizarre transformation, even a reversal, of their traditional pastoral role.

Enclosure was in the air. This reorganisation of methods of working the land helped reshape the contours of the world in which Shakespeare grew up and lived, and on a national scale constituted part of a drive towards what we might now call cost-effectiveness. Essentially, it involved the amalgamation of the ancient medieval strips of land, farmed by individual tenants, into much larger units farmed more profitably by fewer people. To 'enclose' land was to consolidate its resources in the name of efficiency. Frequently the aim of the landowner was to produce by this method larger units of pasture-land for the grazing of sheep. And with a smaller number of shepherds tending the flock, the profits from the sale of wool would be correspondingly greater.[7] Enclosure also buttressed the master–servant relationship because it helped to flush out the 'multiplicity of beggars' and other masterless men known to congregate on unenclosed 'common' land. In 1610 James I encouraged the House of Commons to adopt a programme of enclosure that would rid such land of the numerous cottages that acted as 'nurseries and receptacles of thieves, rogues and beggars'. Enclosure could thus be regarded, Christopher Hill reports, 'as a national duty, a kindness in disguise to the idle poor'.[8]

Unfortunately, enclosure also required the dispossession of a large number of small tenant farmers who accordingly became, as we might say, redundant. Effectively, then, the investment in sheep turned out to be a major factor in the growth of a particular phenomenon: one that we have had to recognise as a continuing feature of the modern world heralded by the enclosure movement. Christopher Hill points out that a major consequence of that movement was that it forced its victims into 'sole dependence on wage labour'.[9] Wage labour involves a concept of work as a quantifiable activity, engaging specific services for a specific period and for a specific purpose. For some the justification of enclosure lay in its power to coerce its victims, however unwilling, into an acceptance of that model. As Adam Moore writes in 1653, enclosure 'will give the poor an interest in toiling, whom terror never yet could enure to travail'.[10] And Hill indicates that by 1663 enclosure was in some quarters pronounced successful on just those grounds: 'people were added to the manufacturing population who previously did not increase the store of the nation but wasted it'.[11]

If we call that notion of work *employment*, we can see it as an outgrowth of a number of sixteenth- and seventeenth-century developments in which enclosure was prominent, and we can also recognise it as an innovation to be set against an older concept of work involving an entire way of life which does not distinguish 'toil' as a quantifiable entity from a broad range of other activities. And in its shadow we can see the outline of a concomitant innovation with whose later complexities we are wholly familiar: *unemployment*. To create the one is to create the other.

Of course, this immediately makes problematical a set of inherited polarities nominating work as good, idleness as bad, since it transfers the principle of enforcement from the one to the other. The prospect of an enforced, involuntary and unwilling idleness clearly eats away at and contradicts the moral imperatives invested in Prospero's and Ferdinand's notion of work.

In short, and despite the prevailing pastoral mode, we might begin to wonder just what those nibbling sheep in *The Tempest* were effectively nibbling at. For to Sir Thomas More even in the previous century they had conjured up a vision precisely the opposite of pastoral in mode: a nightmarish spectacle in which, where once men devoured sheep, now sheep devoured men.

If it seems fanciful to propose that *The Tempest* shared the conceptual horizons or the discursive 'field' of the enclosure movement, it may be helpful to recall one aspect of its author's contemporary context. Like Prospero, he had recently become a landlord.

On 24 July 1605 Shakespeare invested £440 in a half-interest in the tithes deriving from the hamlets of Old Stratford, Bishopton and Welcombe. In September 1614 the landowners Arthur Mainwaring and William Replingham proposed the enclosure of an area of land in close proximity to Stratford, specifically at Welcombe. Shakespeare and other tithe-owners, including Thomas Greene the town clerk of Stratford, were offered assurances that any loss of income to them resulting from the enclosure would be recompensed by the landowners. In return, they were asked not to oppose the move, and possibly to give it their support. For its part, the Stratford corporation vehemently opposed the enclosure, expressing considerable concern about the hardship this would inflict on the tenants and their dependants. They required their town clerk, Greene, to represent these views both to the landowners and to Shakespeare, in an effort to dissuade the former and to persuade the latter to throw his influence (and perhaps artistic fame) behind them. Greene visited Shakespeare and his son-in-law, Dr John Hall, in London, and records their efforts to calm him and the corporation by assurances that the landowners 'meane in Aprill to servey the Land & then to gyve satisfaccion & not before & he & Mr Hall say they think there will be nothyng done at all'. Later Greene reports an unsuccessful attempt to confront the landowners at Shakespeare's house in Stratford, and speaks of letters written to them and to Shakespeare which describe the 'Inconvenyences which wold grow by the Inclosure'.

The affair escalated when William Combe, another wealthy local landowner, joined in the movement to enclose, and arranged for the digging of a ditch on his land as an initial stage in marking the enclosure. Corporation officials tried to prevent this, and violence ensued. Combe persisted and something of a local riot followed. The ghost of Caliban confronted the spirit of Prospero as women and children from Stratford and Bishopton marched out and filled in the ditch as a demonstration of their views. There was further violence, and feelings ran high. Shakespeare seems to have made no move to support the corporation and his involvement in the affair reaches an appropriate climax in a brief but deeply mysterious text. This is an entry in Thomas Greene's diary which records: 'Sept. W. Shakspeares tellyng J. Greene that J was not able to [word deleted] beare the encloseinge of Welcombe'.

Plurality invests all texts of course, but none more so than this. Its very subject guarantees it a talismanic, even votive status in our culture which offers to propel the words beyond the mere page. They seem to present, after all, a record of oral utterance, of actual speech on the Bard's part which, at this date, might almost lay claim to the aura of last words, significant beyond the context of their saying.

Certainly the diary itself projects the entry into a peculiar timeless prominence, since it was clearly made outside the usual temporal sequence characteristic of diaries. The manuscript shows it to be a later insertion, a 'retrospective memorandum' as its editor calls it, of an event whose significance is thereby greatly increased.[12] 'J. Greene' probably refers to John Greene, the brother of the diarist. But the second 'J' who was 'not able to beare the encloseinge of Welcombe' presents an unresolvable ambiguity, a complex *aporia* of broad implication. For the peculiarities of Thomas Greene's handwriting permit the sign here lamely recorded as 'J' to function as 'J' or 'I' or even 'he'. Thus an entire spectrum of potential meaning offers itself since the reference could be to any of the three persons involved. So the entry can indicate that 'J' (i.e. John Greene) was unable to bear the enclosing of Welcombe, or that 'I' (i.e. Thomas Greene) was unable to bear it or, more poignantly, that 'he' (i.e. Shakespeare) was in that situation.

A further complexity resides in the word 'beare'. A contemporary range of potential meaning for the word extends from our modern sense of 'endure', through 'justify' and 'support', to the rather more problematical, even opposite sense of 'promote' or 'carry through' or even 'bear the cost'. The fact that Greene evidently deleted what looks like the beginning of a different word before 'beare' indicates that it may have given him pause too.

Scholars will of course habitually select specific readings of texts and defend them, to the point of rejecting or denying the fruitfulness which this sort of undecidability brings. My argument nevertheless suggests that the ambiguities complicating the entry in Greene's diary serve to fissure that text well beyond the level of its surface, and help to establish that, like all texts, it has no claim to be autotelic, prescribing its own boundaries, determining the limits of its own meaning. Its own historical 'moment' cannot confine it (indeed, by the standards of the diary genre its subsequent insertion marks it as 'out of' sequential time), nor is its range of signification determined by its ostensible concern with a particular matter of real estate. The issue of Elizabethan land enclosure generated questions which potentially obtruded into the discourse of morality, politics and economics both at that time and subsequently. The text of Greene's diary concerning the enclosure of Welcombe also enters and operates within those fields: it links up with a 'network' of discourses running in and out of a variety of other texts as part of a process of *intertextuality* which enables all texts to signify not discretely, by themselves, but structurally, by means of their relationship to each other.[13]

This principle suggests that the magisterial figure of the landlord who confidently parades and enforces established notions of work and idleness in *The Tempest* must be set against – and be made far more complex by – the rather more querulous figure (whoever 'J' is) glimpsed at Shakespeare's elbow in Greene's diary. And the 'brutishness' which colours Caliban's militancy in that play must be perceived through – and also be made more complex by – the sense the same text gives of the compulsions propelling the wretched women and children of Stratford and Bishopton, as they marched on Welcombe.

For the burden of unemployment, our latter-day experience should tell us, is as hard to bear as the burden of work. The range of meaning open to the word 'beare' in Shakespeare's day extends disconcertingly from Prospero's confident promotion of Caliban's dispossession on the one hand (he can 'support', 'justify', 'carry it through') to the evident waning of confidence and resolution experienced by some of its proponents unable to cope with the opposition of the citizens of Stratford to the enclosure of Welcombe. It would be misleading and even falsely reassuring to try to resolve the ambiguities of any of the texts which come to us from the years between 1610 and 1614 when, living in Stratford, writing *The Tempest*, Shakespeare was also involved in a developing relationship with his fellow citizens for which the available discourses offered a specific and contradictory set of positions and oppositions. But we can try to recognise what those ambiguities and contradictions involved and the discursive process of which they formed part. As with Prospero, the situation yields a play-maker who is also a power-broker in a setting in which playing reinforces a master–servant relationship based on the social currency of a particular concept of work. Play thus means work, or enables work to mean.

That the creator of Prospero and Caliban should find this contradiction unbearable is not beyond belief. Ideology works to efface contradiction, and the effect of that is to make any sustained contemplation of its implications both alienating and insupportable. But in any case the extent and degree of Shakespeare's purely personal involvement is not in question here. It is the textual and contextual ambiguities and contradictions in and around *The Tempest* that speak of it as a battleground in a contest whose contours prove instructive when viewed from our own arena. And if Shakespeare or his contemporaries found the contradictions of enclosure difficult to bear, we might reflect on our own situation in respect of a cognate economic climate and its fruit.

CAL

If the 'beare' pursues us, the sheep do not. One of the ironies of Stratford's development lies in the fact that the growth of the fame and influence of its playwright son eventually brought that particular wheel full circle. E. K. Chambers records the sixteenth- and seventeenth-century use of the common pasture at the centre of the town for the purpose of grazing sheep.[14] The area was known as Bank Croft. The modern visitor, stepping on to what is now called Bancroft Gardens, encounters in place of the sheep the majestic pile of the Royal Shakespeare Theatre. It is attended by quite a different flock. First people devoured sheep, then sheep devoured people and finally, in Stratford it appears, Shakespeare has devoured everything.

Whether the women and children who stormed the fields at Welcombe would have approved of the development is another matter. Would they even, we can wonder, recognise the landscape they lived in and fought over, once it had been Shakespearianised in our century's characteristic mode?

> About a mile out of the town at Longbridge the road bifurcates, the way to the left going through Barford and Wellesbourne, where there is a turn to Charlecote, that to the right going up Sherborne Hill, past Coplow Hill, leaving Snitterfield on the right, and then descending through park-like lands, past the mansion of Welcombe, backed by low hills, till it skirts the level meadows through which the Avon flows, and so enters the town of Stratford-upon-Avon.
>
> The little town of Stratford-upon-Avon, built on the river banks, and surrounded on all sides by meadows and green fields, like a coral island set in an emerald sea, is one of the pleasantest places of the earth.
>
> (*Picturesque Warwickshire*, 1906, pp. 68–9)

That can be called enclosure with a vengeance. The ruthless amalgamation, consolidation and reduction of a complex topography by means of a teleological bulldozer forces it to become the ground of a massive industry.

The ideological mode of the Shakespeare industry can be said to be centripetal, integrating. In the middle, geographically and metaphorically, of a potentially tempestuous and certainly volatile industrialised society, not thirty miles from concrete conurbations the size and nature of Birmingham and Coventry, the guidebook casts us upon an enchanted coral island, set in an emerald sea. Organic in its social structure – the clientele who attend the 'bijou theatre beside the Avon' balanced by the crowds who throng the annual fair where 'a very different scene is enacted' (p. 72) – the island is full of noises, resounding to the

> cries of the stall-keepers and screams of laughter from youths and girls bent on enjoyment. ... In every street oxen and pigs are being roasted whole, and the air is filled with the savour of dainties dear to rustic appetites.
>
> (ibid., p. 73)

And as the pageant develops, a Prospero-like voice unfolds the full binding and knitting-together purpose of the revels over which, magus-like, it appears to preside.

The pious enthusiasm which of old led men and women to visit the shrines of saints and martyrs in these days has another outlet. ... The cottage in Henley Street, now guarded with care as great as that once extended to the sacred flame in the temple of Vesta, the chaste goddess of the hearth, is the great meeting-place for all familiar with the English tongue, exactly as in Roman days Vesta's temple was the sanctuary which united the citizens into one large family. The simile may be carried even further. In those ancient times the hearth in every home was regarded as a symbol of the chaste goddess; we feel sure that no English home is worthy of the name where a copy of Shakespeare's Works cannot be found. To us these mighty poems represent the embodiment of our national spirit. They show us the path of virtue, and how evil-doing carries with it its Nemesis: they teach us patriotism, the love of our fellow-men, and our love of Nature.

(ibid., pp. 73–4)

Fortunately, the latter-day Calibans whose 'rustic appetites' required them to be instructed in the path of virtue were not without a voice. We even have a kind of access now to a number of those English homes, located in Stratford at precisely this time, where aspects of the national spirit were indeed embodied. One of them, situated not a hundred yards from what was then called the Shakespeare Memorial Theatre, was the home of a formidable woman called Caroline Cook. A twentieth-century Prospero might not unreasonably quail at the thought of teaching her about the Nemesis that dogged her so-called evil doings. And we can be fairly sure that no copy of Shakespeare's works was to be found in her cottage at the corner of Sheep Street and Waterside. She was known, after all, as 'Cal'.

In fact, Cal Cook's home is redolent less of a vague, rusticised 'national spirit' than of something that Ronald Blythe has termed 'the air of a cheerful, dreadful England which would do for you if it could'. Her use of the 'English tongue' in response to those pressures has inevitable recourse to the same linguistic structures as that of Caliban, whose only 'profit' from learning it was that he learned 'how to curse' (I.ii.366). As her protégé George Hewins tells us, the magistrates before whom Cal was hauled on a charge of using 'profane and obscene language' immediately recognised its brutish origins: 'We think it is the most 'orrible, beastly an' brutal language as can be used by one human bein' to another.' Refusing to pay her fine on this occasion, she served a spell in Warwick gaol.[15]

And yet nobody reading Hewins's penetrative story in *The Dillen* can be repelled by these descendants of the women and children who marched out to halt the Welcombe enclosures of three hundred years earlier. And no one can fail to respond to their situation and what it represents. Shakespeare, Combe and their fellow enclosers may have failed to achieve their ends in the past, but success of a much more substantial nature awaited them in the future. By the early twentieth century, embodied in his Memorial Theatre, Shakespeare was a major Stratford landlord. In ideological terms he was a major British one: fount of the national culture, spring of the national spirit, *fons et origo* of patriotism, love of fellow men, love of nature, and most other precepts of a world view which systematically made Prosperos of the few and Calibans of the many.

In Stratford itself the irony naturally had a fine edge. For the bulk of its citizens, as *The Dillen* makes clear, the dominating features of life seemed to have nothing at all to do with the Bard, and centred on the difficulties of getting adequate food, shelter and money. The central features of life for these citizens were the police and the workhouse. Fear of the latter went deeper than anything represented by the former.

In due course, we learn how Cal's family acquired a new landlord. His name, intriguingly, seemed also to rise from within a literary discourse. Indeed, it had a fine Dickensian ring: Salt Brassington. And appropriately enough, in addition to being a landlord, he also fancied himself as an author. The words quoted above which describe Stratford and the rustic lineaments of our national spirit were in fact written by Salt Brassington and are taken from his book *Picturesque Warwickshire*, one of a number of works in which he introduced the splendours of his native heath to a wider world. It is worth remembering that the mellifluous, expansive phrases which list the beauties of the borough and the duties which they involve –

> unless some measures are taken to preserve the ancient character of the buildings, Stratford will lose the quaint old-world appearance so dear to artists and antiquaries, so highly appreciated by American and Colonial visitors. ... To me it seems to be a sacred duty to preserve the ancient characteristics of Stratford[16]

– are those of a landlord. And it is no less salutary to reflect that the man who speaks, Prospero-like, in favour of the redemptive nature of work and in praise of the 'picturesque' features of the Stratford almshouses –

> Here twelve poor men and twelve poor women spend the last years of
> their lives, if not in luxury, at least in comfort. Long may such institu-
> tions flourish and increase, that those who have worked hard in their
> younger days may entertain the lag end of their lives with quiet hours.[17]

– brought eviction and the dreaded workhouse closer to his own
tenants by a ruthless programme of raising the rent. As the final
irony it is only necessary to add that Salt Brassington was an official
of the Shakespeare Memorial Theatre and acted as its Librarian.

Once again, power seems to lie with the makers of plays: those
who control the dramatic symbolisation of social relationships also
control a relationship based on work. George Hewins's account
leaves us in no doubt that the issue is of that order, with its stress on
work's structured, penalising absence:

> That winter and the next was terrible hard, terrible. The men had no
> work, no dole. The women couldn't go mangeling, they couldn't pull
> the mangels up, they was froze in the ground. They got chilblains on
> their hands; those as went washing or charring like Widow Bayliss
> came home crying where the soda had got in the cracks. Old folks
> died of the cold. The young uns like us with families growing had to
> scratch their heads to know how they was going to live.

But Shakespeare's librarian (the image of Prospero intensifies)
remains unmoved:

> To start with, our rent was three shillings and threepence. We'd got a
> new landlord – Salt Brassington, he was Librarian at the Theatre – and
> he put it up from half-a-crown a week to *three-and-three*! If you didn't
> pay the rent you was chucked out. Folks as couldn't pay – if they was
> old or there was illness in the family – they ended up in the workhouse.
> Old Bill Hinton went in – Brassington upped his rent from three bob to
> five-and-six! – and the Rowe family off the street. They couldn't pay. It
> was a sad sight to see them go. The landlord sold their stuff – put the
> bailiffs in to get the money for the rent. Cal had two mats off them.
> (*The Dillen*, pp. 71–2)

If we set Hewins's vivid, rebarbative account of life in Stratford
against the measured prose of Salt Brassington, and thus set a
'native' guide to the borough against an official 'planter's' version,
the social map it draws presents an alternative set of dimensions.
They can be discerned right from the beginning, in Hewins's account
of the hearing held to establish who his real father might be (he was
born illegitimate). The Mayor of Stratford, Charles Edward Flower

no less, presided as magistrate, and gave judgement in the case with
a dispatch not unconnected with another birth in which neither
paternity nor legitimacy were in dispute:

> He was busy laying plans for the opening of the new Theatre, just a
> few days hence, on Shakespeare's birthday. He'd given the land for it,
> and a lot o' money asides, and it was going to be a really posh occa-
> sion. All the toffs would be there – nobility! Stratford was going to
> get *tone*. ... 'The defendant can pay three bob a week for the babby'
> he said, 'and all the costs!'.
>
> (ibid., p. 7)

Whether the mayor realised it or not, the two 'babbies' over whose
birth fate had given him jurisdiction were to prove emblems of a
new polarity: one in which Flower's role as a magistrate merged
fittingly with his role as promoter of drama. For where the world of
the magistracy would focus on the Playhouse, that of their servants
would focus on the Workhouse. And in truth much of the actual
'tone' of Stratford seemed to derive from that structural opposition.
   We follow the fate of the Rowe family:

> I was doing a job at the workhouse, slating the roof. It was a bitter
> cold morning when we started, frost was in the air and I reckoned it
> could be my last chance o' work for a while. The door opens and the
> slummocky roadster woman they'd got for a nurse brings the babbies
> out, one by one. They'd messed themselves. She peels their clothes
> back and swills them under the pump like so many winter savoys.
> November and ice-cold water! They screamed! Those screams echoed
> round that square yard, hit the high brick walls o' the workhouse –
> and the roof, where I was.
>   The older kiddies starts to congregate. Who should I see but Hilda
> Rowe and Violet. They'd had their hair chopped off, weared long
> holland pinnas with big red letters: STRATFORD-ON-AVON
> WORKHOUSE. They did some sort o' drill, then they was marched
> in a straight line to the National School across the road. The babbies'
> screams and those red letters haunted me all day. If I weren't hearing
> the one I was seeing the other. When I got home I told the missus but
> she said: 'It's to *distinguish* em.'
>
> (ibid., p. 72)

The story of the hapless Rowes, evicted because of their inability to
pay Salt Brassington's rent, hints at a symbiotic relationship between
Playhouse and Workhouse. And any attempt to 'distinguish' the one
institution, as the big red letters try to do, fails to suppress the hint

that perhaps it represents the price paid for the other institution, with its eye firmly on 'distinction' of another sort. That the play-house, and those rustic English cottages in which copies of Shakespeare's mighty poems embody the national spirit, could only be sustained by harsh rent increases and the looming workhouse suggests a contradiction that the best might find difficult to bear. Once again, play seems to mean work. The ironies locked into that situation and their precise location in Salt Brassington's dual in-volvement should not be lost on us. They were certainly not lost on George Hewins. They were part of the rent he paid:

> Well, we was behind with it, but not badly.
> 'I'll make it up,' I said, 'Didn't you tell er? When I gets work.'
> She plonked herself down on the chair. She was near her time.
> 'Er says e wants to see you now,' she said. 'I told er to bugger off. I knows it bain't er fault – but it made me feel better!'
> We looked at each other and laughed, cos there seemed nothing else to do.
> 'I'll go an see Cal.'
> 'No!' said the missus. She and Cal didn't get on. 'There must be summat else. I could ask Kate.' Kate Tappin was her elder sister. They was well off, but they'd got kiddies of their own.
> 'I can see Tommy forkin out for our rent!'
> I had an idea, so I said: 'If that's what e wants – I'll go and see ole Brassington!' I went to the Theatre and there was Salt Brassington sat at a desk with a pen in his hand. He didn't look up.
> 'Yes?'
> I held my tongue – and my temper. It was an effort, I can tell you. 'There ain't no work at present – you can see for yourself – it's snowed up.' Still he didn't meet my eye.
> 'I'm a bricklayer by trade – but I can whitewash, and do odd jobs, plumbin an gas, set my hand to *any*thin,' (*to pay the rent*, I thought) 'and I'm good wi a spade. I knows I didn't pay last week ...'
> 'No,' he said.
> '... But I could make it up. I could work for you! I'd be cheap! Handy for you!'
> That did it! Salt Brassington looked at me: 'Fit man, are you?' He looked long and hard at me, took in every detail. 'Alright!' he said. 'You can clean my windows – you knows where I live, up Rowley Crescent – paint my house for me inside and out. I want some frames for my plants and a gate makin so's to cut off a corner and when spring comes you can mow my lawn –'
> He smiled: 'I'm writin a book,' he said, 'on the cottages of England.'
>
> (ibid., pp. 76–7)

THE TALE OF TWO LANDLORDS

No Prospero ever made the point more clearly to his log-bearing Caliban. And while it may be inherently unfair to compare any man with the Bard, it seems not unreasonable to set these two Stratford landlords side by side for a moment. When we do so, what becomes immediately, astonishingly clear is that William Shakespeare and William Salt Brassington share a common role. They are tellers of tales. More, the tales that they tell in Stratford, Shakespeare's *The Tempest*, Brassington's book *Picturesque Warwickshire* and other works, are not at all dissimilar, for a common discourse inhabits and governs both. Both speak of nature and of culture. Both examine closely knit cultural groups. Both can be read as indicating a clear preference for a particular social relationship in that group, a magistracy under whose terms the roles of master and servant, landlord and tenant are willingly undertaken and dutifully sustained as in a play. Both depict a sympathetic landscape on a magical island as an appropriate context for this play. Both see the play, and its container the playhouse, as the magisterial bearer of culture to an otherwise unredeemed nature. Both advocate a deferential relationship as the basis of that culture, one cemented by a common commitment to manual work as the outward and manifest sign of subservience. Prospero's relation to Caliban –

> We cannot miss him: he does make our fire,
> Fetch in our wood, and serves in offices
> That profit us.
>
> (I.ii.313–15)

– makes clear a discursive and so political principle in which, across the centuries, George Hewins's children find themselves swiftly schooled:

> They was too famished to learn much. After school, to make a few pence, they got wood from the timber yard and went round Stratford selling sticks, to anybody who wanted firewood.
>
> (*The Dillen*, p. 120)

It follows that to challenge that principle is to find oneself excluded from the social realm constructed by the 'play', from the 'house' of the society in which it is enacted, and even from the almshouse and the 'quiet hours' it promises. It is, as the Rowe family, as Hewins's mother, and as Cal herself finally discovered, to enter a house of quite a different kind.

Of course, the actualities of material existence have a complexity that no fiction can match. The women and children who tried to fill in the encloser's ditch at Welcombe can hardly be embodied in a Caliban. Nor can the grateful accepting souls who inhabit the almshouses of which Salt Brassington so fondly writes reflect the ribald sardonic tenantry to be found in Cal Cook and her brood at the corner of Waterside and Sheep Street. Neither could form part of any tale of picturesque Warwickshire.

But that is why such tales exist. Human beings cannot bear very much reality. The attraction of tales lies in their capacity to present a reality that human beings *can* bear: to paper over the cracks, resolve, explain and make coherent the contradictions. It is what tales are for.

And so the argument is not that Shakespeare was in any way simply dramatising his personal experience: the fact that the events at Welcombe occurred a good five years after the writing of *The Tempest* tends to dispose of that. Instead, the causal sequence might be emphatically reversed, particularly if we think of 'personal' experience as necessarily embedded in and moulded and transmitted by the shaping forces of literary or cultural discourse. That is what enables it to be experienced. It is not that the enclosure at Welcombe underlies *The Tempest*. It is that the discursive categories and stratagems which *The Tempest* inherited and developed perhaps underlie the enclosure at Welcombe. Thus the question to be asked is not the rather naïve one posed by Edward Bond's play *Bingo*: how could the man who wrote the great tragedies behave as he did in the face of suffering humanity? The more probing enquiry asks how could he not?

In the case of Salt Brassington, similar conclusions are appropriate. It is the discourse of 'country cottages' which enables, justifies even, the actions of the rack-rent landlord, as the interchange with Hewins quoted above makes clear. The work Hewins is charged to do as a way of paying off his obligations supports the writing of the book on country cottages, and is responsive to that book's demands: Brassington's performance as landlord reproduces the presuppositions of the guidebook discourse and is shaped by its categories and its teleological imperatives.

If the spectacle is one in which both Stratford landlords effectively operate within and by means of a pre-established framework, then a final irony inheres in our own shorthand account of the mode of that discourse as 'Shakespearian'. For while this places Brassington in a well-established tradition of latter-day 'users' of the Bard, it also suggests that the first user of that discourse, its first prisoner, was Shakespeare himself.

That the Prospero–Caliban relationship should offer itself across the years as a model for subsequent social and political alignments is not surprising: it confirms the potency of the figure. Trevor R. Griffiths reports that the first 'overtly republican' Caliban appears in the production of William and Robert Brough's *The Enchanted Isle* in 1848. Uttering anti-slavery slogans, this monster entered to the strains of the *Marseillaise* 'with a Cap of Liberty on his head' and 'a red flag in one hand'. His ultimate surrender to Prospero acknowledges through its absurdities the serious political issues at stake in that year:

> Governor, we surrender at discretion,
> And to your government send in adhesion.
> We own that this a just and fair defeat is
> So take these chains off and let's sign some treaties.

The American civil war generated a Caliban in a *Punch* cartoon of 1863 who in the guise of 'Sambo' offered a 'nigger translation' of *The Tempest* tailored to fit that conflict, and throughout the later nineteenth century numbers of theatrical productions featured a Darwinian 'missing link' Caliban who was also the 'undeveloped' native in need of control by the civilising colonialist intellect.[18]

It will be clear that I take Brassington, seen in the round both as landlord and as custodian of the archives of the Shakespeare Memorial Theatre, as a symbol for a larger enterprise: one which involves our society's recuperation and sentimentalisation of a moment in its own history of four hundred or so years ago. That moment is sensed as crucial, and it will be the purpose of the subsequent essays in this book to examine some of the ways in which the twentieth century puts it to use. In so far as both in himself and in his actions Brassington embodied polarities which our century has seemed unquestioningly to accept – on the one hand a notion of re-demptive Culture, on the other a notion of brutish Nature, Playhouse and Workhouse – he remains a remarkable and richly significant figure, fit to be juxtaposed with his fellow citizen under the aegis of the giant modern industry which both ultimately served.

The ironies generated by that industry lie all about us and perhaps we hardly need the nudging of which Hewins proves himself slyly capable. Yet the spectacle of his progress, by now severely wounded in the Great War, without work of course and reduced to begging from door to door in Stratford, has its telling moments:

> 'Wait there' said one bloke. I thought I was in luck. He gave me a book: *The Complete Works of William Shakespeare*. A *book*! Somebody had writ inside: 'It is hoped that this will always keep you in mind of the true greatness and glory of the cause for which you have fought and suffered.'
>
> (*The Dillen*, p. 159)

To step back finally into generalities, it would be misleading to present what I have obviously conceived of as an archetypal encounter between Prospero and Caliban as if it were a straightforward confrontation of polarities and to leave it at that. Culture and Nature are not the simple opposites we tend to presuppose in our covert preference for one over the other, and convincing arguments exist to persuade us that what we call 'nature' is really just a special case, if not a deliberate invention, of what we term 'culture': that Prospero actively constructs Caliban as part of a complex self-establishing process perhaps recorded in his admission, 'this thing of darkness I acknowledge mine'.[19]

Certainly, leaning on the lock-gate at the point where the Stratford canal (preserved these days, weed-strewn and rustic, by the National Trust) becomes the river Avon (surely one of the major 'cultural' constructs of an English-speaking world), a confusing confluence becomes self-evident. It should be added that while to my left there certainly stands the relatively new cultural edifice of the Royal Shakespeare Theatre (the building so dear to Salt Brassington having succumbed to natural forces, a fire, in 1926) the establishment that confronts it to my right, the fish-and-chip shop, has little enough claim to be a spontaneous popular outgrowth of the town's English inheritance. Several ironies invest it. First, it stands exactly on the site of Cal Cook's cottage at the corner of Waterside and Sheep Street. Second, it now rejoices in the name of *Dillen's Fishery*, after Hewins's successful book (published by the Oxford University Press) and thus exhibits discursive dimensions no less literary or prestigious than those of the establishment to which I have opposed it. The whirligig of Time brings in his revenges. The opposition, in which one citizen of Stratford (William Shakespeare) confronts another (George Hewins), is as complex as those other oppositions in which Playhouse confronted Workhouse in the early years of the century, or enclosers confronted women and children three hundred years before that. And it is certainly no less complex than the opposition in which Prospero confronted Caliban or cultured Elizabethan planters confronted brutish Indian natives in the Virginia colonies in North America.

Indeed, the highest level of complexity was perhaps reached when George Hewins and his wife found themselves, at the urging of Salt Brassington, working respectively as 'super' (i.e. extra) and dresser at the Shakespeare Memorial Theatre. It was the result of further 'difficulties' connected with the rent, of course, and the work exacted finally did establish the sort of symbiotic link between Playhouse and Workhouse that has been proposed above. We can note that Frank Benson, the resident company's leading actor, found it amusing to speculate that some of the Stratford aboriginals might even be descendants of Shakespeare. He had an interest in savagery after all, being famous for his portrayal of Caliban. Constance Benson tells us that he spent 'many hours watching monkeys and baboons in the zoo, in order to get the movements in keeping with his "make-up"'. He also carried a real fish in his mouth, and an eyewitness of his performances between 1900 and 1924 records that 'It added to the realism of his missing-link Caliban that he could clamber nimbly up a tree and hang head downwards from a branch, chattering with rage at Prospero.'[20] Critical insights of this order ensured that the representative of Culture in Stratford was in no doubt of the place in the scheme of things occupied by the natives: they could only be instances of unredeemed Nature: '"Course," 'e says, "they'll be *bastards*, Harry – bound to be!" We all laughed.' (*The Dillen*, p. 124).

It was almost the last laugh. Because if Benson's initiative resulted in the paradox of a bastard Hewins/Caliban who finally knew *Hamlet* legitimately 'by heart, without a book' and could recite chunks of it (ibid., p. 123), that was only the prelude to an ultimate irony when, in 1983, the Royal Shakespeare Company presented a dramatised version of *The Dillen*, not in the theatre but in a series of 'actual' locations in the town of Stratford itself, using present-day townspeople in the performance.[21]

But by then, the long four-hundred-year process which saw Stratford completely colonised by its playwright Prospero was virtually over. The ditches dug to define the theatre's province had extended far beyond Bancroft Gardens to undermine the very phonetics of local speech. And as, at the corner of Waterside and Bridge Street, not a hundred yards from Cal Cook's cottage, the old *Anchor Inn* finally dwindled into the new *Encore Inn*, the full stratagems of a conclusive play-maker/power-broker amalgamation revealed themselves, intent on subsuming all Stratford houses, not to say English-speaking culture at large, in its magisterial, Shakespearianising theatricality. The complications and scale of that sort of enclosure generate a sizeable speculative burden. If we find it difficult to bear, we might reflect that at least, once, we were in distinguished company.

From Terence Hawkes, *That Shakespeharian Rag* (London, 1986), pp. 1–26.

NOTES

[Terence Hawkes does not offer a reading of *The Tempest* but rather a cultural materialist argument concerning Shakespeare's place in English cultural history. The parallel passages in the play where Caliban and Ferdinand respectively complain about the labours Prospero imposes upon them raise questions about work, employment (and unemployment) and relationships between master and servant, landlord and tenant. Hawkes points out that Shakespeare, when he wrote *The Tempest*, was a landlord in Stratford who was enigmatically involved in an attempt to enclose land which would have created poverty and unemployment in the area. (Shakespeare's part is obscure.) The dramatist was also the cultural figure who unwittingly changed the whole socio-economic nature of the Warwickshire town. A comparison with the draconian actions of a later landlord, Salt Brassington, the librarian at the Shakespeare Memorial Theatre who wrote a book, *Picturesque Warwickshire*, is taken as symptomatic of the way in which culture is a colonising and a class force, determining the nature of social relationships. Prospero's isle provides an analogy for the logic and the process which Hawkes sees as happening to England, not only in the seventeenth century but also in the twentieth. Quotations are from *The Tempest*, ed. Frank Kermode (Arden edition, London, 1954) Ed.]

1. Frank Kermode (ed.), *The Tempest*, Arden edition (London, 1954), p. xxiv.

2. See Trevor R. Griffiths, '"This Island's Mine": Caliban and Colonialism', *The Yearbook of English Studies*, 13 (1983), 159–80.

3. George Chapman, 'De Guiana, Carmen Epicum' (1596) in *The Poems of George Chapman*, ed. Phyllis Brooks Bartlett (New York, 1941), pp. 353–4.

4. See the argument of Francis Barker and Peter Hulme, '"Nymphs and Reapers heavily vanish": the discursive con-texts of *The Tempest*' in John Drakakis (ed.), *Alternative Shakespeares* (London, 1985), pp. 191–205 [essay 2 above – Ed.].

5. See Christopher Hill, 'Masterless Men' in *The World Turned Upside Down*, Penguin edn (Harmondsworth, 1975), pp. 39–56; A. L. Beier, *Masterless Men: the vagrancy problem in England 1560–1640* (London, 1985); and Paul Brown, '"This thing of darkness I acknowledge mine": *The Tempest* and the discourse of colonialism' in Jonathan Dollimore and Alan Sinfield (eds), *Political Shakespeare* (Manchester, 1985), pp. 48–71.

6. Louis Adrian Montrose, '"Eliza, queene of Shepheardes" and the Pastoral of Power', *English Literary Renaissance*, 10 (1980), 153–82.

7. See Peter J. Bowden, *The Wool Trade in Tudor and Stuart England* (London, 1962).

8. Hill, 'Masterless Men', p. 51.

9. Ibid., 53.

10. Ibid., 52.

11. Ibid., 51.

12. C. M. Ingleby (ed.), *Shakespeare and the Enclosure of Common Fields at Welcombe: being a fragment of the Private Diary of Thomas Greene, Town Clerk of Stratford upon Avon 1614–1617* (Birmingham, 1885), pp. v–vi.

13. On the concepts of intertextuality and discourse and how these may be fruitfully applied to *The Tempest*, see Barker and Hulme, 'Nymphs and Reapers' [essay 2 above – Ed.].

14. E. K. Chambers, *William Shakespeare, a study of facts and problems* (Oxford, 1930), 1, 9.

15. Angela Hewins (ed.), *The Dillen: Memories of a man of Stratford-upon-Avon* (Oxford, 1982), p. 4. For Ronald Blythe's comment, see p. v.

16. W. Salt Brassington, *Notes on the Old Houses in Stratford-upon-Avon* (privately published: the Walsall Press, 1899), p. i.

17. W. Salt Brassington, *Picturesque Warwickshire* (London, Edinburgh and Dublin, Valentine and Sons, 1906), p. 80.

18. See Trevor R. Griffiths, 'This Island's Mine'.

19. See Paul Brown, '"This thing of darkness" and also Stephen Greenblatt, 'Invisible bullets: Renaissance authority and its subversion' in *Political Shakespeare*.

20. Trevor R. Griffiths, 'This Island's Mine', 166–8.

21. In 1985, Angela Hewins edited a volume of memoirs by Mary, George Hewins's daughter, entitled *Mary, After the Queen* (Oxford, 1985). As part of its summer season in that year, the Royal Shakespeare Company presented a dramatisation of the book, to run in tandem with a revival of *The Dillen*.

4

Subtleties of the Isle: *The Tempest*

RUTH NEVO

> Out of the isle, but not of any isle.
> Close to the senses there lies another isle
> And there the senses give and nothing take,
>
> The opposite of Cythere, an isolation
> At the centre ...
> (Wallace Stevens, 'An Ordinary Evening
> in New Haven', XXI)[1]

The Tempest begins with a shipwreck and ends with an enigma. Neither is what it seems and both are 'outside' the dramatic events exhibited during the play, upon the enchanted island. What is 'outside', and what is 'inside', is indeed one of the matters which is put into question in *The Tempest*, as is the matter of genre itself, and of 'play' itself. Unlike its companion romances, which reveal while concealing unconscious shaping fantasies, *The Tempest*, with its magician protagonist, is overtly, manifestly fantastic. It is not the unconscious of the text that the text solicits us to understand, but the consciousness of its wizard stage manager, who gives us advance notice of the nature of the wish fulfilment fantasy he engineers into existence before our eyes.

The fourth and last of the romances brings Shakespearean tragi-comedy to its meridian. It is useful to remember that the German word for comedy is *Lustspiel*, or pleasure play, as Freud pointed out in *Creative Writers and Daydreaming*; for tragedy, *Trauerspiel*, or mourning play. Comedy, exorcist in its function, remedial of errors and follies, obeys the pleasure principle in its gratification of wishes for an imagined happiness, at least an amelioration of human bondage. It provides what is lacking – a mate, wisdom, a community; good luck, good humour, good will. Tragedy presses beyond the pleasure principle to encounter, even to embrace death, yet also to affirm the value of an individual consciousness, dying in its own way. *The Tempest* is a pleasure play, surely? Yet its undercurrent is deeply melancholy, its ending elegiac – 'despair', for Prospero, the epilogue says, 'Unless [he] be reliev'd by prayer'. What is the nature of this momentum in the play towards death – 'Every third thought ... my grave' (V.i.311) synchronic with its movement towards, and fulfilment of, a rejoicing 'Beyond a common joy' (l. 207)?

The Tempest invites reflection upon the relation between Freud and Shakespeare at a number of points of convergence. It is possible to construct a kind of intertextual dialogue between these two ob-servers of the human scene. The dialogue I have in mind is not, however, with Freud the exegetical detective, diagnostician and therapist, but rather with Freud the meta-psychologist, the anthro-pologist and philosopher of civilisation and its discontents. *The Tempest* is corrective of the negative thrust of *Creative Writers and Daydreaming*, containing what the latter lacks in its failure to credit the artist's creation with more than the provision of diversionary pleasure to distract the secondary, reality-testing processes of the mind, while the primary processes of autistic fantasy can be safely released, and dispelled. *The Tempest* exhibits fantasy neither as merely libidinous nor as defensive, but as heuristic; and it is never deluded. *The Tempest* imagines a process of maturation, of sublima-tion, of renunciation; the relinquishing of needs, passions, bonds, possessivenesses which are regressive and enslaving, for the attaining of eudaemonic ends; but it also imagines the struggle of their attain-ing, and its limits.

What does this pleasure play tell us of pleasure, of power, safety, liberty, the quest of all its dramatis personae? Prospero found these in a cell in Milan, where his library was 'dukedom large enough' (I.ii.110) until his deputy brother usurped his place and cast him out to sea; Alonso found them in regal power, until the loss of his son. Antonio, who would 'have no screen between this part he play'd / And him he play'd it for' and must be therefore 'Absolute Milan' (ll.107–9), in narcissistic aggrandisement; Gonzalo, provider of food, fresh water, garments, beloved books to the castaways, found them in charity; Miranda and Ferdinand in love; Stephano and Trinculo in the oblivion and the intoxication of the bottle; Caliban in creature comforts, the immediate gratification of the primal instinctual cravings; and Ariel in a cowslip. The animating fantasy of *The Tempest* is itself embedded in Prospero's name: it is a grand design for happiness snatched out of disaster, not least the disaster of being born human. The shipwreck figures disaster, but Prospero's conjuring trick shipwreck constitutes a rebirth for the survivors, who believe themselves rescued. 'Not so much perdition as a hair' (l.30) is suffered by any of the voyagers, not so much as a blemish is to be seen upon their sustaining garments when they find themselves alive and ashore. Dazed, amazed, bewitched by strange sounds and sweet airs, by apparitions and hallucinations, they pursue, like banished Kent, their old courses in a country new, but this time under a monitoring eye, and wand.

This – Prospero's magicianship – is the secondary organising fantasy of *The Tempest*, a fantasy of omnipotence, whereby the crooked shall be made straight and all manner of things be well. Isaiah's redemptive latter-day fantasy (and Noah's, another survivor) hovers over the language of *The Tempest* in many places even if Ariel's name did not come from chapter 29. Charles K. Hofling[2] makes the interesting point that the King James Bible was completed in 1611, and that in addition to the name Ariel, nine thematically relevant phrases, images and ideas that occur in Isaiah 29, such as vengeance, a familiar spirit, storm and tempest, a flame of devouring fire, dream, drunkenness and deep sleep recur in *The Tempest*. One could add a sealed book of wisdom, and the doing of a marvellous work. If Shakespeare was reading or rereading the Bible, as well as the Bermuda pamphlets, in 1611, and thinking perhaps about Noah, he might well have remembered the story of Noah's daughters, who, for lack of any alternative on the desert island of Ararat, knew their father. Other biblical daughters had occurred to him in the past: Jephtah's, for instance, in *Hamlet*, and Leah, married to Jacob through a bed-trick, it will be recalled, in *The Merchant*.

The beauty of *The Tempest* is that the fantasy is reality-tested within its own confines. Prospero's civilising enterprise on Sycorax' island is brought face to face with its own discontents, its own mal-contents.

Let us examine Prospero's grand design.

Prospero, we are informed, was never a man ambitious for worldly power. Already in Milan he had neglected 'worldly ends' for the 'secret studies' which would further 'the bettering of [his] mind'

(I.ii.89–90) while Antonio was given the office of his deputy. Insulated – enisled – in the quest for the mind's power 'to liberate the soul from the passions',[3] Prospero believes that his own defection from ducal responsibility awoke the 'evil nature' in his ambitious brother, whose native malice and arrogance, however, we have already glimpsed in the crisis of the storm. The island magnifies and clarifies the attributes of both these manipulative, if dialectically opposed sibling rivals. The island events are their designs for living writ large.

For fifteen years in this island sanctuary Prospero has lived in intimate seclusion with his daughter, a seclusion untroubled and uninterrupted save by the island creature Caliban's attempt upon her. This daughter, whose presence as a babe in the rotten bark saved him from despair, whom he has bred and loved and taught, now presents him with a drastic double bind. She must now herself be saved (they both must be) from the loveliest of all fantasies. To live thus, father and daughter, alone and together, with no rival to challenge, no rebellion to threaten, no sexual turmoil to overthrow the beatific enjoyment of beauty, of obedience, of affection, of consideration (she really is the perfect daughter!) in loving reciprocity and perfect harmony – what is this but the wishful fantasy of a Lear, who would sing like a bird in a cage in prison with Cordelia, or the fantasy of any parent: a revivified, reintensified primal unity with the child who replaces his or her own lost good parent. It might amuse one to reflect that such would have been, presumably, the wishful fantasy of all the thwarting and defied fathers in the Terentian comedies, had the plots of those plays allowed them to figure in their own right, as it were, rather than simply as an obstacle to the mating of the young.[4] However, as Barber pointed out long ago (1969), where the early comedies are designed to free sexuality from the bonds of family, the romances are engaged in freeing parental love from the threat of sexuality. So even on Prospero's island, particularly on Prospero's civilised island, these revels must come to an end; for Miranda is fifteen, nubile and marriageable, and Prospero's time, under the shadow of the threat, under the shadow of Caliban's constant reminder, is running out. He must find a match for his daughter. He must end what he longs to prolong.

The famous first dialogue between Prospero and Miranda, in which he nags for her attention, neatly provides necessary information but also dramatises Prospero's sense of urgency, of a moment which is now ripe, and of a hidden import of the nature of which he cannot enlighten his interlocutor.[5] The stars in their courses have brought about a propitious conjunction – his 'zenith' (etymologically road, way or path) depends upon a 'most auspicious star' (I.ii.181–2). The King of Naples is on his way home from his daughter's marriage. In Prospero's mind a plan has crystallised, a transcendent design for the resolution of all problems, moral and practical. He will marry his daughter to no other than the son of the King of Naples, who, since Antonio's betrayal, is the overlord of Milan. He will thus undo, and outdo, Antonio's treachery: his heirs, not Antonio's, will rule Milan. Gonzalo, rejoicing 'beyond a common joy' at the play's conclusion, makes the point: 'Was Milan thrust from Milan, that his issue / Should become kings of Naples?' (V.i.205–7). This marriage, then, between Miranda and Ferdinand will be the sweetest and subtlest of all possible matches and revenges, hoisting Antonio with his own petard and yet sanctified by its obviously beneficent purpose. Is it revenge? Or is it revenge so sublimated as to lose the name of revenge? It is no wonder that he is excited, that he relishes every detail of the smooth execution, is delighted with the performance of his 'brave spirit' Ariel, is still more delighted when 'it works', his plan, and Miranda and Ferdinand are instantly attracted to each other. When he then plays the classic *senex*, staging a tyrannical ferocity, throwing suspicion upon Ferdinand, magically disarming him of his sword, enslaving him to log-chopping, he announces these impositions as tests of Ferdinand's character, 'lest too light winning / Make the prize light' (I.ii.452–3). However, it is not difficult to perceive in these metaphorical castrations the symbolic enactment of what, albeit repressed, will still out: a possessive father's hostility to his usurper rival.

Prospero's progress throughout the play is a Herculean contest with himself, with ambivalence. What he does, with regard to Miranda's betrothal, he would dearly love to undo. What he forgives, with regard to Antonio's usurpation, he would dearly love to avenge. Prospero does not suddenly discover that 'the rarer action is / In virtue than in vengeance' (V.i.27–8), for this, as an enlightened prince, he knows from the start. It is a communal, and his own, ideal of conduct. What he has to do is to realise his knowledge in action and feeling, but he is filled with love for his beloved daughter, and he is filled with rage against his perfidious brother. These are imperious passions, as hard to subdue as Caliban is to tame; the primal energies, erotic and vindictive. Simply, massively, to repress them, as a man of strict and icy conscience, would make of Prospero an Angelo, an armour-plated, fragile and unhappy man. Simply to indulge them would reduce the great project of civility to naturalist abandon, and make of him another Antonio.

Prospero, unlike Duke Vincentio, his precursor, has supernatural power at his disposal, and spirits to command. He is entirely in charge. He can stage-manage events, create storms at sea, conjure up visions, manipulate situations and people. His actions, therefore, are his wishes, his wishes his actions; but it doesn't always quite work out according to plan. His captives get a little out of hand at times, putting *him* to the test, and this is the course of the play's dramatic tension: formal artifice – shows, emblems, didactic object lessons are constantly destabilised by unpremeditated contingencies, spontaneity which occurs despite the magical control. Total power is exhibited and defeated at once.

Structurally, *The Tempest* is a play within a play: Prospero's, within Shakespeare's, or, one is sometimes tempted to fancy, Shakespeare's within Prospero's. The embedding of play within play dissolves representational boundaries so that the audience is required to suspend its attention, to negotiate a constant interchange between fictional reality and fictional illusion: Prospero creates happenings by having the volatile and tricksy spirit, Ariel, bewilder, placate or punish his captives with shows, which are illusions. The island's enchantments are Prospero's inventions but they are realities for the play's personae; the beings who inhabit the island are indeterminately human and phantasmagoric, as the absurdities of the comic passages ludicrously underline. *The Tempest's* mingled yarn dramatises heuristic fantasy: *The Tempest* is a day-dream in which Prospero, spectator at his own show, remembers and reconstructs, recalls past threats (which then repeat themselves, once in deadly earnest, once in comic parody) and fantasises (or realises?) a reordering of his life. Only in the wedding entertainment is the show overtly, and with the knowledge of the play-spectators, a masque, and that, as we shall see, is dissolved, as were masques in real life, into the realities of the final recognition scenes.

In dreams, as we know, opposites obtain. Going is coming, finding is bringing, banishment may represent a deep wish for flight, log-chopping displaces a threat of castration; and opposites are split off internal objects, or imagos. Prospero found Ariel and Caliban on the island which was Sycorax's, but the embedding of narration within narration makes the journey to that fabulous location a journey into a psychic interior and we readily understand them as representing some emotional or mental aspect of Prospero himself.

Prospero replaced the witch Sycorax (a reincarnation of Circe, transformer of men into beasts, according to the Arden editor [p. 26]) – his own malign double. She too, like himself, was banished, with a child, and abandoned upon the island; her black sorcery is the barbarous counterpart to his theurgic magic. Releasing Ariel, 'too delicate / To act her earthy and abhorr'd commands' (I.ii.272–3) from imprisonment in a cloven pine, he incarcerates her favoured son Caliban and imposes upon him (as later upon Ferdinand) log-bearing slavery. Replacing the bad mother, he is a father to them both, scolding, castigating, punishing, teaching. Prospero turns ferociously upon Ariel when the latter objects to yet another task. 'Malignant thing', he scolds, 'dull thing' (ll.257, 285), and threatens punishment of exactly the kind meted out by Sycorax: 'I will rend an oak / And pen thee in his knotty entrails till / Thou hast howl'd away twelve winters' (ll.294–6). The antithetical symmetries of the symbolic foursome are central to Shakespeare's invention, which, I suggest, performs nothing less than the figuring forth of what we now call the unconscious. These imaginative creations embody desires, memories, impulses not available to cognitive conceptualisation, but only to an intuition of primary tensions, primary duality. Through them a path is opened into the infinite regress of repetition compulsion, of amnesia, 'the dark backward and abysm of time' (l.50) as Prospero memorably puts it.[6]

Shakespeare had precursors in the allegorical personification of the psyche: Marlowe's good and evil angels, the whole of Spenser's master work, the medieval allegorists; and he has had successors, in Jung, and in Freud, who have capitalised, each in his own way, upon his insights. However, his own is its unique and inimitable self, and is not collapsible into any other. Let us attempt to elucidate the allegories of Ariel and Caliban.

The temptation to construe Prospero as ego and Ariel and Caliban as superego and id (or anima and animus/animal)[7] replaces the more traditional readings of the kind formulated by Marjorie Garber, namely Prospero as mankind or poet, Ariel imagination, Caliban natural or instinctive man. It has been taken up by several psychoanalytically oriented interpreters,[8] recently by Meredith Skura. 'Freud internalised Shakespeare's dramas', she says. His metapsychological theories resemble Shakespeare's plays 'since they anthropomorphise the parts of the mind, as does Shakespeare ... Ariel and Caliban may be seen as walking portraits of "the conscious" and the "unconscious"'.[9] There is something troubling about these ascriptions however. It is easy to see the mastering, controlling, adaptational ego-functions in Prospero, and an id-figure in the idle, lustful, piggish, resentful (and enslaved) Caliban, who exhibits what the Renaissance would have regarded as a natural profanity needing constantly to be tamed and restrained in the degree that it cannot be enlightened,[10] but superego demands, strictures, moral imperatives seem to belong more to Prospero than to the pliant and metamorphic, playful and freedom-loving Ariel. The attempt to cut Shakespeare's cloth precisely according to Freudian specification meets with too many obstacles in the dramatisation of *The Tempest* to be anything but procrustean. Shakespeare's 'other scene' was not Freud's. Freud's discoveries can rediscover for us much that is embodied in Shakespeare's; but Shakespeare's, in their turn, can amplify Freud's.

Prospero's fantasy of omnipotence, his dialogue with Miranda suggests, included the desire to be an onlie begetter, prolific and nourishing. Antonio 'new created / The creatures that were mine' (I.ii.81–2) he says resentfully; Antonio became an ivy which 'sucked my verdure out' (l.87). Such grandiose omnipotence, psychoanalytical theory tells us, is a defence against its obverse, the infantile terror of total dependency, therefore it requires the fantasied destruction of maternal power. Miranda, it will be recalled, sees no mother figure in the dim past of her memory, only vague women attendants; later she says that she remembers 'no woman's face' save her own in her mirror (III.i.49–51). There is, indeed, a notable absence, or repression, of mothers in *The Tempest*. 'The mother aspect of woman is under a peculiar tabu', says Abenheimer[11] who sees both Miranda and Ariel as fantasised beneficent surrogate feminine presences. But this absence of mothers would be true of the middle comedies too, with their resourceful and adventurous heroines. In *The Tempest* there is a mother – the witch-mother Sycorax – 'with age and envy / ... grown into a hoop' (I.ii.257–8), a female claw, an evil female dominance which is annihilated, since she dies before the opening of the play. Is Sycorax then a derivative of infantile fantasy, a bad mother upon whom the helpless rage and terror of separation is projected? In this connection we note the imagery of the oceanic, pervasive in *The Tempest*, especially in the echoing, haunting compounds – sea-sorrow, sea-storm, sea-swallowed, sea-change – which are peculiar to this play, and, though subdued to an undertone by comparison with *Pericles* – for Prospero is endowed with a power over storms at sea rather than a Gower to narrate his proneness to fall a victim to them – the swallowing and belching sea is, from the first graphic scene of the wreck, a constant verbal evocation. It is possible to read in *The Tempest* polyphonic variations upon the theme of a lifetime's contest with the oceanic.

But to return from the ego of Prospero to his pair of servitors: if we try to map the Freudian metapsychology upon the Shakespearean, we can see that the latter extends the range of meanings implicit in the former as generally received. Ariel, rather than being a superego (with the connotations, not only of 'ego-ideal' but of a censorious, critical and punitive function), or 'the conscious' (for what is then left to ego?), represents, I suggest, the urge towards sublimation, and Caliban the drift towards regression – a Shakespearean Eros and Thanatos respectively – and it is the struggle between these two cardinal impulses that structures the progress of the play, and can mediate our understanding of it, especially of the angers of Prospero, which have proved a stumbling block to interpreters.

His vituperation of Ariel – 'Malignant thing ... dull thing' (I.ii.257, 285) occurs after the capturing of the ship's party has been splendidly accomplished with 'not a hair perish'd'; the next step in Prospero's project is, significantly, the leading of Ferdinand to Miranda, crux of the renunciation that he must effectuate. If Ariel fails him now his entire project crumbles. The moment Ariel has capitulated and flown off to become the water-nymph whose invisible beguilements will bring Ferdinand from the sea-shore where he sits mourning his father's loss, we are introduced to Caliban, the 'poisonous slave got by the devil himself' (I.319), 'hagseed', 'freckled whelp', 'filth', 'earth', once the recipient of Prospero's affection, and guide to the island's fertile bounty, now object of his unmitigated hatred and contempt. The wonderfully imagined pair, linked and opposed, loved and hated, recalcitrant and obedient, mirror Prospero's complex ambivalence: he both wills to annul or to transcend the natural craving for destructive revenge, to transform and so in some way to preserve the naturally exclusive attachment to Miranda, and is tempted to yield to that which is to be transformed and transcended.

Both Prospero's creatures are marvellously imagined: Ariel, spirit of transformation, invisible to the audience except in his various transformations, sublimated agent of Prospero's grand scheme of sublimations, and regressive Caliban, stubbornly a presence precivilised, uninhibited, abhorred and feared, hence object of Prospero's own sadistic rage. Ariel, all air and fire – elements of sublimation in alchemy – Prospero's 'Delicate Ariel' (I.ii.442), his 'bird' (IV.i.184), is etherealised, spiritualised, hermaphrodite; Caliban, earth and fen-water, half brute half demon, is grossly, aggressively male, but rendered impotent under Prospero's domination. Sexuality is strictly under guard on Prospero's island, as he warns Ferdinand, repeatedly. It was precisely Caliban's attempt to rape Miranda, it will be recalled, which lost him Prospero's original affection and earned instead the cramps and aches and pinches and blisters with which he is tormented, by, among other means, creatures appropriately spiky and snaky ('hedgehogs which / Lie tumbling in my barefoot way, and mount / Their pricks at my footfall ... adders, who with cloven tongues / Do hiss me into madness' [II.ii.10–14]).

Norman Holland[12] has picked out the imagery suggestive of infantile libido in his analysis of Trinculo's discovery of the 'deboshed fish' Caliban in the monster shape on the shore: 'Yond same black cloud, yond huge one, looks like a foul bumbard that would shed his liquor' (II.ii.20–2) parodies in advance, he says, Caliban's dream of a sensorily soporific, pleasure-providing environment: 'Be not afeard', Caliban says to Stephano, his fellow conspirator made nervous by Ariel's audible invisibility:

> the isle is full of noises,
> Sounds, and sweet airs, that give delight and hurt not.
> Sometimes a thousand twangling instruments
> Will hum about mine ears; and sometimes voices,
> That if I then had wak'd after long sleep,
> Will make me sleep again, and then in dreaming,
> The clouds methought would open, and show riches
> Ready to drop upon me, that when I wak'd
> I cried to dream again.
>
> (III.ii.135–43)

This fantasy is surely derivative – a palimpsest of a child between sleep and waking with his thumb in his mouth. Trinculo crawls under the shape's fishy-smelling gaberdine, only to be discovered by Stephano as a fourlegged monster with two mouths, one before and one behind, into both of which he happily pours his bottle of 'riches' (II.ii.88–93). 'In effect', says Holland, 'shortly before Caliban tells his new-found masters his recurring dream, they have recited and acted out for him a "black", "foul", smelly, and backward – in short, anal – version of that dream' (l.526). The drunken butler and his jester colleague (themselves childish) uncover, from an alienated adult but comically good-tempered point of view, the primordial infant in the primitive savage with the voracious name.

Upon Prospero Caliban hurls malignant curses which are reciprocated with punitive vindictiveness, for they are engaged in mortal combat, these two, as a man with his most inward and intimate threat. It is the threat of a return of the repressed, of the *bête noir*, the thing of darkness which accounts for Prospero's rage at the height of the festivities when he recalls the 'foul conspiracy / Of the beast Caliban and his confederates' (IV.i.139–40), an episode which has seemed superfluous and unaccountable to many commentators. It is a far cry from innocent orality or anality, even from less innocent greed and lust to the raw uninhibited pursuit of murder and rape, however disabused of actual menace these may be; but the latter are what he has to contend with as he walks away 'to still [his] beating mind' (l.163). It 'beats in his mind'. The phrase recurs like a pulse.

If Caliban is imagined as infantile, shape-changing Ariel, affectionate, docile, playful, volatile, is childlike, representing a wishful fantasy rooted in the same primal soil. Ariel's 'sweet airs' allay the fury and the passion of Ferdinand, 'weeping again the King [his] father's wrack' (I.ii.391, 393–4). 'Come unto these yellow sands' invites its dancers to curtsy, kiss, and 'foot it featly' while the 'wild waves' are calmed, the sun shines, the protective watch-dog barks and the barnyard cock crows (ll.375–87). If this is an invitation to the dance, proleptic of Ferdinand's fortunes on the island, it is also a nursery rhyme. Ariel's final song, in Act V, scene i, as he anticipates his freedom, is a kind of lullaby in its evocation of ease and safety, its transformation of womb or breast into a cowslip's bell, its intimacy, the delicate eroticism of its miniscule cowslips and blossoms, and its friendly creatures:

> Where the bee sucks, there suck I,
> In a cowslip's bell I lie;
> There I couch when owls do cry.
> On the bat's back I do fly
> After summer merrily.
> Merrily, merrily shall I live now,
> Under the blossom that hangs on the bough.
> (ll.88–94)

'Full fathom five', the most haunting of these lyrics of recreation, transforms death itself, refashions mortal remains, watches the never-surfeited sea metamorphose skeletons into coral and eyeballs into pearls, forbids mourning:

> Full fathom five thy father lies,
>   Of his bones are coral made:
> Those are pearls that were his eyes:
>   Nothing of him that doth fade,
> But doth suffer a sea-change
> Into something rich and strange.
> Sea-nymphs hourly ring his knell.
>   (I.ii.397–403)

These pearls and corals – transitional objects which defend against grief, loss, dissolution – are apotropaic. They preserve and immortalise, by the transformations of a mythic natural alchemy. Themselves the work of the sea's living organisms, they are a trope, says Marjorie Garber, 'for the activity of artistic creation'.[13] It has been my argument that that trope is itself a trope, in *The Tempest*, for the activity of psychic reformation. It is upon himself that Prospero works his wizardry, and it is the vicissitudes of the creative imagination that Ariel and Caliban illuminate.

Anne Barton claims that *The Tempest* 'is an extraordinarily secretive work of art ... deliberately enigmatic ... [seeming] to hide as much as it reveals' and depending to a 'surprising' extent upon 'the suppressed and the unspoken', upon fragmentary and disjointed glimpses of 'a vitally important past' that the dramatist 'did not choose to elucidate. ... It provokes imaginative activity on the part of its audience or readers ... demand[s] interpretation and expansion'.[14] To the extent that these observations apply to all great works of literature they apply to *The Tempest*, but the inner dimension of *The Tempest* is actually less veiled or occulted than in the other romances because we are privy to the protagonist's will and intentions from the outset, at least from scene ii. Other plays provide screens for fantasies which reveal themselves in devious ways. Here Prospero announces his wishful intention from the start, which, since it depends upon his possession of magic powers is necessarily already in the realm of fantasy. The apparitions, mysteries, 'strangenesses' are experienced as such by the manipulated dramatis personae, not the audience, who are, with Prospero, in the know. Nevertheless we have still to read, to spell out, Prospero's fantasy as the play's dynamic articulates it.

We can understand Antonio as a figure out of a fifteen-year-old past who reappears and is re-encountered, in a re-enactment of his original malfeasance; but we can also understand him as Prospero's *alter ego*. Like other sibling rivals in Shakespeare, including Alonso and Sebastian in this very play, they are split, antithetical, decomposed parts of a psychic whole. Both sought power, one by grasping, one by withdrawing. Both would be 'absolute Milan' (I.ii.109), but one renounces, or sublimates, one ruthlessly fulfils the passions and appetites of the mind. Antonio's 'sleepy language' to Sebastian (II.i.211) parallels Prospero's enchantments in that both are machiavellian and manipulative, both seek the end of contemplative magic, namely, to cause changes in consciousness by the exercise of will; but Prospero is good, and Antonio is evil – in psychological terms, one represents the compensatory, reparative urge, the other the envious and destructive. There are few villains in Shakespeare more heartlessly, chillingly cynical than Antonio and Sebastian. If the exhibition of Antonio's villainy is a test for Prospero, audiences are certainly enabled to sympathise. What auditor has not wished something very unpleasant, and quite unsublimated, to happen to the jeering pair?

The five scenes of Acts II and III divide symmetrically between the court party sophisticates and the fools, with the scene between the lovers, watched by Prospero, forming the apex of a triangle: court-party, fools, lovers, fools, court-party. The courtiers appear in Act II, structurally the phase which articulates the terms of the drama's psychomachia. They anchor the contest between the better and the worse human possibilities in the concrete actualities of political behaviour, just as Gonzalo's Montaignean Golden-Age dream of effortless natural bounty, security, untroubled and perpetual plenitude translates Caliban's dream, and Ariel's, into terms of property and polity. Gonzalo is mercilessly mocked by the cynics, but the conspiracy of Antonio and Sebastian is itself mocked by Stephano's parody of a plot, as is their intoxication by the foolish glee of the inebriated and self-enslaved Caliban. Shakespeare's employment here of fool parody is a return to his high mastery of the mode in the mature comedies: the fools' doings ridicule the aspirations of the middle characters, while enhancing those of the higher – in this case morally rather than socially higher – protagonists.[15] Stephano floating ashore on his wine-butt is a survivor of the tempest, like Noah-Prospero, and a coloniser-king (to Caliban), which mocks the would-be usurpers. The villains have their banquet

– another dream of satiety – ludicrously snatched from them at the play's reversal. Note, however, the modulation of register that follows:

> You fools! I and my fellows
> Are ministers of Fate ...
>   your swords ... may as well
> Wound the loud winds, or with bemock't-at stabs
> Kill the still-closing waters, as diminish
> One dowle that's in my plume.
>
>   (III.iii.60–5)

The fierce female bird-monster's denunciation of the 'three men of sin' (l.53) precipitates, at least in Alonso, a gnawing remorse which exacerbates his grief for his son till he can only desire to end his own life, 'mudded' – no sea-change here – in the ooze where his son is bedded.

Whether sinister, or comic, or solemn, the alternations of Acts II and III, and the central scene of the lovers' vows are a sustained dramatic meditation upon the themes of subservience and mastery, guilt and liberation, the better and the worse of the human possibilities. Three times in these scenes is a coupling watched. The tipsy Stephano, who later takes the mooncalf under his fatherly wing, observes the extremely strange coupling of two mouths and four legs in the composite 'monster' under the gaberdine (II.ii.89). The villainous brothers watch the sleeping pair of vulnerable older figures, Alonso and Gonzalo, related anagrammatically as they are related by guilt and goodness respectively, and plan their speedy demise (II.i.198–296); and Prospero watches the love-exchange between Miranda and Ferdinand, the crown of his scheme, with a complex ambivalence. 'Poor worm, thou art infected' (III.i.31) he says, but also, 'Fair encounter / Of two most rare affections! Heavens rain grace / On that which breed between 'em!' (ll.74–6). There is a wry self-awareness in the balance-sheet of his summing up:

> So glad of this as they I cannot be,
> Who are surpris'd [withal] but my rejoicing
> At nothing can be more.
>
>   (ll.92–4)

By Act IV Prospero's design and the foiling of the villains is all but completed. It remains to 'bestow upon the eyes of [the] young couple / Some vanity of [his] art' (IV.i.40–1), before the discovery of the truth which will bring about the recuperation of the repentant sinners, and the conclusion of his project. Re-creation, renunciation, recognition, regeneration, and then return. Prospero's morality play is faultlessly conceived and worked out; his self-congratulation surely justified; but the play is not finished, and it is not a play. Prospero, as has been noted, is himself tested by the drama he has imagined.

In a sense the whole of *The Tempest*, the enchanted island itself, represents a version of the pastoral restorative 'other place' of liberating fantasy in which Shakespearean comedy is rooted. The remedial fantasy comes to a culmination in the fourth act nuptial masque with its imagery of natural abundance, rural labour and well-being – Prospero works hard at his project of guiding, checking, ordering and re-forming:

> Ceres, most bounteous lady, thy rich leas
> Of wheat, rye, barley, fetches, oats, and pease;
> Thy turfy mountains, where live nibbling sheep,
> And flat meads thatch'd with stover, them to keep;
> Thy banks with pioned and twilled brims,
> Which spungy April at thy hest betrims,
> To make cold nymphs chaste crowns
> (IV.i.60–6)

This is a nourishing and nourished land, fertile in contrast to its 'sea-marge, sterile and rocky-hard' (l.69). True, the nymphs are cold, and the bachelors 'lass-lorn' (l.68), but this could be seen as a temporary and necessary stage in the life-history of the young. The question which has been found most troublesome is Prospero's sudden vexation during the betrothal masque in Act IV, which is signalled by 'strange, hollow and confused noise' and the vanishing into thin air of the masquers. Miranda has never seen him so 'touch'd with anger, so distemper'd' (l.145). He calls off the 'revels' and retires to his cell to 'still [his] beating mind' (l.163). What beats in Prospero's mind?

Let us first consider the masque itself, which he has composed and which therefore will speak his meaning. The three deities are carefully chosen for the nuptial that Prospero has conceived and brought about: Juno, goddess of the rain-bestowing sky, Ceres of the receiving earth, and Iris, the rainbow messenger who joins above and below with promise of a postdiluvian regeneration, a return of the natural cycle of seedtime and harvest. But what of the goddess of Love, whose absence is queried by Ceres herself?

This is after all a wedding ceremony, Venus should surely have a part to play, but Venus and Cupid, who 'thought to have done / Some wanton charm' upon the bridal couple, are not among the sponsors of this masque. 'Mars's hot minion' was seen safely 'cutting the clouds towards Paphos' with her 'waspish-headed son' who 'has broke his arrows, / Swears he will shoot no more, but play with sparrows / And be a boy right out' (ll.93–101, passim). Chaste fertility was a Renaissance commonplace, premarital sex firmly out of bounds. There is nothing here that is in the least unconventional. Yet the interdict on Venus, and the refusal to contemplate an adult Cupid is emphatic. A fertility ritual which bans sex is odd, and therefore expressive, we may infer, of Prospero's need to ward off sexuality even in the celebration of his daughter's marriage, or particularly in the celebration of his daughter's marriage. 'So rare a wond'red father and a wise / Makes this place Paradise' (ll.123–4) says Ferdinand, picking up his father-in-law's own theme of another Genesis. Prospero taught Caliban, it will be recalled, 'how / To name the bigger light, and how the less, / That burn by day and night' (I.ii.334–6); Prospero, survivor and maker of floods, entertains the fantasy of a second creation, a new-made world which will be without libido, or will have mastered its force. But the mature and benign fantasy gives way at a moment of crisis to the persecutory anxiety of an earlier desperation.

The masque is disrupted. It breaks off, its spell broken, just at the moment of the dance of the river Naiads with the Reapers. Reapers gather in the harvest, but they are tearers and renders, actually and etymologically, and immemorial signifiers of death. Prospero remembers Caliban, who would have violated his daughter and would do so again if his conspiracy succeeds. And Prospero experiences an upsurge of almost uncontrollable rage.

Prospero's perturbation reveals the core of his emotional problem, as a reading of the symbolic sequence can make clear. The 'sunburn'd sicklemen', with their intimations of mortality, and of castration (the scythe of Father Time, Panovsky reminds us, was originally Saturn's castrating sickle before Kronos/Saturn and Chronos/Time were conflated),[16] precipitate the recall of 'a born devil, on whose nature / Nurture can never stick' (IV.i.188–9). How can we read this but as a stubborn return of the repressed, of the utterly tabooed, of his own unacknowledged desire, together with the terror that accompanies it and is then unleashed in rage upon Caliban? Caliban is the rock upon which the fantasy of omnipotence and the fantasy of sublimation both founder. The dispiriting fact that Prospero now faces, at this culminating moment, is that he is not, after all, master in his own house. He glimpses beyond the three daughters of Eros, Iris, Juno and Ceres, the three faces of Thanatos: lust and rage and death, that no fantasy can abolish, no mastery control.

He recaptures the self-possession of a host: 'You do look, my son, in a mov'd sort, / As if you were dismay'd: be cheerful, sir' (IV.i.146–7); but the whole of the famous speech that ends the revels is a struggle for composure:

> Our revels now are ended. These our actors
> (As I foretold you) were all spirits, and
> Are melted into air, into thin air,
> And like the baseless fabric of this vision,
> The cloud-capp'd tow'rs, the gorgeous palaces,
> The solemn temples, the great globe itself,
> Yea, all which it inherit, shall dissolve,
> And like this insubstantial pageant faded
> Leave not a rack behind. We are such stuff
> As dreams are made on; and our little life
> Is rounded with a sleep. Sir, I am vex'd;
> Bear with my weakness, my old brain is troubled.
> Be not disturb'd with my infirmity.
> If you be pleas'd, retire into my cell,
> And there repose. A turn or two I'll walk
> To still my beating mind.
>
> (ll.148–63)

It needs no more than an actor's gesture to make the apparently superfluous repetition: 'the baseless fabric of this vision', 'this insubstantial pageant', refer disjunctively to world and to theatre and then to deny the difference. The speech collapses the levels of representation with which *The Tempest* has juggled: the globe that is the world, the Globe that was the theatre, fantasy, reality, dream, all are one, a little life islanded in an ocean of non-existence. 'It seems strange', says Northrop Frye, 'that a melancholy elegy on the dissolving of all things in time should be the emotional crux of the play.'[17] But is it so strange? The lament for the passing of time is so poignant that it obscures the radical narcissism of which it is the expression. The world disappears with the observing eye only if

the I is everything. 'They told me I was every thing', said Lear
(IV.vi.104), whose very accents can be heard in the last lines of
the speech. The speech is as poignant as it is because it captures the
primary narcissism of Everyman, with whom and for whom the
world begins and ends; the primary yearning, always destined to
defeat, for total possession of the beloved other who is also and at
once oneself.

Ariel can dowse the would-be conspirators in pools of horse-piss,
bedazzle them (the civilised ones, at least) with trumpery, and
hound them from the stage, but he (or his master) cannot transform
the Caliban in himself:

> A devil, a born devil, on whose nature
> Nurture can never stick; on whom my pains,
> Humanely taken, all, all lost, quite lost;
> And as with age his body uglier grows,
> So his mind cankers.
> (IV.i.188–92)

The lament opens upon an abyss of dismay. It is his own old age, as
much as Caliban's, that is envisaged. So he punishes Caliban and
company, sadistically, not only with goblin pinches, but with aches
and pains from within an ageing body:

> Go, charge my goblins that they grind their joints
> With dry convulsions, shorten up their sinews
> With aged cramps, and more pinch-spotted make them
> Than pard or cat o'mountain.
> (ll.258–61)

In terms of tragic structure this is Prospero's moment of despair,
the surrender of his will to make sublimation prevail; but in the
recognition scenes of Act V Ariel again comes into his own, when
Prospero's captives, entirely in his power, are saved and forgiven.

Then Prospero solemnly dismisses his puppet-elves, buries his
staff, drowns his book. He renounces his fantasy of omnipotent
domination of nature and men, sets Ariel, 'his diligence', his 'chick'
free. Why? Has he no more need of a sublimating discipline? Of
Art? Is happiness so firmly secured as to need no further maintaining? Or is it because Caliban is an ineluctable fact of life, Ariel an
evanescent grace? We are not, certainly, asked to believe in a transformation of Antonio, a pat repentance. He is obstinately, or grimly,
silent. It is also to be noticed that he (together with Sebastian) is

now within Prospero's (natural) power, a permanent hostage to good behaviour. 'Were I so minded', Prospero addresses his 'brace of lords', 'I here could pluck his Highness' frown upon you / And justify you traitors. At this time / I will tell no tales' (V.i.126–9). Nor are we required to share Miranda's admiration of 'the goodly creatures' of her 'brave new world' (V.i.182–3). Prospero, would-be maker of a brave new world, speaks with a total absence of illusion when he says, dryly, 'Tis new to thee' (l.184). Is then the final note of *The Tempest* tragic rather than comic? Have the innumerable commentators who have found *The Tempest* the acme of serenity been, perhaps wishfully, deluded?

Yet Prospero has triumphed. Who can deny it? Prospero's fantasy, his Eros design for human amelioration, for human regeneration has achieved its end. He wished to be set free – from his island, from obsessive memories, hatreds, from the past, from the problem of a loved young daughter cut off from human society. All these ends are magnificently accomplished. Yet when he returns to Milan his every third thought will be the grave. He is stirred, unhappy, in a way that suggests that the beating in his mind is unassuaged; and at the end, in the famous epilogue, which unmasks the fictional protagonist to reveal the professional actor pleading for the plaudits of an actual audience and which recognises the play's make-believe, its consolatory fantasy, by drawing attention to it, he pleads, as if all is to be done again, to be set free. Why, and from what 'bands' does he now long to be released?

Prospero, with a great effort of renunciation, has created the conditions for happiness on his island but he cannot, as cynical Sebastian knows, 'carry this island home in his pocket, and give it his son for an apple' (II.i.91–2). Prospero knows what the cynics know, and more. He knows that his triumph is a triumph because, and in so far as the perennial force of the instinctual – of what he has overcome – is recognised. 'This thing of darkness I acknowledge mine' (V.i.275) is his acknowledgement of the primitive, the infantile, the unreconstructed libidinous in himself, but it is not merely or only a general, mandatory Christian humility confessing to the frailties of the worser self that speaks in

> And my ending is despair,
> Unless I be relieved by prayer,
> Which pierces so, that it assaults
> Mercy itself, and frees all faults.

Prospero's melancholy at the end of his immense effort to conquer and to sublimate is perhaps, at one very realistic level, no more than the collapse into depression of the euphoric, creatively imaginative moment. But I think we read the play's fantasy more fully if we read in it more than a reflex lassitude. It is the wound of Narcissus, the pain both of renunciation itself and of the knowledge of the dark backward and abysm of love. Every man is an island, or an ark, severed from its continent, doomed to lack what is most loved, to sail nowhere but to death.

The Tempest is therefore Shakespeare's most indissolubly tragi-comic drama. Prospero's restitutive project – 'to please' – was of the highest human value. For its success the 'gentle breath' of audience empathy, the clapping of their – our – 'good hands' is required. But the liberation for which Prospero begs the audience's 'indulgence' is the freedom, now that all is over, to mourn.

From Ruth Nevo, *Shakespeare's Other Language* (London and New York, 1987), pp. 130–60.

NOTES

[Ruth Nevo presents the play in terms of psychoanalysis – an approach acknowledged as significant by other critics in this volume. *The Tempest* becomes a 'Freudian metapsychology', where not only is there a textual unconscious but also an explicit allegorisation of the ego and the id. Dream, that state which interested Freud and Jung so much, becomes an analogy for the artistic representation or fantasy, at once concealing and revealing psychic impulses and finally sublimating them in the closure. Quotations are from the *Riverside Edition*, ed. G. Blakemore Evans (Boston, 1974) Ed.]

1. Reprinted from *The Collected Poems of Wallace Stevens* by permission of Alfred A. Knopf, Inc. and Faber and Faber Ltd.

2. Charles K. Hofling, 'Psychological Aspects of Shakespeare's *Tempest*', *Psychoanalytic Review*, 61 (1974).

3. On the philosophy of magic as a discipline of the soul see Frank Kermode (ed.), *The Tempest*, Arden edition (London, 1962), p. xviii.

4. Ludwig Jekels, 'On the Psychology of Comedy', *Imago*, xii (1926), de-velops the notion of courtship comedy as essentially oedipal from the son's point of view.

5. Kermode (p. 18) points out how 'the imagery of Prospero suddenly changes, becoming conceited and Italianate ('To cry to th'sea that roar'd to us; to sigh / To th'winds, whose pity, sighing back again, / Did us but loving wrong' [I.ii.149–51]), when, in the dialogue with Miranda, he shifts from 'reality', the level of the 'probable and natural', to the level of the 'miraculous'.

6. The genitive 'of', always ambiguously indicative of part or whole, makes 'the dark backward and abysm' either the whole passage of time itself, or some part or aspect of time, i.e. the inevitable loss of memory caused by the passage of time.

7. K. M. Abenheimer, 'Shakespeare's *Tempest*, A Psychological Analysis', *Psychoanalytic Review*, 33 (1946), takes this Jungian view, but he sees the play as a dramatic representation of Prospero's failure to overcome 'inflated loneliness, paranoid isolation' and 'archaic and magical fantasies about women as either horrible witches or Mirandas' (p. 515). Such a reading fails to take into account Prospero's manifest successes. One would have thought Prospero's acceptance of his 'shadow', Caliban, would have met with the approval of a Jungian.

8. Among others, Theodore Reik, *Fragment of a Great Confession* (New York, 1949); Leo Lowenthal, *Literature and the Image of Man* (Boston, 1957); Charles K. Hofling, 'Psychological Aspects of Shakespeare's *Tempest*', *Psychoanalytic Review*, 61 (1974); and Morton Kaplan and Robert Kloss, *The Unspoken Motive* (New York, 1973). For Garber, see note 13 below.

9. Meredith Skura, *The Literary Use of the Psychoanalytic Process* (New Haven, CT, 1981), pp. 36–7.

10. On the complex Renaissance conceptions of nature, see Kermode, pp. xxxiv–xliii.

11. Abenheimer ('Shakespeare's *Tempest*', Faber edn), p. 515.

12. Norman Holland, *Psychoanalysis and Shakespeare* (New York, 1964), pp. 522ff.

13. Marjorie B. Garber, *Dreams in Shakespeare: From Metaphor to Metamorphosis* (New Haven, CT, 1974), p. 141.

14. Anne Barton (ed.), *The Tempest*, New Penguin edition (Harmondsworth, 1980), pp. 12–26, passim.

15. See Richard Levin, *The Multiple Plot in English Renaissance Drama* (Chicago, 1971).

16. See Erwin Panovsky, *Studies in Iconology* (New York, 1962), p. 74. Jeffrey Mehlman refers to this iconology in his discussion of the Lacanian emphasis upon the notion of the fragile narcissistic ego as

opposed to the Freudian ego, agent of synthesis, mastery, integration, and adaptation. See 'The "floating signifier": from Lévi-Strauss to Lacan', *Yale French Studies*, 48 (1972).

17. Northrop Frye, 'Introduction', *The Tempest* (Harmondsworth, 1959), p. 10.

5

Martial Law in the Land of Cockaigne

STEPHEN GREENBLATT

I

When near the close of his career Shakespeare reflected upon his own art with still greater intensity and self-consciousness than in *Measure for Measure*, he once again conceived of the playwright as a princely creator of anxiety. But where in *Measure for Measure* disguise is the principal emblem of this art, in *The Tempest* the emblem is the far more potent and disturbing power of magic. Prospero's chief magical activity throughout *The Tempest* is to harrow the other characters with fear and wonder and then to reveal that their anxiety is his to create and allay. The spectacular storm in the play's first scene gives way to Miranda's empathic agitation: 'Oh! I have suffered / With those that I saw suffer. ... O, the cry did knock / Against my very heart.' 'The direful spectacle of the wrack,' replies Prospero,

> which touch'd
> The very virtue of compassion in thee,
> I have with such provision in mine art
> So safely ordered that there is no soul –
> No, not so much perdition as an hair
> Betid to any creature in the vessel
> Which thou heardst cry, which thou saw'st sink.
> (I.ii.26–32)

97

Miranda has been treated to an intense experience of suffering and to a still more intense demonstration of her father's power, the power at once to cause such suffering and to cancel it. Later in the play the threat of 'perdition' – both loss and damnation – will be concentrated against Prospero's enemies, but it is important to recall that at the start the management of anxiety through the 'provision' of art is practised upon Prospero's beloved daughter. Her suffering is the prelude to the revelation of her identity, as if Prospero believes that this revelation can be meaningful only in the wake of the amazement and pity he artfully arouses. He is setting out to fashion her identity, just as he is setting out to refashion the inner lives of his enemies, and he employs comparable disciplinary techniques.

With his daughter, Prospero's techniques are mediated and softened: she suffers at the sight of the sufferings of unknown wretches. With his enemies the techniques are harsher and more direct – the spectacle they are compelled to watch is not the wreck of others but of their own lives. In one of the play's most elaborate scenes, Prospero stands above the stage, invisible to those below him, and conjures up a banquet for Alonso, Antonio, Sebastian, and their party; when they move toward the table, Ariel appears like a Harpy and, with a clap of his wings and a burst of thunder and lightning, makes the table disappear. Ariel then solemnly recalls their crimes against Prospero and sentences the guilty in the name of the powers of Destiny and Fate:

> Thee of thy son, Alonso,
> They have bereft; and do pronounce by me
> Ling'ring perdition (worse than any death
> Can be at once).
> (III.iii.75–8)

Prospero is delighted at Ariel's performance:

> My high charms work,
> And these, mine enemies, are all knit up
> In their distractions. They now are in my pow'r.
> (III.iii.88–90)

To compel others to be 'all knit up / In their distractions', to cause a paralysing anxiety, is the dream of power, a dream perfected over bitter years of exile.[1] But as we have already seen, the artful manipulation of anxiety is not only the manifestation of aggression;

it is also a strategy for shaping the inner lives of others and for fashioning their behaviour. Hence we find Prospero employing the strategy not only upon those he hates but upon his daughter and upon the man whom he has chosen to be his daughter's husband. Ferdinand and Miranda fall in love instantly – 'It goes on, I see, / As my soul prompts it' (I.ii.420–1), remarks Prospero – but what is missing from their love is precisely the salutary anxiety that Prospero undertakes to impose: 'this swift business / I must uneasy make, lest too light winning / Make the prize light' (I.ii.451–3). To Miranda's horror, he accuses Ferdinand of treason and employs his magic charms once again to cause a kind of paralysis: 'My spirits', exclaims Ferdinand, 'as in a dream, are all bound up' (I.ii.487). The rituals of humiliation and suffering through which Prospero makes Ferdinand and Miranda pass evidently have their desired effect: at the end of the play the couple displayed to the amazed bystanders are revealed to be not only in a state of love but in a state of symbolic war. The lovers, you will recall, are discovered playing chess, and Miranda accuses Ferdinand of cheating. The deepest happiness is represented in this play as a state of playful tension.

Perhaps the supreme representation of this tension in *The Tempest* is to be found not in Prospero's enemies or in his daughter and son-in-law but in himself. The entire action of the play rests on the premise that value lies in controlled uneasiness, and hence that a direct reappropriation of the usurped dukedom and a direct punishment of the usurpers has less moral and political value than an elaborate inward restaging of loss, misery, and anxiety. Prospero directs this restaging not only against the others but also – even principally – against himself. That is, he arranges for the re-enactment in a variety of registers and through different symbolic agents of the originary usurpation, and in the play's most memorable yet perplexing moment, the princely artist puts himself through the paralysing uneasiness with which he has afflicted others. The moment to which I refer is that of the interrupted wedding masque. In the midst of the climactic demonstration of Prospero's magical powers, the celebration of the paradisal 'green land' where spring comes at the very end of harvest, Prospero suddenly starts, breaks off the masque, and declares that he had 'forgot that foul conspiracy / Of the beast Caliban and his confederates / Against my life' (IV.i.139–41).

In recalling the conspiracy, Prospero clearly exhibits signs of extreme distress: Ferdinand is struck by the 'passion / That works him strongly', and Miranda says that 'never till this day' has she seen him 'touch'd with anger, so distemper'd' (IV.i.143–5). Noticing that Ferdinand looks 'in a mov'd sort', as if he were 'dismay'd', Prospero tells him to 'be cheerful' and informs him that 'Our revels now are ended.' The famous speech that follows has the effect of drastically evacuating the masque's majestic vision of plenitude. 'Let me live here ever,' the delighted Ferdinand had exclaimed, enchanted by the promise of an aristocrat's equivalent of the Land of Cockaigne:

> Honor, riches, marriage-blessing,
> Long continuance, and increasing,
> Hourly joys be still upon you!
> (IV.i.106–8)

But Prospero now explains that the beneficent goddesses 'Are melted into air, into thin air' (IV.i.150). What had seemed solid is 'baseless'; what had seemed enduring ('the great globe itself')

> shall dissolve,
> And like this insubstantial pageant faded
> Leave not a rack behind.
> (IV.i.154–6)

Prospero offers this sublime vision of emptiness to make Ferdinand feel 'cheerful' – secure in the consciousness that life is a dream. It is difficult to believe in the effectiveness of these professed attempts at reassurance: like Duke Vincentio's religious consolations in *Measure for Measure*, they seem suited more to heighten anxiety than to allay it. The ascetic security Prospero articulates has evidently not stilled his own 'beating mind':

> Sir, I am vex'd;
> Bear with my weakness, my old brain is troubled.
> Be not disturb'd with my infirmity.
> (IV.i.158–60)

Since Prospero's art has in effect created the conspiracy as well as the defence against the conspiracy, and since the profession of infirmity comes at the moment of his greatest strength, we may conclude that we are witnessing the practice of salutary anxiety operating at the centre of the play's world, in the consciousness of Prospero himself, magician, artist, and prince. This does not mean that Prospero's anxiety about the conspiracy, about his enemies and servants and daughter, about his own inward state is not genuinely felt, nor does it mean that he is in absolute, untroubled control either of the characters whom he has brought onto the island or of himself. Rapt in his own magical vision of bounteousness, he has forgotten a serious threat to his life: 'The minute of their plot / Is almost come' (IV.i.141–2). But it is important to take seriously his deep complicity in his present tribulations, for only by actively willing them can he undo the tribulations that he unwillingly and unwittingly brought about years before. At that time, absorbed in his occult studies, he had been unaware of the dangers around him; now as the condition of a return to his dukedom, he himself brings those dangers to the centre of his retreat. This centre, whether we regard it as emblematic of the dominant religious, aesthetic, or political institution, is not the still point in a turbulent world but the point at which the anxieties that shape the character of others are screwed up to their highest pitch. Precisely from that point – and as a further exemplification of the salutary nature of anxiety – reconciliation and pardon can issue forth. This pardon is not a release from the power in which Prospero holds everyone around him but, as with Latimer and James I, its ultimate expression.[2]

Shakespeare goes beyond Latimer and James, however, in envisaging a case in which anxiety does not appear to have its full redeeming effect, a case in which the object of attention refuses to be fashioned inwardly, refuses even to acknowledge guilt, and yet is pardoned. The generosity of the pardon in this instance is inseparable from a demonstration of supreme force. 'For you, most wicked sir', Prospero says to his brother Antonio,

> whom to call brother
> Would even infect my mouth, I do forgive
> Thy rankest fault – all of them; and require
> My dukedom of thee, which perforce, I know
> Thou must restore.
>
> (V.i.130–4)

Antonio's silence at this point suggests that he remains unrepentant, but it also expresses eloquently the paralysis that is the hallmark of extreme anxiety. It has been argued convincingly that the truculence of the villains at the close of the play marks the limit of Prospero's power – as Prospero's failure to educate Caliban has already shown, the strategy of salutary anxiety cannot remake the inner life of everyone – yet at the very moment the limit is marked,

the play suggests that it is relatively inconsequential. It would no
doubt be preferable to receive the appropriate signs of inward gratitude from everyone, but Prospero will have to content himself in the
case of Antonio with the full restoration of his dukedom.³

II

What I have been describing here is the theatrical appropriation and
staging of a sixteenth- and seventeenth-century social practice. But
the strategy of salutary anxiety is not simply reflected in a second-
hand way by the work of art, because the practice itself is already
implicated in the artistic traditions and institutions out of which this
particular representation, *The Tempest*, has emerged. Latimer may
have been indifferent or hostile to the drama and to literature in
general, but his tale of the Cambridge prisoner seems shaped by literary conventions, earlier tales of wronged innocence and royal
pardons. And if the practice he exemplifies helps to empower theatrical representations, fictive representations have themselves
helped to empower his practice.⁴ So too Dudley Carleton, watching
men about to go to their deaths, thinks of the last act of a play, and
when a pardon is granted, the spectators applaud. This complex circulation between the social dimension of an aesthetic strategy and
the aesthetic dimension of a social strategy is difficult to grasp
because the strategy in question has an extraordinarily long and
tangled history, one whose aesthetic roots go back at least as far as
Aristotle's *Poetics*. But we may find a more manageable, though still
complex, model in the relation between *The Tempest* and one of
its presumed sources, William Strachey's account of the tempest
that struck an English fleet bound for the fledgling colony at
Jamestown.⁵

Strachey's account, with its bravura description of a violent storm
at sea and its tale of Englishmen providentially cast ashore on an uninhabited island rumoured to be devil haunted, is likely, along with
other New World materials, to have helped shape *The Tempest*. The
play was performed long before Strachey's narrative was printed in
Purchas's *Pilgrims* as 'A true reportory of the wrack, and redemption of Sir Thomas Gates Knight', but scholars presume that
Shakespeare read a manuscript version of the work, which takes the
form of a confidential letter written to a certain 'noble lady'.⁶ My

interest is not the particular verbal echoes, which have been painstakingly researched since Malone in 1808 first called attention to them, but the significance of the relation between the two texts, or rather between the institutions that the texts serve. For it is important to grasp that we are dealing not with the reflections of isolated individuals musing on current events but with expressions whose context is corporate and institutional.

William Strachey was a shareholder and secretary of the Virginia Company's colony at Jamestown; his letter on the events of 1609–10 was unpublished until 1625, not for want of interest but because the Virginia Company was engaged in a vigorous propaganda and financial campaign on behalf of the colony, and the company's leaders found Strachey's report too disturbing to allow it into print. Shakespeare too was a shareholder in a joint-stock company, the King's Men, as well as its principal playwright and sometime actor; *The Tempest* also remained unpublished for years, again presumably not for want of interest but because the theatre company resisted losing control of its playbook. Neither joint-stock company was a direct agent of the crown: despite the legal fiction that they were retainers of the monarch, the King's Men could not have survived through royal patronage alone, and they were not in the same position of either dependence or privilege as other household servants; the crown had deliberately withdrawn from the direction of the Virginia Company. Royal protection and support, of course, remained essential in both cases, but the crown would not assume responsibility, nor could either company count on royal financial support in times of need. Committed for their survival to attracting investment capital and turning a profit, both companies depended on their ability to market stories that would excite, interest, and attract supporters. Both Strachey and Shakespeare were involved in unusually direct and intricate ways in every aspect of their companies' operations: Strachey as shareholder, adventurer, and eventually secretary; Shakespeare as shareholder, actor, and playwright. Because of these multiple positions, both men probably identified intensely with the interests of their respective companies.

I want to propose that the relation between the play and its alleged source is a relation between joint-stock companies.[7] I do not mean that there was a direct, contractual connection.[8] As we have already seen with Latimer, the transfer of cultural practices and powers depends not upon contracts but upon networks of resemblance. In the case of Strachey and Shakespeare, there *are*, in point of fact, certain intriguing institutional affiliations: as Charles Mills Gayley observed many years ago, a remarkable number of social and professional connections link Shakespeare and the stockholders and directors of the Virginia Company; moreover, Strachey in 1605 wrote a prefatory sonnet commending Jonson's *Sejanus* and in 1606 is listed as a shareholder in an acting company known as the Children of the Queen's Revels, the company that had taken over the Blackfriars Theatre from Richard Burbage.[9] Still, I should emphasise that these affiliations do not amount to a direct transfer of properties; we are dealing with a system of mimetic rather than contractual exchange. The conjunction of Strachey's unpublished letter and Shakespeare's play signals an institutional circulation of culturally significant narratives. And as we shall see, this circulation has as its central concern the public management of anxiety.

Strachey tells the story of a state of emergency and a crisis of authority. The 'unmerciful tempest' that almost sank Sir Thomas Gates's ship, the *Sea Venture*, provoked an immediate collapse of the distinction between those who labour and those who rule, a distinction, we should recall, that is at the economic and ideological centre of Elizabethan and Jacobean society: 'Then men might be seen to labour, I may well say, for life, and the better sort, even our Governour, and Admiral themselves, not refusing their turn. ... And it is most true, such as in all their life times had never done hours work before (their minds now helping their bodies) were able twice forty eight hours together to toil with the best' (in Purchas, 19:9–11). 'The best' – the violence of the storm has turned Strachey's own language upside down: now it is the common seamen, ordinarily despised and feared by their social superiors, who are, as the Romans called their aristocrats, the *optimi viri*, the best of men.[10] Indeed the storm had quite literally a levelling force: while the governor was 'both by his speech and authority heartening every man unto his labour', a great wave 'struck him from the place where he sat, and groveled him, and all us about him on our faces, beating together with our breaths all thoughts from our bosoms, else then that we were now sinking' (p. 10).

Even after the ship had run aground in the Bermudas and the one hundred and fifty men, women and children on board had been saved, the crisis of authority was not resolved; indeed it only intensified then, not because of a levelling excess of anxiety but because of its almost complete absence in the colonists. The alarm of the rulers makes itself felt in quirks of Strachey's style. He reports, for example, that many palmettos were cut down for their edible tops, but the report has a strange nervous tone, as the plants are comically turned into wealthy victims of a popular uprising: 'Many an ancient Burgher was therefore heaved at, and fell not for his place, but for his head: for our common people, whose bellies never had ears, made it no breach of Charity in their hot bloods and tall stomachs to murder thousands of them' (p. 19).

The strain registered here in the tone stands for concerns that are partially suppressed in the published text, concerns that are voiced in a private letter written in December 1610 by Richard Martin, secretary of the Virginia Company in London, to Strachey, who was by then in Jamestown. Martin asks Strachey for a full confidential report on 'the nature & quality of the soil, & how it is like to serve you without help from hence, the manners of the people, how the Barbarians are content with your being there, but especially how our own people do brook their obedience, how they endure labor, whether willingly or upon constraint, how they live in the exercise of Religion, whether out of conscience or for fashion, And generally what ease you have in the government there, & what hope of success.'[11]

Here the deepest fears lie not with the human or natural resources of the New World but with the discipline of the English colonists and common seamen. And the principal questions – whether obedience is willing or forced, whether religious observance is sincere or feigned – suggest an interest in inner states, as if the shareholders in the Virginia Company believed that only with a set of powerful inward restraints could the colonists be kept from rebelling at the first sign of the slippage or relaxation of authority. The company had an official institutional interest in shaping and controlling the minds of its own people. But the Bermuda shipwreck revealed the difficulty of this task as well as its importance: set apart from the institutional and military safeguards established at Jamestown, Bermuda was an experimental space, a testing ground where the extent to which disciplinary anxiety had been internalised by the ordinary venturers could be measured.

The results were not encouraging. As Strachey and others remark, Bermuda was an extraordinarily pleasant surprise: the climate was healthful, the water was pure, there were no native inhabitants to contend with, and, equally important, there was no shortage of food. Tortoises – 'such a kind of meat, as a man can neither absolutely call Fish nor Flesh' (p. 24)[12] – were found in great number, and the skies were dark with great flocks of birds:

> Our men found a pretty way to take them, which was by standing on
> the Rocks or Sands by the Sea side, and hollowing, laughing, and
> making the strangest out-cry that possibly they could: with the noise
> whereof the Birds would come flocking to that place, and settle upon
> the very arms and head of him that so cried, and still creep nearer
> and nearer, answering the noise themselves: by which our men would
> weigh them with their hands, and which weighed heaviest they took
> for the best and let the others alone.
>
> (Purchas, 19:22–3)

Even to us, living for the most part in the confident expectation
of full bellies, this sounds extraordinary enough; to seventeenth-
century voyagers, whose ordinary condition was extreme want and
who had dragged themselves from the violent sea onto an unknown
shore with the likely prospect of starvation and death, such extrava-
gant abundance must have seemed the fantastic realisation of old
folk dreams of a land where the houses were roofed with pies and
the pigs ran about with little knives conveniently stuck in their pre-
cooked sides. In this Land of Cockaigne setting, far removed not
only from England but from the hardships of Jamestown, the authority of Sir Thomas Gates and his lieutenants was anything but
secure. For the perception that Bermuda was a providential deliverance contained within it a subversive corollary: why leave? why
press on to a hungry garrison situated in a pestiferous swamp and in
grave tension with the surrounding Algonquian tribesmen?[13]

According to Strachey, Gates was initially concerned less about
his own immediate authority than about the possible consequences
of his absence in Virginia. The *Sea Venture* had come to grief in the
tempest, but Gates thought (correctly, as it happened) that the other
two vessels might have reached their destination, and this thought
brought not only consolation but anxiety, which focused, in characteristic Renaissance fashion, on the ambitions of the younger generation. Fearful about 'what innovation and tumult might happily
[haply] arise, among the younger and ambitious spirits of the new
companies to arrive in Virginia' (p. 26) in his absence, Gates wished
to construct new ships as quickly as possible to continue on to
Jamestown, but the sailors and the colonists alike began to grumble
at this plan. In Virginia, they reasoned, 'nothing but wretchedness
and labour must be expected, with many wants and a churlish en-
treaty'; in Bermuda, all things 'at ease and pleasure might be
enjoyed' (p. 29) without hardship or threatening. There is, at least
as Strachey reports it, virtually no internalisation of the ideology of

colonialism; the voyagers appear to think of themselves as forced to endure a temporary exile from home. As long as 'they were (for the time) to lose the fruition both of their friends and Country, as good, and better it were for them, to repose and seat them where they should have the least outward wants the while' (p. 29). And to this dangerous appeal – the appeal, in Strachey's words, of 'liberty, and fulness of sensuality' (p. 35) – was added a still more dangerous force: religious dissent.

Arguments against leaving Bermuda began to be voiced not only among the 'idle, untoward, and wretched number of the many' (p. 29) but among the educated few. One of these, Stephen Hopkins, 'alleged substantial arguments, both civil and divine (the Scripture falsely quoted) that it was no breach of honesty, conscience, nor Religion, to decline from the obedience of the Governour, or refuse to go any further, led by his authority (except it so pleased themselves) since the authority ceased when the wrack was committed, and with it, they were all then freed from the government of any man' (pp. 30–1). Hopkins evidently accepted the governor's authority as a contractual obligation that continued only so long as the enterprise remained on course. Once there was a swerve from the official itinerary, that authority, not granted a general or universal character, lapsed, and the obedience of the subject gave way to the will and pleasure of each man.[14] We cannot know, of course, if Hopkins said anything so radical, but this is how his 'substantial arguments, both civil and divine', sounded to those in command. In Strachey's account, at least, the shipwreck had led to a profound questioning of authority that seems to anticipate the challenge posed by mid-seventeenth-century radicals like Winstanley. What are the boundaries of authority? What is the basis of its claim to be obeyed? How much loyalty does an individual owe to a corporation?

When the seditious words were reported to Gates, the governor convened a martial court and sentenced Hopkins to death, but the condemned man was so tearfully repentant that he received a pardon. This moving scene – the saving public display of anxiety – evidently did not settle the question of authority, however, for shortly after, yet another mutiny arose, this time led by a gentleman named Henry Paine. When Paine was warned that he risked execution for 'insolency', he replied, Strachey reports, 'with a settled and bitter violence, and in such unreverent terms, as I should offend the modest ear too much to express it in his own phrase; but its contents were, how that the Governour had no authority of that quality, to justify upon any one (how mean soever in the colony) an action of that nature, and therefore let the Governour (said he) kiss, &c.' (p. 34). When these words, 'with the omitted additions', were reported, the governor, 'who had now the eyes of the whole Colony fixed upon him', condemned Paine 'to be instantly hanged; and the ladder being ready, after he had made many confessions, he earnestly desired, being a Gentleman, that he might be shot to death, and towards the evening he had his desire, the Sun and his life setting together' (p. 34). 'He had his desire' – Strachey's sarcasm is also perhaps the representation of what those in authority regarded as an intolerable nonchalance, a refusal to perform those rituals of tearful repentance that apparently saved Hopkins's life. In effect Paine is killed to set an example, condemned to die for cursing authority, for a linguistic crime, for violating discursive decorum, for inadequate anxiety in the presence of power.

In his narrative, Strachey represents the norms Paine has challenged by means of his '&c.' – the noble lady to whom he is writing, like Mr Kurtz's intended, must be sheltered from the awful truth, here from the precise terms of the fatal irreverent challenge to authority. The suppression of the offending word enacts in miniature the reimposition of salutary anxiety by a governor 'so solicitous and careful, whose both example ... and authority, could lay shame, and command upon our people' (p. 28). The governor is full of care – therefore resistant to the lure of the island – and he manages, even in the midst of a paradisal plenty, to impose this care upon others. When the governor himself writes to a fellow officer explaining why all of the colonists must be compelled to leave the island, he invokes not England's imperial destiny or Christianity's advancement but the Virginia Company's investment: 'The meanest in the whole Fleet stood the Company in no less than twenty pounds, for his own personal Transportation, and things necessary to accompany him' (p. 36). On the strength of this compelling motive, new ships were built, and in an impressive feat of navigation, the whole company finally reached Jamestown.[15]

Upon their arrival Gates and his people found the garrison in desperate condition – starving, confused, terrorised by hostile and treacherous Indians, and utterly demoralised. In Gates's view, the problem was almost entirely one of discipline, and he addressed it by imposing a set of 'orders and instructions' upon the colony that transformed the 'government' of Jamestown 'into an absolute command'. The orders were published in 1612 by Strachey as the

Laws Divine, Moral, and Martial, an exceptionally draconian code by which whipping, mutilation, and the death penalty might be imposed for a wide range of offences, including blasphemy, insubordination, even simple criticism of the Virginia Company and its officers. These orders, the first martial law code in America, suspended the traditional legal sanctions that governed the lives of Englishmen, customary codes based on mutual constraints and obligations, and instituted in their stead the grim and self-consciously innovative logic of a state of emergency. The company's claim upon the colonists had become total. The group that had been shipwrecked in Bermuda passed from dreams of absolute freedom to the imposition of absolute control.

Such then were the narrative materials that passed from Strachey to Shakespeare, from the Virginia Company to the King's Men: a violent tempest, a providential shipwreck on a strange island, a crisis in authority provoked by both danger and excess, a fear of lower-class disorder and upper-class ambition, a triumphant affirmation of absolute control linked to the manipulation of anxiety and to a departure from the island. But the swerve away from these materials in *The Tempest* is as apparent as their presence: the island is not in America but in the Mediterranean; it is not uninhabited – Ariel and Caliban (and, for that matter, Sycorax) were present before the arrival of Prospero and Miranda; none of the figures are in any sense colonists; the departure is for home rather than a colony and entails not an unequivocal heightening of authority but a partial diminution, signalled in Prospero's abjuration of magic.

> I'll break my staff,
> Bury it certain fadoms in the earth,
> And deeper than did ever plummet sound
> I'll drown my book.
>   (V.i.54–7)

If the direction of Strachey's narrative is toward the promulgation of the martial law codes, the direction of *The Tempest* is toward forgiveness. And if that forgiveness is itself the manifestation of supreme power, the emblem of that power remains marriage rather than punishment.

The changes I have sketched are signs of the process whereby the Bermuda narrative is made negotiable, turned into a currency that may be transferred from one institutional context to another. The changes do not constitute a coherent critique of the colonial discourse, but they function as an unmooring of its elements so as to confer upon them the currency's liquidity. Detached from their context in Strachey's letter, these elements may be transformed and recombined with materials drawn from other writers about the New World who differ sharply from Strachey in their interests and motives – Montaigne, Sylvester Jourdain, James Rosier, Robert Eden, Peter Martyr – and then integrated in a dramatic text that draws on a wide range of discourse, including pastoral and epic poetry, the lore of magic and witchcraft, literary romance, and a remarkable number of Shakespeare's own earlier plays.

The ideological effects of the transfer to *The Tempest* are ambiguous. On the one hand, the play seems to act out a fantasy of mind control, to celebrate absolute patriarchal rule, to push to an extreme the dream of order, epic achievement, and ideological justification implicit in Strachey's text. The lower-class resistance Strachey chronicles becomes in Shakespeare the drunken rebellion of Stephano and Trinculo, the butler and jester who, suddenly finding themselves freed from their masters, are drawn to a poor man's fantasy of mastery: 'the King and all our company else being drown'd, we will inherit here' (II.ii.174–5). Similarly, the upper-class resistance of Henry Paine is transformed into the murderous treachery of Sebastian, in whom the shipwreck arouses dreams of an escape from subordination to his older brother, the king of Naples, just as Antonio had escaped subordination to his older brother Prospero:

> **Sebastian**   I remember
>   You did supplant your brother Prospero.
> **Antonio**   True.
>   And look how well my garments sit upon me,
>   Much feater than before. My brother's servants
>   Were then my fellows, now they are my men.
>   (II.i.270–4)

By invoking fratricidal rivalry here Shakespeare is not only linking the Strachey materials to his own long-standing theatrical preoccupations but also supplementing the contractual authority of a governor like Sir Thomas Gates with the familial and hence culturally sanctified authority of the eldest son. To rise up against such a figure, as Claudius had against old Hamlet or Edmund against Edgar, is an assault not only on a political structure but on the moral and natural order of things: it is an act that has, as Claudius says, 'the primal eldest curse upon't'. The assault is magically thwarted by Ariel, the indispensable agent of Prospero's 'art'; hence that art, potentially a force of disorder, spiritual violence, and darkness, is confirmed as the agent of legitimacy. Through his mastery of the occult, Prospero withholds food from his enemies, spies upon them, listens to their secret conversations, monitors their movements, blocks their actions, keeps track of their dealings with the island's native inhabitant, torments and disciplines his servants, defeats conspiracies against his life. A crisis of authority – deposition from power, exile, impotence – gives way through the power of his art to a full restoration. From this perspective Prospero's magic is the romance equivalent of martial law.

Yet *The Tempest* seems to raise troubling questions about this authority. The great storm with which the play opens has some of the levelling force of the storm that struck the *Sea Venture*. To be sure, unlike Strachey's gentlemen, Shakespeare's nobles refuse the boatswain's exasperated demand that they share the labour, 'Work you then', but their snarling refusal – 'Hang, cur! hang, you whoreson, insolent noisemaker!' (I.i.42–4) – far from securing their class superiority, represents them as morally beneath the level of the common seamen.[16] Likewise, Shakespeare's king, Alonso, is not 'groveled' by a wave, but – perhaps worse – he is peremptorily ordered below by the harried boatswain: 'What cares these roarers for the name of king? To cabin! silence! trouble us not' (I.i.16–18). And if we learn eventually that these roarers are in fact produced *by* a king – in his name and through his command of a magical language – this knowledge does not altogether cancel our perception of the storm's indifference to the ruler's authority and the idle aristocrat's pride of place.

The perception would perhaps be overwhelmed by the display of Prospero's power were it not for the questions that are raised about this very power. A Renaissance audience might have found the locus of these questions in the ambiguous status of magic, an ambiguity deliberately heightened by the careful parallels drawn between Prospero and the witch Sycorax and by the attribution to Prospero of claims made by Ovid's witch Medea. But for a modern audience, at least, the questions centre on the figure of Caliban, whose claim to the legitimate possession of the island – 'This island's mine by Sycorax my mother' (I.ii.331) – is never really answered, or rather is answered by Prospero only with hatred, torture, and enslavement.[17]

Though he treats Caliban as less than human, Prospero finally expresses, in a famously enigmatic phrase, a sense of connection with his servant-monster, standing anxious and powerless before him: 'this thing of darkness I / Acknowledge mine' (V.i.275–6). He may intend these words only as a declaration of ownership, but it is difficult not to hear in them some deeper recognition of affinity, some half-conscious acknowledgement of guilt. At the play's end the princely magician appears anxious and powerless before the audience to beg for indulgence and freedom.

As the epilogue is spoken, Prospero's magical power and princely authority – figured in the linked abilities to raise winds and to pardon offenders – pass, in a startling display of the circulation of social energy, from the performer onstage to the crowd of spectators. In the play's closing moments the marginal, vulnerable actor, more than half-visible beneath the borrowed robes of an assumed dignity, seems to acknowledge that the imaginary forces with which he has played reside ultimately not in himself or in the playwright but in the multitude. The audience is the source of his anxiety, and it holds his release quite literally in its hands: without the crowd's applause his 'ending is despair' (Epilogue, 15). This admission of dependence includes a glance at the multitude's own vulnerability:

> As you from crimes would pardon'd be,
> Let your indulgence set me free.
> (Epilogue, 19–20)

But it nonetheless implicates the prince as well as the player in the experience of anxiety and the need for pardon.

Furthermore, even if we may argue that such disturbing or even subversive reflections are contained within the thematic structure of the play, a structure that seems to support the kind of authority served by Strachey, we must acknowledge that the propagandists for colonisation found little to admire in the theatre. That is, the most disturbing effects of the play may have been located not in what may be perceived in the text by a subtle interpreter – implied criticisms of colonialism or subversive doubts about its structures of authority – but in the phenomenon of theatrical representation itself. In 1593 Sir Thomas Smith reminded each captain in Virginia that his task was 'to lay the foundation of a good and ... an eternal colony for your posterity, not a May game or stage play'.[18] Festive, evanescent, given over to images of excess, stage plays function here as the symbolic opposite to the lasting colony. So too in a sermon preached in London in 1610 to a group of colonists about to set out for Virginia, William Crashaw declared that the enemies of the godly colony were the devil, the pope, and the players – the latter angry 'because we resolve to suffer no Idle persons in Virginia.'[19] Similarly, at the end of the martial law text, Strachey records an exceptionally long prayer that he claims was 'duly said Morning and Evening upon the Court of Guard, either by the Captain of the watch himself, or by some one of his principal officers'. If Strachey is right, twice a day the colonists would have heard, among other uplifting sentiments, the following: 'Whereas we have by undertaking this plantation undergone the reproofs of the base world, insomuch as many of our own brethren laugh us to scorn, O Lord we pray thee fortify us against this temptation: let *Sanballat*, & *Tobias*, Papists & players, & such other *Ammonites* & *Horonites* the scum & dregs of the earth, let them mock such as help to build up the walls of Jerusalem, and they that be filthy, let them be filthy still.'[20] Even if the content of a play seemed acceptable, the mode of entertainment itself was the enemy of the colonial plantation.

III

What then is the relation between the theatre and the surrounding institutions? Shakespeare's play offers us a model of unresolved and unresolvable doubleness: the island in *The Tempest* seems to be an image of the place of pure fantasy, set apart from surrounding discourses; and it seems to be an image of the place of power, the place in which all individual discourses are organised by the half-invisible ruler. By extension art is a well-demarcated, marginal, private sphere, the realm of insight, pleasure, and isolation; and art is a capacious, central, public sphere, the realm of proper political order made possible through mind control, coercion, discipline, anxiety, and pardon. The aesthetic space – or, more accurately, the commercial space of the theatrical joint-stock company – is constituted by the simultaneous appropriation of and swerving from the discourse of power.

And this doubleness in effect produces two different accounts of the nature of mimetic economy. In one account, aesthetic representation is unlike all other exchanges because it takes nothing; art is pure plenitude. Everywhere else there is scarcity: wretches cling to 'an acre of barren ground, long heath, brown furze, any thing' (I.i.66–7), and one person's gain is another's loss. In works of art, by contrast, things can be imitated, staged, reproduced without any loss or expense; indeed what is borrowed seems enhanced by the borrowing, for nothing is used up, nothing fades. The magic of art resides in the freedom of the imagination and hence in liberation from the constraints of the body. What is produced elsewhere only by intense labour is produced in art by a magical command whose power Shakespeare figures in Ariel's response to Prospero's call:

> All hail, great master, grave sir, hail! I come
> To answer thy best pleasure; be't to fly,
> To swim, to dive into the fire, to ride
> On the curl'd clouds. To thy strong bidding, task
> Ariel, and all his quality.
>
> (I.ii.189–93)

This account of art as pure plenitude is perhaps most perfectly imaged in Prospero's wedding masque, with its goddesses and nymphs and dancing reapers, its majestic vision of

> Barns and garners never empty;
> Vines with clust'ring bunches growing,
> Plants with goodly burthen bowing.
>
> (IV.i.111–13)

But the prayer at the end of the marital law code reminds us that there is another version of mimetic economy, one in which aesthetic exchanges, like all other exchanges, always involve loss, even if it is cunningly hidden; in which aesthetic value, like all other value, actively depends upon want, craving, and absence; in which art itself – fantasy ridden and empty – is the very soul of scarcity. This version too finds its expression in *The Tempest* in the high cost Prospero has paid for his absorption in his secret studies, in Ariel's grumblings about his 'pains' and 'toil', and in the sudden vanishing – 'to a strange, hollow, and confused noise' – of the masque that had figured forth plenitude and in Prospero's richly anxious meditation on the 'baseless fabric' of his own glorious vision.

It is this doubleness that Shakespeare's joint-stock company bequeathed to its cultural heirs. And the principal beneficiary in the end was not the theatre but a different institution, the institution of literature. Shakespeare served posthumously as a principal shareholder in this institution as well – not as a man of the theatre but as the author of the book. During Shakespeare's lifetime, the King's Men showed no interest in and may have actually resisted the publication of a one-volume collection of their famous playwright's work; the circulation of such a book was not in the interests of their company. But other collective enterprises, including the educational system in which this study is implicated, have focused more on the text than on the playhouse.

For if Shakespeare himself imagined Prospero's island as the great Globe Theatre, succeeding generations found that island more compactly and portably figured in the bound volume. The passage from the stage to the book signals a larger shift from the joint-stock company, with its primary interest in protecting the common property, to the modern corporation, with its primary interest in the expansion and profitable exploitation of a network of relations. Unlike the Globe, which is tied to a particular place and time and community, unlike even the travelling theatre company, with its constraints of personnel and stage properties and playing space, the book is supremely portable. It may be readily detached from its immediate geographical and cultural origins, its original producers and consumers, and endlessly reproduced, circulated, exchanged, exported to other times and places.[21]

The plays, of course, continue to live in the theatre, but Shakespeare's achievement and the cult of artistic genius erected around the achievement have become increasingly identified with his collected works. Those works have been widely acknowledged as the central literary achievement of English culture. As such they served – and continue to serve – as a fetish of Western civilisation, a fetish Caliban curiously anticipates when he counsels Stephano and Trinculo to cut Prospero's throat.[22]

> Remember
> First to possess his books; for without them
> He's but a sot, as I am; nor hath not
> One spirit to command: they all do hate him
> As rootedly as I. Burn but his books.
> (III.ii.91–5)

I want to close with a story that provides an oddly ironic perspective on Caliban's desire and exemplifies the continued doubleness of Shakespeare in our culture: at once the embodiment of civilised recreation, freed from the anxiety of rule, and the instrument of empire. The story is told by H. M. Stanley – the journalist and African explorer of 'Doctor Livingstone, I presume?' fame – in his account of his journeyings through what he calls 'the dark continent'. In May 1877 he was at a place called Mowa in central Africa. I will let him tell the story in his own words:

> On the third day of our stay at Mowa, feeling quite comfortable amongst the people, on account of their friendly bearing, I began to write down in my note-book the terms for articles in order to improve my already copious vocabulary of native words. I had proceeded only a few minutes when I observed a strange commotion amongst the people who had been flocking about me, and presently they ran away. In a short time we heard war-cries ringing loudly and shrilly over the table-land. Two hours afterwards, a long line of warriors, armed with muskets, were seen descending the table-land and advancing towards our camp. There may have been between five hundred and six hundred of them. We, on the other hand, had made but few preparations except such as would justify us replying to them in the event of the actual commencement of hostilities. But I had made many firm friends amongst them, and I firmly believed that I would be able to avert an open rupture.
>
> When they had assembled at about a hundred yards in front of our camp, Safeni [the chief of another tribe with whom Stanley had become friendly] and I walked up towards them, and sat down midway. Some half-dozen of the Mowa people came near, and the shauri began.
>
> 'What is the matter, my friends?' I asked. 'Why do you come with guns in your hands in such numbers, as though you were coming to fight? Fight! Fight us, your friends! Tut! this is some great mistake, surely.'
>
> 'Mundelé,' replied one of them, … 'our people saw you yesterday make marks on some tara-tara' (paper). 'This is very bad. Our country will waste, our goats will die, our bananas will rot, and our women will dry up. What have we done to you, that you should wish to kill us? We have sold you food, and we have brought you wine, each day. Your people are allowed to wander where they please, without trouble. Why is the Mundelé so wicked? We have gathered together to fight you if you do not burn that tara-tara now before our eyes. If you burn it we go away, and shall be friends as heretofore.'
>
> I told them to rest there, and left Safeni in their hands as a pledge that I should return. My tent was not fifty yards from the spot, but while going towards it my brain was busy in devising some plan to foil this superstitious madness. My note-book contained a vast number of valuable notes; plans of falls, creeks, villages, sketches of localities, ethnological and philological details, sufficient to fill two octavo volumes – everything was of general interest to the public.

I could not sacrifice it to the childish caprice of savages. As I was rummaging my book box, I came across a volume of Shakespeare (Chandos edition), much worn and well thumbed, and which was of the same size as my field-book; its cover was similar also, and it might be passed for the note-book provided that no one remembered its appearance too well. I took it to them.

'Is this the tara-tara, friends, that you wish burnt?'

'Yes, yes, that is it!'

'Well, take it, and burn it or keep it.'

'M-m. No, no, no. We will not touch it. It is fetish. You must burn it.'

'I! Well, let it be so. I will do anything to please my good friends of Mowa.'

We walked to the nearest fire. I breathed a regretful farewell to my genial companion, which during many weary hours of night had assisted to relieve my mind when oppressed by almost intolerable woes, and then gravely consigned the innocent Shakespeare to the flames, heaping the brush-fuel over it with ceremonious care.

'Ah-h-h', breathed the poor deluded natives, sighing their relief. 'The Mundelé is good – is very good. He loves his Mowa friends. There is no trouble now, Mundelé. The Mowa people are not bad.' And something approaching to a cheer was shouted among them, which terminated the episode of the Burning of Shakespeare.[23]

Stanley's precious notebook, with its sketches and ethnographic and philologic details, survived then and proved invaluable in charting and organising the Belgian Congo, perhaps the most vicious of all of Europe's African colonies. As Stanley had claimed, everything was indeed of general interest to the public. After Stanley's death, the notebooks passed into the possession of heirs and then for many years were presumed lost. But they were rediscovered at the time of the Congo independence celebrations and have recently been edited. Their publication revealed something odd: while the notebook entry for his stay at Mowa records that the natives were angry at his writing – 'They say I made strong medicine to kill their country' – Stanley makes no mention of the burning of Shakespeare.[24] Perhaps, to heighten that general interest with which he was so concerned, he made up the story. He could have achieved his narrative effect with only two books: Shakespeare and the Bible. And had he professed to burn the latter to save his notebook, his readers would no doubt have been scandalised.

For our purposes, it doesn't matter very much if the story 'really' happened. What matters is the role Shakespeare plays in it, a role at once central and expendable – and, in some obscure way, not just expendable but exchangeable for what really matters: the writing that more directly serves power. For if at moments we can convince ourselves that Shakespeare *is* the discourse of power, we should remind ourselves that there are usually other discourses – here the notes and vocabulary and maps – that are instrumentally far more important. Yet if we try then to convince ourselves that Shakespeare is marginal and untainted by power, we have Stanley's story to remind us that without Shakespeare we wouldn't have the notes. Of course, this is just an accident – the accident of the books' resemblance – but then why was Stanley carrying the book in the first place?

For Stanley, Shakespeare's theatre had become a book, and the book in turn had become a genial companion, a talisman of civility, a source not of salutary anxiety but of comfort in adversity. The anxiety in his account – and it is not salutary – is among the natives, and it is relieved only when, as Caliban had hoped, the book is destroyed. But the destruction of one book only saves another, more practical, more deadly. And when he returned to London or New York, Stanley could always buy another copy (Chandos edition) of his genial companion.

From Stephen Greenblatt, *Shakespearean Negotiations: The Circulation of Social Energy in Renaissance England* (Oxford, 1988), pp. 142–63.

NOTES

[Stephen Greenblatt places *The Tempest* in a longer argument concerning 'the staging of anxiety', the arousing, representing and manipulating of anxiety in the theatre: Prospero manages the insecurity of those at his mercy, and Shakespeare implicates the audience through his technique. As a self-styled 'new historicist', Greenblatt links up this characteristic of Shakespeare with power in the political world ('mind control, coercion, discipline, anxiety, and pardon'). The paradox of theatre (and later, literature, when Shakespeare's works were published and fetishised) is that it is both an image and enactment of this political discourse while simultaneously being pure fantasy and an act from the power of the imagination. Edition of Shakespeare used is *The Riverside Shakespeare*, ed. G. Blakemore Evans (Boston, 1974). Ed.]

1. Recall Carleton's description of the expression on the faces of the Bye Plot conspirators as they were assembled together on the scaffold. Dudley Carleton's letter, dated 11 December 1603, is reprinted in Thomas Birch, *The Court and Times of James the First*, 2 vols (London,

1849), 1:27–32. Carleton suggests that Sir Walter Ralegh, who had also been convicted in the Bye Plot, was the particular object of the king's techniques of anxiety arousal.

2. On the significance of pardon as a strategy in Renaissance monarchies, see Natalie Zemon Davis, *Fiction in the Archives* (Stanford, CA, forthcoming). Davis's wonderful book, which she graciously allowed me to read in manuscript, shows that the system of pardons in France generated a remarkable range of narratives. Though the English legal system differed in important ways from the French, pardon played a significant, if more circumscribed, role. Shakespeare seems to have deliberately appropriated for *The Tempest* the powerful social energy of princely pardons.

3. In this regard Prospero resembles less a radical reformer like Latimer than a monarch like Queen Elizabeth: a ruler who abjured the complete inquisitorial control of the inner life and settled when necessary for the outward signs of obedience.

   For a brilliant discussion of Prospero's relations with Antonio, see the introduction to the Oxford Shakespeare edition of *The Tempest*, ed. Stephen Orgel (Oxford, 1987). Throughout this chapter, I have profited from Orgel's introduction, which he kindly showed me in advance of its publication.

4. I am trying to resist here the proposition that Latimer's story is the actual practice that is then represented in works of art, and hence that in it we encounter the basis in reality of theatrical fictions. Even if we assume that the events in Cambridge occurred exactly as Latimer related them – and this is a large assumption based on a reckless act of faith – those events seem saturated with narrative conventions. It is not only that Latimer lives his life as if it were material for the stories he will tell in his sermons but that the actions he reports are comprehensible only if already fashioned into a story.

5. On Strachey's career, see S. G. Culliford, *William Strachey, 1572–1621* (Charlottesville, VA, 1965). See also Charles Richard Sanders, 'William Strachey, the Virginia Colony, and Shakespeare', *Virginia Magazine*, 57 (1949), 115–32. Sanders notes that 'many of the eighteenth and nineteenth century Stracheys became servants of the East India Company' (118).

6. William Strachey, in Samuel Purchas, *Hakluytus Posthumus or Purchas His Pilgrimes*, 20 vols (Glasgow, 1905–7), 19:5–72. [All further references are given in parentheses in the text. Ed.] It seems worth remarking the odd coincidence between this circumstance and Latimer's presenting his sermon also to a noble lady. Men in this period often seem to shape their experiences in the world to present them as instruction or entertainment to powerfully placed ladies. The great Shakespearean exploration of this social theme is *Othello*.

7. On joint-stock companies in the early modern period, see William Robert Scott, *The Constitution and Finance of English, Scottish, and Irish Joint-Stock Companies to 1720*, 3 vols (Cambridge, 1912). On the theatre and the marketplace, see the excellent book by Jean-Christophe Agnew, *Worlds Apart: The Market and the Theater in Anglo-American Thought, 1550–1750* (Cambridge, 1986).

8. Indeed the demand for such connections, a demand almost always frustrated in the early modern period, has strengthened the case for the formalist isolation of art.

9. Charles Mills Gayley, *Shakespeare and the Founders of Liberty in America* (New York, 1917); William Strachey, *The Historie of Travell into Virginia Britania* (1612), ed. Louis B. Wright and Virginia Freund, Hakluyt Society 2d ser., no. 103 (London, 1953), p. xix.

10. Detestation of the sailors is a common theme in the travel literature of the period. One of the strongest elements of an elitist utopia in *The Tempest* is the fantasy that the sailors will in effect be put to sleep for the duration of the stay on the island, to be awakened only to labour on the return voyage.

11. Quoted in the introduction to *The Historie of Travell into Virginia Britania*, p. xxv.

12. I quote these lines because they may have caught Shakespeare's attention: 'What have we here?' asks Trinculo, catching sight of Caliban, 'a man or a fish? dead or alive? A fish, he smells like a fish' (II.ii.24–6). Prospero in exasperation calls Caliban a tortoise (I.ii.316).

13. The promotional literature written on behalf of the Virginia Company prior to the voyage of 1609 makes it clear that there was already widespread talk in England about the hardships of the English colonists. No one on the *Sea Venture* is likely to have harboured any illusions about conditions at Jamestown.

14. The office of governor was created by the royal charter of 1609. The governor replaced the council president as the colony's chief executive. He was granted the right to 'correct and punishe, pardon, governe, and rule all such the subjects of us ... as shall from time to time adventure themselves ... thither', and he was empowered to impose martial law in cases of mutiny or rebellion (quoted in *The Three Charters of the Virginia Company of London, with Seven Related Documents, 1606–1621*, ed. S. F. Bemiss, Jamestown 350th Anniversary Historical Booklet 4 [Williamsburg, VA, 1957], p. 52). See Warren M. Billings, 'The Transfer of English Law to Virginia, 1606–1650', in *The Westward Enterprise: English Activities in Ireland, the Atlantic, and America, 1480–1650*, ed. K. R. Andrews, N. P. Canny, and P. E. H. Hair (Liverpool, 1978), pp. 214ff.

15. Leaving the island is not in itself, as is sometimes claimed, an abjuration of colonialism: as we have seen in the case of Bermuda, the enforced departure from the island signals the resumption of the colonial enterprise. On the other hand, insofar as *The Tempest* conflates the Bermuda and Virginia materials, the departure for Italy – and by implication England – would necessitate abandoning the absolute rule that had been established under martial law.

16. The noblemen's pride is related to the gentlemanly refusal to work that the leaders of the Virginia Company bitterly complained about. The English gentlemen in Jamestown, it was said, preferred to die rather than lift a finger to save themselves. So too when the boatswain urges Antonio and Sebastian to get out of the way or to work, Antonio answers, 'We are less afraid to be drown'd than thou art' (I.i.44–5).

17. For acute observations on the parallels with Sycorax, see Stephen Orgel, 'Prospero's Wife' [essay 1 above – Ed.]; among the many essays on Caliban is one of my own: 'Learning to Curse: Aspects of Linguistic Colonialism in the Sixteenth Century', in *First Images of America: The Impact of the New World on the Old*, 2 vols, ed. Fredi Chiappelli (Berkeley, CA, 1976), 2:561–80.

18. Quoted in Nicholas Canny, 'The Permissive Frontier: The Problem of Social Control in English Settlements in Ireland and Virginia, 1550–1650', in *The Westward Enterprise*, p. 36.

19. William Crashaw, *A sermon preached in London before the right honorable the Lord Lawarre, Lord Governour and Captaine Generall of Virginia ... at the said Lord Generall his leave taking of England ... and departure for Virginea, Febr. 21, 1609* (London, 1610), pp. H1v–H1r. The British Library has a copy of Strachey's *Lawes Diuine, Morall and Martiall* with a manuscript inscription by the author to Crashaw; see Sanders, 'William Strachey, the Virginia Colony, and Shakespeare', p. 121.

20. William Strachey, *For the Colony in Virginea Britannia. Lawes Diuine, Morall and Martiall, &c.* (London, 1612), in Peter Force, *Tracts and Other Papers, Relating Principally to the Origin, Settlement, and Progress of the Colonies in North America, from the Discovery to the Year 1776*, 4 vols (Washington, DC, 1836–46), 3:67.

21. In our century the market for Shakespeare as book has come to focus increasingly upon adolescents in colleges and universities who are assigned expensive texts furnished with elaborate critical introductions and editorial apparatus. On the ideological implications of Shakespeare in the curriculum, see Alan Sinfield, 'Give an account of Shakespeare and Education, showing why you think they are effective and what you have appreciated about them. Support your comments with precise references,' in *Political Shakespeare: New Essays in Cultural Materialism*, ed. Jonathan Dollimore and Alan Sinfield (Manchester, 1985), pp. 134–57.

22. But if Shakespeare's works have become a fetish, they are defined for their possessors not by their magical power to command but by their freedom from the anxieties of rule. They are the emblems of cultivation, civility, recreation, but they are not conceived of as direct agents in the work of empire.

23. Henry M. Stanley, *Through the Dark Continent*, 2 vols (New York, 1878), 2:384–6. I owe this story to Walter Michaels, who found it quoted by William James in a footnote. James's interest was aroused by what he saw as primitive literalism. The natives' oral culture makes it impossible for them to understand writing. They cannot distinguish between books that are reproducible and books that are unique, or for that matter between fiction and field notes, and because of this inability they cannot identify what was at least the immediate threat to their culture. In making the book a fetish they fail to make the necessary distinction between fantasy and truth, a distinction whose origins reside in texts like *The Tempest*, that is, in texts that thematise a difference between the island of art and the mainland of reality.

   It is difficult to gauge how much of this analysis is only James's own fantasy. The natives may not actually have been incapable of making such a distinction. It is interesting, in this regard, that they are said to be carrying muskets, so there must already have been a history of involvement with Arabs or Europeans, a history that Stanley, making much of his role as explorer, represses. It is noteworthy too that as Stanley warms to his story, his natives increasingly speak in the racist idiom familiar from movies like *King Kong*: 'M-m. No, no, no'. And it is also possible, as I have already suggested, to see in Stanley the actual fetishism of the book: the attribution of power and value and companionship to the dead letter. In Stanley's reverie Shakespeare becomes a friend who must be sacrificed (as Stanley seems prepared to sacrifice Safeni) to protect the colonial project. Shakespeare is thus indispensable in two ways – as a consolation in the long painful trials of empire and as a deceptive token of exchange.

24. *The Exploration Diaries of H. M. Stanley*, ed. Richard Stanley and Alan Neame (New York, 1961), p. 187. Many of the journal entries that Stanley professes to transcribe in *Through the Dark Continent* are in fact invented: 'The so-called "extracts from my diary" in *Through the Dark Continent*', the editors remark, 'are hardly more than a device for varying the typeface, for they are quite as deliberately composed as the rest of the narrative' (p. xvi). I should add that the day after the burning of his 'genial companion', Stanley lost his close friend and associate Frank Pocock, who drowned when his canoe overturned. There is an odd sense of a relation between the loss of these two friends, as if Stanley viewed the burning of the one and the drowning of the other as linked sacrifices for the cause of empire.

6

'Thought is Free': *The Tempest*

ANNABEL PATTERSON

> Popular men,
> They must create strange monsters and then quell'em
> To make their arts seem something.
> Ben Jonson, *Catiline* (III.i.104–6)

In *Felix Holt: The Radical*, the novel in which George Eliot elaborated her theories of class structure, electoral politics and the deep connections between cultural and political conservativism, her hero, as well as her narrator, cites Shakespeare. In fact, Shakespeare is brought into contest with Milton, as if they were ideologically opposed. In the interview alluded to in the last chapter, between Felix and Mr Lyon, the Nonconformist minister, Felix is reminded of the older meaning of radicalism, of 'the great times when Nonconformity was in its giant youth', the years of the Puritan revolution, and responds by redefining radicalism as sending its roots 'a good deal lower down than the franchise'.[1] What then develops is a debate on priorities, on the relative importance of inner and outer change. As Lyon sees the problem, 'there is a work within which cannot be dispensed with; but it is our preliminary work to free men from the stifled life of political nullity, and bring them into what Milton calls "the liberal air", wherein alone can be wrought the final triumphs of the Spirit.' As Felix sees it, no amount of political liberation or consciousness-raising will have any melioristic effect while the common man remains the common man: '... while Caliban is

123

Caliban, though you multiply him by a million, he'll worship every Trinculo that carries a bottle. I forget, though – you don't read Shakespeare, Mr. Lyon' (pp. 368–9).

This exchange aptly introduces the problem posed by *The Tempest*, not only for this study, but for all of Shakespeare's audiences, directors, readers and critics. What does it mean to be Caliban? This question goes far beyond Shakespeare studies in cognitive range and geographical application; upon its answering more depends, even, than on what we make of *Coriolanus*; and here, as has not been the case with *Coriolanus*, while the dominant tradition of interpretation has agreed, more or less, with George Eliot, its control over the play has been strongly challenged in the twentieth century by a counter-interpretation, in which Caliban, not Prospero, is the rightful spirit at the play's centre. And it was precisely the dominance of the dominant tradition that other accounts of *The Tempest* were designed to resist. I refer here, of course, to appropriations of the play and its central symbols by African and Caribbean writers, partly in response to the provocation delivered by Octave Mannoni's *Psychologie de la Colonisation*, published in Paris in 1950 as a response to the Madagascan uprising of 1947–8. For where Mannoni, correctly diagnosing the uprising as a sign of the death of French colonialism and the birth of African nationalism, reread *The Tempest* as an allegory of colonial relations; and particularly of the psychology of colonial master and slave,[2] his successors effectively reversed the allegory in favour of anti-colonial polemic. Yet for Aimé Césaire, George Lamming and Roberto Fernández Retamar,[3] as also for their commentators,[4] the project was always a reversal, a transgressive reading against the grain that Western cultural and political history had engraved on their lives and their countries.

Not surprisingly, I question their central assumption, that Shakespeare's play was fully complicit in a mythology of benevolent colonialism, of the foreign conqueror's right to the land and labour of native peoples supposedly less civilised than himself. In the list of *Dramatis Personae*, Caliban is introduced in terms that might seem to settle his value for all time, 'a savage and deformed slave'; yet every director has to decide for himself what Caliban shall look like. 'Slave' is, we learn, Prospero's term for Caliban, and accurate in that endless work without wages has been imposed upon him. Miranda's term is 'villain' (villein) which was also Cornwall's term for the servant who intervened against the blinding of Gloucester. 'Monster' is Stephano's term, born of mistaking Caliban and Trinculo, under a single cloak, for a creature with four human legs. But Caliban's own name is a symbolic anagram of race, an allusion to Montaigne's essay 'Of the Cannibales', and at least for Montaigne and his translator Florio virtually an honorific.

Also, simply at the level of character and action there are facts about Caliban and his master that are difficult to square with the critical convention of bestialising the former and idealising the latter. We learn that Caliban loves music, has learned English, speaks as good poetry as the playtext has to offer, and knows something about the laws of inheritance. 'This island's mine, by Sycorax my mother, / Which thou tak'st from me' (I.ii.333–4). Even Coleridge, in his lectures of 1811–12, before the pressures of post-Waterloo England showed him 'the springs of the vulgar in politics' in this play, had responded to the evidence of Caliban's sensibility. And for every intimation of something valuable in Caliban that cannot be controlled stigmatically, there is an aspect of Prospero not fully compatible with ideas of benevolent, providential government. In the 1920s, Lytton Strachey's 'irreverent eye' had already seen him 'as an unpleasantly crusty personage, in whom a twelve year's monopoly of the conversation had developed an inordinate propensity for talking'.[5] And, as Stephen Orgel observed for the new Oxford edition, such scepticism is also to be found in post-World War II productions in Britain.[6]

Orgel continued this line of interpretation, moreover, by focusing on non-characterological problems in the text: the magus's association, by way of his long quotation from Ovid's Medea, with an unmistakably sinister concept of magic; the incompleteness of his reconciliatory and regenerative plan, since Antonio refuses to repent, and nurture will not stick to Caliban's nature; and the startling interruption of the betrothal masque when Prospero recalls the conspiracy of Caliban and his mates. This disruptive moment Orgel connected to his own earlier work on the Jacobean masque as merely the illusion of power, rather than power's effective form in the symbolic order. Yet despite his stress on the play's 'ambivalences', Orgel concluded that it remains at heart benevolent, and so reinscribed the critical enterprise within what he rightly denoted 'Prospero's view' of its meaning.

The inference that Prospero's perspective is the commanding one, the one closest to Shakespeare's own attitude, is structurally related to beliefs that the Thesean aesthetic governs *A Midsummer Night's Dream* and that the politics of Coriolanus sufficiently explain the play that bears his name; but in *The Tempest* the inference is supported, apparently, by autobiographical gesture: Prospero's resignation of his magic, Shakespeare's farewell to the stage. This attractive notion was already in circulation when Dryden produced his Restoration adaptation; it was undoubtedly reinforced, rather than contradicted, by the fact that *The Tempest* has pride of first place in the Folio edition of Shakespeare's *Works*; and it tends to override the factual question of whether, and how much, Shakespeare contributed to *Henry VIII* or *All is True*. The premise that this play is in some sense Shakespeare's last 'Will and Testament' needs, however, to be treated with a certain caution. It does not require us to set Shakespeare himself up as a benevolent spiritual father, asserting the rightful primacy of mind over matter, art over nature, the philosopher over the slave.

It seems inarguable that, by keying his play both to pamphlets describing the colonialist ventures of James's England, and to Montaigne's utopian essay 'Of the Cannibales', Shakespeare intended a contribution to a philosophical debate on colonialism and race relations that was already surfacing in the Europe of his day. Yet it does no dishonour to the anti-colonialist argument to suggest that *The Tempest* speaks to a still more expansive set of problems. Following the focus, though not the opinions of George Eliot, I assume that Caliban has always represented, as well as the racial Other, those underclasses of whose low nature and inclinations Felix Holt is certain. When Shakespeare turned back to the territory of fantasy he had not re-entered since *A Midsummer Night's Dream*, he retained as an essential constituent of that fantasy the idea of the lowest common denominator, unaccommodated man, the base at the bottom of the superstructure. But in Caliban, as was not true even of Bottom, and certainly not of the Roman plebeians, this idea is rendered in absolute, mythic, terms. To show that he had not forgotten his earlier sociopolitical analyses, the text of *The Tempest* is filled with the ideologemes of popular culture; but they now reverberate as echoes from another world of more or less realistic mimesis. In *The Tempest*, instead, we move in the territory of philosophical allegory.

One can perhaps see this coming, by way of the increasingly non-realistic 'romances'. In *The Winter's Tale*, especially, the popular tradition had resurfaced in clearly festive terms, signalled by Perdita's unserious imitation of 'Whitsun pastorals' (IV.iv.134); the subversive impulse in the popular tradition was there divided between pre-Homeric trickster and Elizabethan clown, Autolycus whose ballads are hawked as trinkets, the shepherd's son whose echoes of Lear's fool ('I was a gentleman born before my father'

[V.ii.148–9]) are confidently ludic, whose social satire is authorised by unexpected gentrification. Controlling them both is the premise of fictionality embedded in the play's title, 'a winter's tale' being proverbial for popular fictions in the oral tradition; while allegory's coming is announced by Time's appearance as master of ceremonies, in the long midway breach that makes nonsense of chronological realism.

In *The Tempest*, from the start, the allusions to popular culture come from the more threatening territory of protest and resistance. The play opens with a challenge from below: the Boatswain announces that physical danger from the elements makes nonsense of social hierarchy, and equates personal worth with the willingness to work.[7] But the equation between waves and rioters – 'What care these roarers for the name of King?'[8] – is one that objectifies elemental turmoil, while relegating the political to mental (metaphorical) space.

Likewise, *The Tempest* reintroduces one of the central problems of populism: what is the role of education in political society, and what does it contribute to social justice? Caliban's famous statement, so often quoted in anti-colonialist polemic – 'You taught me language, and my profit on it is, I know how to curse' – clearly relates also to the vexed status of literacy in the history of popular protest. Shakespeare's Jack Cade had confusedly grasped hegemony's central dilemma – that while the educational system and its central symbol, *the book*, normally works to keep the underprivileged unenlightened, it occasionally produces, precisely by making them articulate, effective popular spokesmen. Caliban has also learned the power of the book, and instructs Stephano and Trinculo to begin their insurrection by seizing Prospero's library; yet because we also know that the books are those of a Neoplatonic magus, that their content is literally magic, the political point is raised to a level of high abstraction.

What Shakespeare did *not* do in *The Tempest* was done for him in a nakedly political appropriation of his play, the late nineteenth-century adaption by Ernest Renan, *Caliban: Suite de la Tempête*, published in Paris in 1878 in the aftermath of the Paris Commune. As Robert Fernández Retamar observed in his own *Caliban*, Renan was one of those French humanists who savagely denounced the Commune, and who believed that the future lay with a philosophical elite who would govern the world by possessing the secrets of science.[9] Rewriting *The Tempest* according to this agenda, Renan represented Caliban as a French populist *citoyen*, who leads a successful insurrection against Prospero, but who, once in power, gradually finds himself adopting the beliefs and alliances of the deposed aristocracy. Significantly, Renan's agenda could only be accomplished by removing both master and slave from their insular, allegorical space and by returning them to Italy, where Caliban's monstrosity disappears in 'cette grande école de canaille populaire qui s'appelle Milan' (p. 18); and where Shakespeare's Caliban knows only that Prospero's books are the mysterious source of his power, Renan's Caliban knows precisely how the social structure is supported by an elitist, obscurantist education:

> War against books! They are the worst enemies of the people. Those who possess them hold power over their equals. The man who knows Latin rules other men. Down with Latin![10]

And in an important statement of his own principles of interpretation and adaptation, Renan put into the mouth of Ariel an account of his own move to realism:

> I will explain it to you ... It is Alonzo and those like him who were susceptible to our magic ... When Alonzo saw the tempest, he believed that the waves speak, that the winds growled, that the tempest murmured, that the thunder, that 'deep and dreadful organ-pipe', reproached him in its deep voice for the crime which he had committed against you. The people admit nothing of the kind ... The magic no longer works. Revolution, that is realism.[11]

Despite or because of his extreme antidemocratic bias, Renan provides remarkable insight both into *The Tempest* and into the critical tradition, which has deeply invested in the play's projection of idealisms – neo-platonism, providentialism, benevolent rule, the redemptive power of forgiveness.[12] Renan's nineteenth-century conviction that all idealisms are magic (that is to say, ideological phantasms that the underclasses have become immune to) reveals the unspoken equation in *The Tempest* between art and ideology and, more important, that Shakespeare leaves it unspoken. 'What is to be done', Renan's Ariel asks (in *Caliban* he is explicitly idealism's representative) 'when the people have become positivists?' But *Caliban* itself makes positive what *The Tempest* only makes conceivable; and it shows more clearly than can *The Tempest* alone, or in contrast to the earlier plays, the political implications of a realist mimesis that is here, unmistakably, avoided.

Must we, then, draw the conclusion that after *Coriolanus*, in which Shakespeare challenged the very structure of his society, he retreated to the philosophical aristocracy of which, according to Coleridge, he had always been a member? Is the allegorical ambience of *The Tempest* precisely the sign of the 'prevalence of the abstracting and generalising habit' that Coleridge saw in Hamlet and himself, the habit not only of doing philosophy but of aiming it against the 'general' in the other sense? Not necessarily; for by the same autobiographical ruse that invites the conflation of Shakespeare's attitudes and 'Prospero's view' *The Tempest* warns us against that easy assumption of superiority, and suggests that Prospero, and hence Shakespeare himself, are not the masters of all they command, but the slaves of peculiar circumstance.

By having his Caliban open the 'Suite' with a soliloquy on liberty and the inalienable rights of man, Renan's *Caliban* also underlines *The Tempest's* insistence on ideas of freedom and servitude. In Shakespeare's play, however, it is impossible to prove (though not to claim) how the Master-Slave dialectic connects to historical circumstances. While it is possible to align the play with developments in James's England, and particularly with the increasing emphasis on political liberties that appears in the records of the 1610 parliament, the fact remains that Shakespeare virtually prohibits a topical response like that produced (I assume) by *Coriolanus*. And as in the 1610 parliament Sir Francis Bacon had warned that 'questions which concern the power of the king and the liberty of the subject should not be textual, positive and scholastical, but slide in practice silently',[13] Shakespeare slid into the text of *The Tempest* a discourse of liberty and servitude that is, if not silent, deeply mysterious. For not only is Caliban a slave to Prospero, but so also is Ariel, whose servitude is in no sense penal; and in the epilogue, so vital to the assumption that Prospero speaks for Shakespeare himself, he too claims to be on the wrong side of the Master-Slave dynamic, likely to end his days in a penal colony:

> I must be here confin'd by you
> Or sent to Naples ...
>   Now I want ...
> Spirits to enforce, Art to enchant;
> And my ending is despair,
> Unless I be reliev'd by prayer,
> Which pierces so, that it assaults
> Mercy itself, and frees all faults.
>   As you from crimes would pardon'd be,
>   Let your indulgence set me free.

What can this mean (beyond the conventional actor's appeal for applause) if not that Shakespeare, at the end of his career, found himself in the carceral space of his own intelligence and its limits, partly self-imposed, partly the constraints of time, place, profession and belief. The effect of the Epilogue, then, is to situate the Master-Slave dynamic *within* the problematic of intellectual freedom, which also includes artistic independence, the question of agency, and, in a religious context, which the Epilogue certainly invokes, the role of the 'Will' – Shakespeare's personal signature. But to broaden the question does not necessarily weaken the force of any component; and for Shakespeare, in his own time, place, and especially as a popular dramatist, the premise of thought's freedom would have retained a sociopolitical charge.

In 1601, in the wake of the Essex rebellion, one of the many published comments on that event was E. Nisbet's *Dialogue or A Familiar Communication containing the first Institution of a Subject, in allegiance to his Soveraigne.* It is only nominally a dialogue, in the sense that the outcome has already been decided by the title, while the contributions of each speaker (a father and his son) and their respective claims to authority, have been equally predetermined by age, relationship and the educational premise. At times that relationship sounds more like that of priest to catechumen; and the pamphlet would be utterly undistinguished in its confirmation of patriarchal ideology were it not for one detail: that in the course of the son's education in hegemony he cites, with a hopeful curiosity, a question that would seem to endanger the governing hypothesis – that political insubordination will always fail because surveillance is total.

> Shall not Thought be free?
> (p. 23)

Mysteriously attributed here to John 4:14, whereas in fact it has not biblical but proverbial origins, the phrase appears twice in Shakespeare's canon. Once, in *Twelfth Night*, when Maria is teasing Sir Andrew Aguecheek (I.iii.68):

> Now, Sir, 'thought is free'; I pray you, bring your hand to the buttery bar and let it drink.

and once in *The Tempest*, where also in the context of drunken festivity, Stephano sings a popular song:

> Flout 'em and cout 'em,
> And scout 'em and flout 'em;
> Thought is free.
> (III.ii.119–21)

It is worth noting that Caliban already knows this song, and complains that it is sung to the wrong tune, whereupon Ariel, who has been invisibly observing the group as they plan their revolt against Prospero, supplies the right one. He therefore gives approximately the same answer (though rendered musically) to the question ('Shall not Thought be free?') as was given by the father in Nisbet's pamphlet, who advised his son that thought is always exposed to God: 'he need not goe farre for an informer' (p. 25). For Ariel's presence in the air is the ultimate representation of surveillance.

In Sir John Hayward's notorious *Life* of Henry IV, to which Shakespeare's company was connected at least by association, the bishop of Carlisle, who represents the voice of order and moderation, speaks against the deposition of Richard as follows: 'It is a common saying, thought is free: free indeede from punishment of secular lawes, except by worde or deed it breake foorth into action: Yet the secret thoughts against the sacred maiesty of a Prince, without attempt, without endeavour, have been adiudged worthy of death.'[14] The political context of this 'common saying', and its evident absorption by a tradition of resistance, is unmistakable in Hayward's text even as its speaker, ventriloquising the popular tradition, attempts to deny its optimistic claim: that there is always an interior freedom (a Will) immune from external coercion. Shakespeare passes this popular wisdom on, not, as one might have supposed, to Caliban, but to Stephano, 'a drunken butler'.

But there it stands, nevertheless, the common saying released by the common players on to the stage at Whitehall in the spring of 1613, and probably at the Blackfriars, as Dryden attested in the preface to his own adaptation, *The Tempest, or The Enchanted Island* (1674). The thought that thought is free must have been always on Shakespeare's mind when he wrote for the Elizabethan and Jacobean stages, knowing that his own powerful work was contributing to what was thinkable. When Prospero aligns his 'so potent Art' with Medea's magic – calling forth 'mutinous winds' and opening the graves of history to let out their sleepers – he speaks perhaps for Shakespeare, who may also have wished to abjure such 'rough magic' (V.i.42–51) as renders baseless, if not actually rends, the visionary social fabric (IV.i.151). If so, he surely confessed as much to the *other* temptation, to impose on resistant human material an idealised, fantastic, allegorical resolution.

When Dryden adapted the *The Tempest* for Restoration audiences, his prologue assumed that Prospero, at least as magician, was Shakespeare's self-characterisation:

> But Shakespeare's Magick could not copy'd be,
> Within that Circle none durst walk but he.
> I must confess t'was bold nor would you now
> That liberty to vulgar wits allow
> Which works by Magick supernatural things:
> But Shakespeare's pow'r is sacred as a Kings.
> (II.19–24)[15]

But even as he established metaphorically an alliance between playwright and ruler, Dryden recorded it as an act of 'bold' social inversion, implying that Shakespeare's own wit was profoundly *vulgar*, claiming for itself the *liberty* to *work*, by magic, on the structure of his world. In the subsequent history of Shakespeare's reception, these are the terms and issues in Shakespeare's plays that have gone insufficiently recognised, while the sacredness of his power, and all of the exclusions that implies, has been at the centre of the enterprise.

From Annabel Patterson, *Shakespeare and the Popular Voice* (Oxford, 1989), pp. 154–62.

NOTES

[Annabel Patterson points out that the appropriation of Shakespeare for cultural and political conservatism analysed by Hawkes (essay 3) was noticed by George Eliot in the mid nineteenth century. However, Patterson resists the assumption that *The Tempest* itself was complicit in mythologies of benevolent employer and colonialism. It is, for example, difficult to bestialise Caliban and idealise Prospero in a consistent way, and picking up Stephano's phrase, 'Thought is free', Patterson argues that the play has a level of populist rebellion against authority which adds a discourse of liberty and servitude. Quotations from *The Tempest*, ed. Frank Kermode (Arden edition, London, 1954). Ed.]

1. George Eliot, *Felix Holt: The Radical*, ed. Peter Coveney (Harmondsworth, 1972), p. 368.

2. Mannoni's ideas were also applied to English colonialism. See Philip Mason, *Prospero's Magic: Some Thoughts on Class and Race* (London, 1962), a deeply ambivalent statement by a colonial employee who defended Mannoni's psychology (and the need for the 'firm hand' of paternalistic government) while seeing himself, with distaste, in Prospero.

3. Aimé Césaire, *Une Tempête: D'Après 'la Tempête' de Shakespeare – Adaptation pour un théâtre nègre* (Paris, 1969); George Lamming, *The Pleasures of Exile* (1960; New York, 1984) and *Water with Berries* (New York, 1971); Roberto Fernández Retamar, 'Caliban. Notes Toward a Discussion of Culture in Our America', first published in Spanish in *Casa de Las Américas*, 68 (1971), tr. Lynn Garafola *et al.*, *Massachusetts Review*, 15 (1974).

4. For accounts of these anti-colonialist interpretations, see Charlotte H. Bruner, 'The Meaning of Caliban in Black Literature Today', *Comparative Literature Studies*, 13 (1976), 240–53; and Rob Nixon, 'Decolonizing, Revaluing: Caribbean and African Appropriations of *The Tempest*', *Critical Inquiry*, 14 (1987), 557–78. For an account of anti-colonial appropriations in Britain, see Trevor R. Griffiths, '"This Island's Mine": Caliban and Colonialism', *Yearbook of English Studies*, 13 (1983), 159–80.

5. Lytton Strachey, *Books and Characters* (1922), p. 68.

6. Stephen Orgel (ed.), *The Tempest* (Oxford, 1987), pp. 82–7.

7. The social implications of this challenge did not escape Coleridge, who in the 1611–12 lectures speaks of the Boatswain as pouring forth 'his vulgar mind' 'when the bonds of reverence are thrown off'. See Samuel Taylor Coleridge, *Lectures 1808–1819*, ed. R. A. Foakes, Vol. 5 in *Collected Works*, 16 vols (Princeton, NJ, 1987), p. 520.

8. References will be to the New Arden edition: *The Tempest*, ed. Frank Kermode (Cambridge, MA, 1954).

9. Retamar, 'Caliban', p. 16.

10. Renan, 'Caliban', p. 48: 'Guerre aux libres! Ce sont les pires ennemis du peuple. Ceux qui les possèdent ont des pouvoirs sur leurs semblables. L'homme qui sait le latin commande aux autres hommes. A bas le latin!'

11. Renan, 'Caliban', pp. 69–70: 'Voici comme je l'explique ... C'est que Alonzo et les siens etaient accessible à nos charmes ... Quand Alonzo vit la tempête, il crut que les vagues parlaient, que les vents grondaient, que la tempête murmurait, que le tonnerre, cet orgue profond et terrible, lui reprochait de sa voix de basse le crime qu'il avait commis contre toi. Le peuple n'admit rien de tout cela ... La magie ne sert plus de rien. La révolution, c'est le réalisme'.

12. For evidence that this view (that is to say, Prospero's view) was critical orthodoxy, see the protest against it (first published in 1969) by Harry Berger, Jr, 'Miraculous Harp: A Reading of Shakespeare's *Tempest*', in *Second World and Green World: Studies in Renaissance Fiction Making* (Berkeley and Los Angeles, 1988), pp. 147–85. For evidence of its persistence, see John S. Mebane, 'Metadrama and the Visionary Imagination in *Dr. Faustus* and *The Tempest*', *South Atlantic Review*, 53 (1988), 25–45, where the claim is made that 'only those who possess a capacity for this kind of vision can respond to Prospero's magical art or participate in the harmonious order that it helps to establish' (p. 34). What is needed to sustain the idealist interpretation is explicitly stated: 'interpersonal faith'.

13. See Elizabeth Read Foster (ed.), *Proceedings in Parliament. 1610*, 2 vols (New Haven, CT, 1966), 2:103.

14. Sir John Hayward, *Life of Henry IIII* (London, 1599), pp. 102–3.

15. For a fine account of Dryden's adaptation, and the difference between its political analysis and that implied by *The Tempest*, see Katharine Maus, 'Arcadia Lost: Politics and Revision in the Restoration *Tempest*', *Renaissance Drama*, 13 (1982), 189–209; and for an account of magic in *The Tempest* as political mystification see Curtis Breight, '"Treason doth never prosper": The Tempest and the Discourse of Treason', an unpublished paper to which I owe this chapter's epigraph.

7

Seizing the Book

ANIA LOOMBA

THE CONTAMINATED TEXT

The Tempest's varied stage and critical history has explicitly fore-grounded the question of appropriations of dominant culture. This history reveals a struggle over textual truth and value, but also alerts us to the problems of 'seizing the book'; hence the following discussion is not a 'conclusion' at all, but more in the nature of a speculation on some of these difficulties.

McLuskie, writing on Shakespeare, quotes Eagleton, writing on ideology: 'The aesthetic is too valuable to be surrendered without a struggle to the bourgeois aestheticians, and too contaminated by that ideology to be appropriated as it is'.[1] It is this 'contamination' which makes appropriation rather than just another interpretation of the text necessary; a demarcation between the two terms is in one sense false, for they spill into one another, and yet it marks the distinction between a criticism that explicitly acknowledges its own partisanship and another that defends itself by claiming that it is ob-jective, and not 'devoted to special purposes' – which is how the *Oxford Illustrated Dictionary* defines 'appropriation'.

So often the first step of our devotion to special purposes is to expose those of others – to treat institutionalised readings as appropri-ations too: 'If Shakespeare can be appropriated by these conservative standpoints, there is scope for intervention also for an oppositional politics'.[2] *The Tempest* lends itself easily to such an exposé.[3] Western criticism and productions of the play have differed from those of *Othello* in their earlier and more explicit acknowledgement of the play's involvement with the colonial theme. One reason for this difference is that Caliban's status (confirmed by the list of *personae* as a 'savage and deformed slave') does not threaten commonsense notions about black people or slaves in the same way as does Othello's emphasised nobility and heroism. While much critical effort was expended to prove both Othello's non-negroid lineage and his moral whiteness – despite abundant references to his blackness – there has been no parallel concern about the precise shade of colouring of Prospero's 'thing of darkness'; even though *The Tempest* is more ambiguous about Caliban's colour and race. Not until 1934 was he represented as black on the British stage, but most previous productions had presented him as animalistic and, after the publication of Darwin's *Origin of the Species* in 1859, as an ape, hideously deformed and grotesque, a sort of 'half monkey, half coco-nut' representing the missing link, half-seal, half-man, fishlike, and so on. Simultaneously he was projected as a colonised native of varying descriptions.[4] Such explicitly social-Darwinist, racist and imperialist productions indicated Caliban's *political* colour as clearly *black*.

It is true that the play's connection with the 'New World' (acknowledged as early as 1808) was, until fairly recently in Western criticism, relegated to background material and not allowed to become part of the play's ideological and historical 'con-texts'.[5] Such a closure negatively acknowledged and actively utilised material which was formally marginalised. Hence in Kermode's introduction to the play, for example, sources are painstakingly logged but kept at bay; we are told that the play is primarily concerned with an opposition between Nature and Art ('as all serious pastoral poetry always is') and that 'there is nothing in *The Tempest* fundamental to its structure of ideas which could not have existed had America remained undiscovered' (p. xxv). Any illusions we might have about the political innocence of such efforts to close off the text from what Barker and Hulme have called 'contextual contamination' are dispelled by what follows:

> If Aristotle was right in arguing that 'men ... who are as much inferior to others as the body is to the soul ... are slaves by nature, and it is advantageous for them to be always under government' ... then the black and mutilated cannibal must be the natural slave of the European gentleman, and *a fortiori*, the savage and deformed Caliban of the learned Prospero.
>
> (p. xlii)

It is no accident that Kermode's text is widely used in India or that in that context its obvious bias is inserted into notions of the play as a romance, an almost mystic piece of enchantment. Although appropriations occur all the time, in every reading or staging of the text, it is only when they become subversive that questions of *authenticity* – historical or thematic 'correctness' – surface sharply.

For example, generations of white Othellos are permitted while a single black Antony provokes an outrage. In a letter to the *Guardian*, Brigid Larmour refers to the paper's disparaging review of her casting a black man as Antony: 'How is authenticity being infringed? Would it be authentic to have an Italian, toga'd Antony and a boy Cleopatra ... Does it strain authenticity to have a blonde Cleopatra like Helen Mirren or a tall one like Vanessa Redgrave?' (30 May 1987). From an editorial in *Plays and Players* entitled 'Multi-racial humbug' it is obvious that theatrical authenticity is a way of holding on to a lost empire:

> Far from taking pride in one of the most complex, consistent and individual cultures in Europe, apologetic Brits are welcoming the (in many cases artificial) grafting of new elements of varying suitability or relevance on to the indigenous growth. Politics, we suspect, have more to do with this than art; quotas rather than quality.

Referring to Hugh Quarshie, a black actor who speaks of Enobarbus being played by a Caribbean actor as 'a real coup', the editor continues: 'Too true, Hugh. It will also be coup when played by a Chinese midget, nude on rollerskates, and just as relevant. Of course, there could be a production (any day now, to judge by the RSC's slavish addiction to updating for dumb dumbs) in which this would be valid' (July 1986, p. 2). It is not entirely accidental that I found this review, which ends by referring to alternative theatre practices as 'the new colonialism', in the library of the British Council at Delhi, nor that a few days later a prominent professor of English literature at Delhi introduced a talk on Shakespeare by declaring that she was 'a diehard conservative' whose love for Shakespeare had distanced her from 'new-fangled theories and writers' in whom her students seemed unfortunately very interested.

To return to *The Tempest*; while social-Darwinist depictions of Caliban as ape-man were greeted with exclamations of wonder at Shakespeare's prophetic anticipation of Darwin's scientific analysis, the *Financial Times* complained after Jonathan Miller's anti-imperialist production that 'colonialism, the dominion of one race (as opposed to one nation) over another, is something that Shakespeare had never heard of'.[6] Caliban stands more clearly and self-consciously in opposition to dominant culture than does Othello. For this reason, it was an easier text to appropriate for anti-imperial purposes; since the early fifties African and Caribbean intellectuals 'chose to utilise (it) ... as a strategy for (in George Lamming's words) getting "out from under this ancient mausoleum of (Western) historic achievement". They seized upon *The Tempest* as a way of amplifying their calls for decolonisation within the bounds of the dominant cultures'.[7]

Whereas Western readings had acknowledged Caliban as 'the core of the play' only in order to concur with Prospero's reading of him as an inherently inferior being 'on whose nature / Nurture can never stick' (IV.i.188–9), this other history seized upon Caliban to articulate its own bondage and rebellion; at the same time it also initiated a debate on the psyche of the colonised subject. Significantly, during the years following Britain's forced retreat from Empire, as such anti-imperialist appropriations became frequent, there were very few productions of the play on the British stage.[8]

The history of *The Tempest*, therefore, clearly reveals a contest over textual truth and value, and exposes dominant Shakespearian criticism as part of that struggle rather than the guardian of some irrefutable core of meaning. That both racist and anti-colonialist appropriations and interpretations of the play exist does not argue for the simultaneous validity of contradictory meanings; pluralism seeks to deflect the fact that 'different readings *struggle* with each other on the site of a text, and all that can count, however provisionally, as knowledge of a text, is achieved through this discursive conflict'.[9]

But what makes it possible for *The Tempest* to be read in these different ways? A recent article by Thomas Cartelli, entitled 'Prospero in Africa',[10] suggests that the reasons why particular readings arise in relation to a specific text are not entirely extraneous to the text itself. Centring his argument on Ngugi Wa Thiong'o's *A Grain of Wheat*, Cartelli argues that the Kenyan writer's association of Prospero with Conrad's Kurtz by combining them in his central character, Thompson, is not a misreading of the play but is historically justified by the inevitable collapse of imperialist 'idealism', which we might identify with Prospero, into coercive brutality, which is so clearly revealed by Kurtz. Prospero's rhetoric of noble intentions combined with his coercive actions was the strategy employed by later colonialists as well.

Recent criticism of the play has been concerned with a historically determined *ambivalence* in the text; Paul Brown's incisive analysis concludes that *The Tempest* 'serves as a limit text in which the characteristic operations of colonial discourse may be discerned – as an instrument for exploitation, a register of beleaguerment and a site of radical ambivalence'; Barker and Hulme have shown that 'Prospero's play and *The Tempest* are not necessarily the same thing'. Cartelli's article suggests that this ambivalence has been central in establishing *The Tempest*'s 'as a privileged text in the history of colonialist discourse'. He maintains that since the play is not 'simply anticolonialist' and allows Prospero a certain privileged status, it is 'a responsible party to its successive readings and rewritings in so far as it has made seminal contributions to the development of the colonial ideology through which it is read'.[11] The text thus becomes, at least partly, the source of the ideological contamination of which Eagleton speaks.

It seems to me, however, that Cartelli emphasises only half the implications of this position, and of recent criticism of *The Tempest*. If there is a connection between the ambivalence of the play and its usefulness for the construction of later paternalistic colonialism, is there also not one between the same ambivalence and anti-colonialist appropriations? Cartelli's article suggests that alternative readings are only possible in relation to the *The Tempest's* original contexts but that later history of the play has unfolded its latent imperialist elements: 'the position which *The Tempest* occupied at its moment of production may not ... have been as decidedly colonialist as Thompson and Ngugi consider it to be at its point of reception'. But here, surely, we are talking about only one, dominant and institutionalised, point of reception. There have been others, as I have indicated by recounting the already well-known features of its African and Carribean appropriations. Because he ignores these, Cartelli goes on posit too drastic an opposition between the original and subsequent contexts of the play:

> For Ngugi, a historically or critically 'correct' reading of *The Tempest* that isolates the play 'at its originating moment of production' would serve merely an antiquarian interest, documenting an alleged 'intervention' in colonialist discourse that made no discernibly positive impact on the subsequent development of colonial practices. His own variety of historicity would, on the other hand, focus less on the text's status as a historically determined literary artifact, now open to a variety of interpretations, than on its subordination to what history has made of it.[12]

If we consider the issues raised by anti-colonialist appropriations alongside those that emerge when we assess the 'originating moment of the play', then a 'historically correct reading' of a text need not be pitted against locating 'what history has made of it': radical readings are not about investing a text with what isn't there at all. Can we suggest, instead, that the struggle over meaning is intensified in the case of a text which is itself polyphonic and that the contradictions within the text and the struggle between its different appropriations are inter-related? This would mean that the difficulties of appropriating the play should be looked at alongside the limits of its 'radical ambivalence'. Moreover, one cannot read the political interests of all oppositional readings, even those that emerge at the same time, as identical. These two propositions need to be examined together, and I shall do so by looking at the ways in which the representation of gender in *The Tempest* marks the limits for its appropriation in the Third World context today.

'THE IMPERISHABLE EMPIRE'

The play's history in India alerts us against reading the encounter of Third World readers with the white text as a uniform one. A recent production of *The Tempest* on the Delhi stage worked hard at excluding the imperial theme. It attempted to make the spectators identify with Prospero instead of Caliban by elaborating the 'magical' effects desired by Prospero so that the Calibans in the audience would be hypnotised into complicity with the colonial closure which is part of the play's contradictory enterprise. Such productions have been largely ignored as semi-amateur, incompetent theatre playing to a relatively small urban elite, but they serve to uncover ways in which different colonised peoples bring varying histories to bear upon their contact with Western literature. If identification with Caliban came strongly for African and Caribbean audiences, it was because their own blackness and racial difference were overtly emphasised by colonial rule. In India, the Aryan myth was invoked to disguise the specifically racist aspects of Empire, and can be seen to 'persuade' the readers/spectators of *The Tempest*, already holding strong colour prejudices that permeate caste and communal politics within India, and unfortunately perceiving themselves as somehow less black than Africans, that in fact they are closer to noble, white Prospero than monstrous, black Caliban.

Moreover, Shakespeare's last plays, and particularly *The Tempest*, had been the focus of Orientalist comparisons of Shakespeare to Kalidasa, the most famous of ancient Sanskrit playwrights. This analogy was picked up by Indian criticism of Shakespeare, which invoked both the stereotype of a spiritual India and dominant assumptions about the universality of art, fixed Indian literary achievement in the distant past, excluded the question of present relevance (or irrelevance) and lifted both dramas from their respective historical contexts. Both Shakespeare and Kalidasa (and by implication all great art) value order, suffering and passivity:

> The theme is more or less the same, destruction of domestic happiness, separation, suffering and finally reconciliation and reunion. In all these plays there is regeneration achieved through patient suffering and repentance ... at the highest level of poetic experience, all barriers that divide peoples disappear, revealing the essential unity of art and unity of poetic experience itself.[13]

An earlier book, written jointly by an Indian, H. H. Anniah Gowda, and an Englishman, Henry W. Wells, claims to be 'a monument to hearts and hands across the seas' on the basis of its comparisons between Shakespeare's last plays and some classical plays of India. A comprehensive critique of these books is tempting but beyond my scope here. Notable, however, are the ways in which they combine an Orientalist conception of India ('with the possible exception of Egypt ... the supreme mother of myth', p. 30), patriarchal identification of female with instinct and male with reason ('both Shakuntala and Miranda represent an instinctive harmony with nature; their lovers the King Dushyanta and Ferdinand, merely add understanding to intuition', pp. 122–3), and an essentialist idealism (these plays deal with the 'basic and outstanding realities in the human condition', p. 65).

It might be argued that such writings are extreme examples, but their assumptions are certainly normative in the Indian classroom. The complex histories behind books such as Wells and Gowda's are also at work when an Indian audience in 1987 is told to accept *The Tempest* as a drama of forgiveness, patience and magic, or research students at Delhi University are asked to study the play as part of 'The Romance Tradition' in English literature, with connections with *Daphnis and Chloe* prioritised to 'erase' the imperial theme. The point, however, is that with varying degrees of sophistication, these histories and pedagogic traditions *underline* the colonial history of the play: they work to ensure what one critic had frankly admitted, that 'the imperishable Empire of Shakespeare will always be with us'.[14]

THE BLACK RAPIST

One of the reasons for the play's declining pertinence to contemporary third world politics has been identified as

> the difficulty of wresting from it any role for female defiance or leadership in a period when protest is coming increasingly from that quarter. Given that Caliban is without a female counterpart in his oppression and rebellion, and given the largely autobiographical cast of African and Caribbean appropriations of the play, it follows that all the writers who quarried from *The Tempest* an expression of their lot should have been men.[15]

It is true that the play poses a problem for a feminist, and especially a nonwestern feminist appropriation, if by 'appropriation' we mean an amplification of the anti-colonial voices within the text. But such a difficulty does not arise simply from the lack of a strong female presence, black or white, in the play, but also from the play's representation of black male sexuality.

Caliban contests Prospero's account of his arrival on the island but not the accusation of attempted rape of Miranda. Identifying the political effects of Prospero's accusation, Paul Brown comments that 'the issue here is not whether Caliban is actually a rapist or not, since Caliban accepts the charge'.[16] On the contrary, I suggest that this acceptance is important for assessing both colonial and anticolonial readings of the play. An article written in 1892, which later became what Griffiths calls 'a standard defence of Caliban' speaks of the rape as 'an offence, an unpardonable offence, but *one that he was fated to commit*',[17] and goes on to see Caliban as unfortunate, oppressed, but 'like all these lower peoples, easily misled'. This implies that sexual violence is part of the black man's inferior nature, a view that amalgamates racist common-sense notions about black sexuality and animalism, and sexist assumptions about rape as an inevitable expression of frustrated male desire.

These notions were complexly employed in the influential *Psychologie de la colonisation* (1948) by Octava Mannoni, who seriously reassessed the play in order to propound a controversial view of the psychology of the colonised subject. Mannoni advocated the notion of the 'Caliban complex' which he analysed as the desire for dependency on the part of the native. Caliban (and the Madagascans, whose uprising of 1947–48 provided the impetus for the work) revolts not against slavery but because he is abandoned by Prospero. Analysing Caliban's speech in Act II, Mannoni came to the conclusion that 'Caliban does not complain of being exploited: he complains of being betrayed'. As other Caribbean and African intellectuals pointed out, Mannoni posited Caliban as an eager partner in his own colonisation.[18] Crucially, Mannoni traces the roots of racism to sexual guilt. The antagonism between Caliban and Prospero hinged on Miranda's presence as the sole woman on the island. Accordingly, a definition of the coloniser's psyche, or what Mannoni called the 'Prospero complex' was based on the notion of racism as a pseudo-rational construct used to rationalise feelings of sexual guilt.

Both dependency and racism by this account are connected to politics of sexual desire, but in a way that preserves the patriarchal exclusion of sexuality from economics as well as the racist assumption that Caliban's subordinate status will naturally lead him to desire (and hence rape) Miranda. The supposed desire of the native for European care has been advanced by nearly every imperialist regime. That Mannoni's theories could be used to legitimise colonisation was demonstrated by the publication of Philip Mason's *Prospero's Magic: Some Thoughts on Class and Race* in 1962.[19] Mannoni was severely criticised for his psychological reductionism by, among others, Frantz Fanon, who pointed out that economic motivations for plunder were omitted in the former's account.

Fanon's own explanation of the sexual encounter between the black man and white woman in *Black Skins, White Masks*, which has already been cited in connection with *Othello*, attributes both sexual insecurity and racist hatred to the white father who is antagonised by the black lover of his daughter. Fanon also describes the ways in which a black man who has internalised the value system of white society may view his liaison with a white woman as a pathway to acceptance (for example, Othello's love for Desdemona). A Fanonian explanation of black men's desire for white women is useful only in specific situations and with some qualifications. Firstly, to extend it to the consciousness of all black men would be to assume 'too readily that black men have necessarily internalised the white man's view of things'.[20] Secondly, in Fanon's account, the white woman is

only an object of the black man's desire; her own subjectivity is
markedly absent. This is a serious limitation of Fanon's work, for
racist common-sense (although from a totally different perspective)
also posits that black men lust after white women, and also erases
the desire of white women. By doing so, racism moves from the
black man's desire to his bestiality and concludes that black men will
seek to *enforce* a liaison upon white women. Hence the myth of the
black rapist. In *Othello*, such a myth hovers on the margins of
Brabantio's accusations, but is undercut by Desdemona's own powerfully articulated desire for Othello.

In *The Tempest*, Prospero's accusation of rape and its corrobora-
tion by Caliban upholds such a myth, which derives from the idea
that, aware of the damage they can do by making sexual advances
towards white women, black men have all conceived 'a peculiar lust
for white womanhood'.[21] Of course, rape has been articulated as a
weapon by black militants: Eldridge Cleaver called it an 'insurrec-
tionary act' against white society. Imamu Baraka wrote: 'Come up,
black dada nihilismus. Rape the white girls. Rape their fathers. Cut
the mother's throats.'[22] If varieties of feminism are guilty of racist
practices, it needs hardly to be detailed here that sexist versions of
anti-racism abound as well. The result of these has strengthened the
fiction, often presented as 'facts', of black animalism. Susan
Brownmiller's influential study of rape, *Against Our Will*, has argued
that black men's historical oppression has placed many of the 'legitimate' expressions of male supremacy beyond their reach, resulting
in their open sexual violence. Quoting Jean McKellar's *Rape: The
Bait and the Trap*, which claims that ninety per cent of all reported
rapes in the United States are by black men, Angela Davis points out
that even official FBI figures place it at forty per cent (p. 179). The
point here is not that black men do not rape, but that their dominant fictional representation has legitimised both patriarchal and
racist myths of female and black sexuality.

Gerda Lerner rightly says that 'the myth of the black rapist of
white women is the turn of the myth of the bad black woman – both
designed to apologise for and facilitate the continued exploitation of
black men and women'.[23] And of white women, one may add – the
construction of the black rapist also includes that of the passive
white woman, whose potential desire for black men is thus effaced.
In *The Tempest*, therefore, we must read Caliban's rapacity as set
against Sycorax's licentious black femininity and the passive purity
of Miranda, whose own desire, like Portia's, corroborates the will of

the father; although Miranda can be seen to 'slip away' from Prospero,[24] this slippage does not erode fatherly authority in the same way as Desdemona's passion for Othello. Moreover, this juxtaposition of Miranda, Sycorax and Caliban focuses both on the economic aspects that were erased by Mannoni, and on the gender politics that have been ignored in some other appropriations.

SYCORAX

Mannoni, significantly, edited out these opening lines of Caliban's version of Prospero's arrival on the island:

> This island's mine, by Sycorax my mother,
> Which thou tak'st from me.
> (I.ii.331–2)

These lines had elicited the first recorded anti-imperialist response to the play in 1904, which found that in them 'the whole case of the aboriginal against aggressive civilisation (was) dramatised before us'.[25] They were also focused by subsequent Caribbean and African appropriations, but although some of these indicated the matrilinear nature of many pre-colonial societies, gender was hardly ever seized upon by anti-colonial intellectuals as a significant dimension of racial oppression.

Sycorax is more than the justification for Caliban's territorial rights to the island – she operates as a powerful contrast to Miranda. Both Prospero and Caliban testify to her power; the former draws upon the language of misogyny as well as racism to construct her as a 'foul witch' (I.ii.258), the latter invokes her strength to express his hatred of his master (I.ii.321–3, 339–40). Prospero's descriptions of Sycorax emphasise both her non-European origins – she's 'from Argier' – and her fertility – 'This blue-ey'd hag was hither brought with child' (I.ii.265, 269). She is also 'so strong / That could control the moon, make flows and ebbs, / And deal in her command without her power' (V.i.269–71). Hence she stands in complete contrast to the white, virginal and obedient Miranda. Between them they split the patriarchal stereotype of woman as the white devil – virgin and whore, goddess (Miranda is mistaken for one by Ferdinand) and witch.

But Sycorax is also Prospero's 'other'; his repeated comparisons between their different magics and their respective reigns of the island are used by him to claim a superior morality, a greater strength and a greater humanity, and hence legitimise his takeover of the island and its inhabitants; but they also betray an anxiety that Sycorax's power has not been fully exorcised, and for Caliban still invokes it for his own rebellion: 'All the charms / Of Sycorax, toads, beetles, bats, light on you!' (I.ii.339–40). As George Lamming pointed out in *The Pleasures of Exile*, while Miranda is like many an African slave child in never having known her mother, 'the actual Caliban of *The Tempest* has the advantage ... of having known the meaning and power of his mother Sycorax'.[26]

Prospero's takeover is both *racial* plunder and a transfer to *patriarchy*. The connections between witches and transgressive women, between witch-trials with the process of capital accumulation, and between the economic, ideological and sexual subordination of native women by colonial rule, are significant. The restructuring of the colonised economy not only involved the export of raw material to factories in England, but also a redefinition of men and women's work, which economically dislocated women, and calcified patriarchal tendencies in the native culture.[27] In Burma, for example, British colonialists acknowledged that Burmese women had property and sexual rights unheard of in England. Accordingly, Fielding Hall, Political Officer in the British Colonial Administration in Burma, suggested that in order to 'civilise' the Burmese people:

1.   The men must be taught to kill and to fight for the British colonialists.
2.   Women must surrender their liberty in the interests of men.[28]

Colonised women were also subjected to untold sexual harassment, rape, enforced marriage and degradation, both under direct slavery and otherwise. Sycorax's illegitimate pregnancy contrasts with Miranda's chastity and virginity, reminding us that the construction of the promiscuity of non-European women served to legitimise their sexual abuse and to demarcate them from white women.

Therefore Prospero as colonialist consolidates power which is specifically white and male, and constructs Sycorax as a black, wayward and wicked witch in order to legitimise it. If Caliban's version of past events prompts us to question Prospero's story, then this interrogation should include the re-telling of Sycorax's story. The distinctions drawn by generations of critics between his 'white magic' and Sycorax's 'black magic' only corroborate Prospero's narrative. African appropriations emphasised the brutality of Prospero's 'reason' and its historical suppression of black culture, but they did not bring out the gender-value of these terms; they read the story of colonised and colonising men but not of colonised and colonising women, which is also told by Miranda's lonely presence on the island.

MIRANDA'S SCHOOLING

It is ironical but not entirely inappropriate that one of the oldest of Delhi's colleges for women should have been called 'Miranda House', after the daughter of the university's colonial founder, Sir Maurice Gwyer. Miranda's schooling in *The Tempest* demonstrates the contradictory position occupied by white women in the colonial adventure. Paul Brown has discussed how 'the discourse of sexuality ... offers the crucial nexus for the various domains of colonialist discourse' and the ways in which control of his subjects' sexuality is crucial for Prospero's exercise of power.[29] Patriarchalism alternately asserts its *knowledge* (the father's wisdom: Prospero's magic, his schooling of Miranda, his civilising of Caliban); its *humanity* (parental concern and love: Prospero's reiteration of his 'care' of Miranda, his liberation of 'my Ariel', and of his 'humanely taken' pains over Caliban); its *power* (the father's authority: Miranda cannot choose but obey Prospero, he can torture both Caliban and Ariel); and often all three together (Prospero's aside to the rebels that he will 'tell no tales' is simultaneously a disclosure of his knowledge of their plans, a favour and a warning). In the colonial situation, patriarchalism makes specific, and often apparently contradictory demands of its 'own' women.

Miranda is the most solitary of Renaissance woman protagonists, and moves on an exclusively male stage – 'I do not know / One of my sex; no woman's face remember' (III.i.48–9) – where references are made to only three other women. She indicates the apparent exclusion of women from the colonial arena, but at the same time, their actual and sinister inclusion, together with other images of femininity in the play, propels the narrative even when posited as an absence. Miranda provides the ideological legitimation of each of Prsopero's actions; at the beginning of the play he tells her that his 'Art' is prompted by his concern for her: 'I have done nothing but in care of thee' (I.ii.16). Next, in the same scene, he claims that his enslavement of Caliban was prompted by the latter's attempted rape of Miranda (I.ii.345–8). Later she is described by him as 'a third of mine own life, / Or that for which I live' (IV.i.3–4); therefore after she is married he will 'retire me to my Milan, where / Every third thought shall be my grave' (V.i.310–11).

Prospero's complaint against Antonio is that he 'new created / The creatures that were mine, I say or chang'd 'em, / Or else new form'd 'em (I.ii.81–3). His own enterprise is precisely the same, and Miranda is the most successful of his creations. For twelve years 'have I, thy schoolmaster, made thee more profit / Than other princess' can, that have more time / For vainer hours, and tutors not so careful' (I.ii.171–4). This education has had two main and diverse purposes. On the one hand it has schooled her to obedience; Prospero proudly affirms that Miranda is 'ignorant of what thou art; nought knowing / Of whence I am'. She obeys in silence and has been taught not to question why, despite the fact that Prospero has left his story tantalisingly incomplete: 'More to know / Did never meddle with my thoughts' (I.ii.17–22). She has therefore been well prepared to accept his version of the past (unlike Caliban, who questions it). Gratitude to her father mingles with a self-depreciation and she repeatedly perceives herself as a nuisance to him (I.ii.63; I.ii.151–2). Prospero never takes this control for granted, however, and is anxious to secure her attention and obedience. His story-telling is punctuated by repeated orders to 'sit down', 'Obey, and be attentive', 'Dost thou attend me', 'I pray thee, mark me', 'Thou attend'st not?', 'Dost thou hear?' (I.ii). Miranda is ordered to sleep, awake, come on, see, speak, be quiet, obey, be silent, hush and be mute. She is his property, to be exchanged between father and husband: 'Then, as my gift, and thine own acquisition / Worthily purchas'd, take my daughter' (IV.i.13–14).

On the other hand, Miranda's schooling calls upon her to *participate* actively in the colonial venture. Although she does not 'love to look upon' Caliban, she must be educated about the economics of the situation:

> We cannot miss him: he does make our fire,
> Fetch in our wood, and serves in offices
> That serve us
>
> (I.ii.311–15)

Editors of *The Tempest* have often sought to transfer Miranda's verbal assault on Caliban beginning 'Abhorred slave' (I.ii.351–62) to Prospero on the grounds that Miranda is too delicate and not philosophical enough to speak so harshly.[30] On the contrary, these lines underline Miranda's implication in the colonialist project. She has been taught to be revolted by Caliban ('abhorred slave'); to believe in his natural inferiority ('thy vile race') and inherent incapacity to be bettered ('which any print of goodness will not take'); to feel sorry for the inferior native ('I pitied thee') and to try and uplift him ('took pains to make thee speak'); and to concur totally in his 'deserv'd ' confinement. Miranda thus conforms to the dual requirements of femininity within the master-culture: by taking on aspects of the white man's burden the white woman only confirmed her own subordination.

'Miranda House' was a school for Indian women and its naming was not a careful colonial conspiracy. I do not want to ignore the contradictions of such institutions, and the space for alternative stances within them; yet the name betrays some of the assumptions underlying female education in the colonies and indicates the effort to create a native *female* intelligentsia which will be schooled to ignore its gendered and racial alienation from the prevailing status quo.[31] Two other women are mentioned in *The Tempest*, and the references to them reinforce racial and sexual power relations. The first of these is Miranda's mother, who is dismissed as 'a piece of virtue' (I.ii.56) and remembered solely for her capacity to ensure the pure descent of the Duke of Milan. Later we hear of Claribel, daughter of Alonzo, King of Naples, who has been married to the King of Tunis. The tempest wrecked the ship while it was returning from the wedding celebrations. While he laments the death of his son, Alonzo is told:

> Sir, you may thank yourself for this great loss,
> That would not bless our Europe with your daughter,
> But rather loose her to an African.
> (II.i.117–19)

Thus women and black men, and particularly a combination of the two, are posited as the cause of misfortune. We are also told that Claribel herself, 'the fair soul', oscillated between 'loathness' at this union and 'obedience' to her father (II.i.123–4). Her marriage is abnormal and the source of ill-luck but she, a true European daughter, is subservient to patriarchal will. The references to the marriage also serve to distinguish between different non-Europeans, between the King of Tunis and Caliban, underlining the way that class positions, power and regional differences can alter the meaning of racial difference. In this respect, one may recall also that whereas Cleopatra's status can allow her frankly to acknowledge her dark colour – 'Think on me, / That am with Phoebus' amorous pinches black' (I.v.27–8)–Zanche as a lowly servant girl must attempt, with a dowry of 'a hundred thousand crowns', to 'wash the Ethiop white' (*The White Devil*, V.iii.256, 259).[32]

A DOOMED DIALECTIC?

The 'rape' amplifies the doomed dialectic which might be detected in Caliban's ability to curse *in the coloniser's tongue*, which exerted the greatest fascination for anti-colonial appropriations and became a symbol both for the internalisation of European values by the African and Caribbean intellectual and for his subversion (hers was not considered) of them. George Lamming's *The Pleasures of Exile* points out that the 'gift' of language is 'not English, in particular, but speech and concept as a way ... (it) is the very prison in which Caliban's achievements will be realised and restricted' (pp. 109–10). Caliban presents the rape as his attempt to 'people ... This isle with Calibans' (I.ii.350–1). But even by positing himself as worthy of duplication, Caliban's revolt boomerangs to confirm the shaping power of dominant culture. Lamming wonders why Caliban is so sure that his children by Miranda would be like him, and not like her or Prospero. But he does not consider the phallocentricism of Caliban's confidence, nor how it is ironically undercut by his subordinate racial position. Moreover, he constantly simplifies both Caliban and Miranda: 'Caliban is in his way a kind of Universal. Like the earth he is always there, generous in his gifts, inevitable, yet superfluous and dumb ... Caliban can never reach perfection, not even the perfection implicit in Miranda's privileged ignorance' (pp. 108–10). The political effect of Prospero's accusation and Caliban's acceptance is to make the potential revolutionary a rapist, and I have tried to suggest that it is crucially interrelated with the other ways in which Caliban's spaces are limited by the boundaries of colonial discourse. Although the connection between Caliban's linguistic and sexual rebellion is hinted at by Lamming, it is not fully developed; this omission is typical of the gender-blindness of many anti-colonial appropriations and criticism.

Can Caliban ever exist outside the territories allowed him by *The Tempest*? Feminists have found the 'masculine will' of disorderly women in Renaissance drama unsatisfactory, and I have tried to show that no other pure feminist consciousness is possible from within the masculine arena available to them. Homi Bhabha writes: 'it is always in relation to the place of the Other that colonial desire is articulated: that is, in part, the fantasmatic space of "possession" that no one subject can singly occupy which permits the dream of the inversion of role'.[33] This implicates both the coloniser and the colonised: while it would be idealist to imagine spaces outside such a dialectic in the colonial situation, the interlocking is increasingly dissatisfying in the post-colonial reality. Even within the colonial struggle, the evocation of native culture has been important – Aimé Césaire, for example, tried to locate his Caliban in indigenous space – he is rooted in African religion and culture and draws on traditions uncontaminated by colonialism.

Here *The Tempest* brings us to the centre of a crucial controversy surrounding current theories of colonial discourse. Benita Parry has suggested that recent work in this area has concentrated on the complexity, ambiguity and 'hybridity' of colonial discourse at the expense of obscuring what Fanon called the 'murderous and decisive struggle between two protagonists'.[34] This problem has been identified in relation to *The Tempest* by Thomas Cartelli. He counterposes those 'who quarrel with the notion of a *Tempest* that speaks the predatory language of colonialism' and 'another non-western interpretative community for whom *The Tempest* has long served as the embodiment of colonial presumption'. As he sees it, the first group 'problematise(s) the traditionally stereotyped critical estimate of the relationship of Prospero and Caliban', while the second resists this 'by recuperating the starkness of the master/slave configuration'.

It is true that the limits of the 'radical ambivalence' of *The Tempest* are marked by the confinement of Caliban to the space structured by the coloniser; the play does not allow him to visualise what Parry calls 'another condition beyond imperialism'. But we can question a simple opposition between the two groups identified by Cartelli by arguing that the play functions as 'the embodiment of colonial presumption' only when the tensions and ambivalence which Brown points to are erased. What do we mean by 'the starkness of the master/slave configuration'? Surely not that either of the two opponents, their stances and psyches, are simple or monolithic? The harshness of the colonial conflict cannot be stressed by ignoring the complexity of the adversaries.

This project has tried to emphasise this point in relation to our own encounter with the European text, including the agenda for its alternative teaching. The colonial conflict intersects with others – those of class, gender, caste and ethnicity and 'the colonial subject' is not a simple being. Moreover, three centuries of colonial history have shaped complex institutions, such as the Indian education system, which cannot be dismantled unless we take into account the interpenetration of colonial, indigenous and patriarchal power structures. But this is precisely the point at which Parry's criticism becomes crucial: she attributes the concentration on 'hybridity' to a 'programme marked by the exhorbitation of discourse and a related incuriosity about the enabling socio-economic and political institutions and other forms of social praxis'.[35] Whereas in *The Tempest* Caliban is simply left on his island, we know that in reality Prospero rarely simply sails away. To curse in 'your language' (I.ii.362) is not to appropriate the European text on its own terms or to limit ourselves to the spaces allowed by it. Not only will it centre around a disclosure of the similarity and dissimilarity, usefulness and irrelevance of the Western text, but it must extend to the economic, sociopolitical and institutional realities in which our academic practice exists.

From Ania Loomba, *Gender, Race, Renaissance Drama* (Manchester, 1989), pp. 142–58.

NOTES

[Ania Loomba reads *The Tempest* as a woman and as somebody educated in English departments in India, so she is acutely aware of the ways by which patriarchal and racist appropriations of the play can be insidious and powerful. She demonstrates the intersection of issues of class, gender, race, caste and ethnicity, not only in the play and the criticism it has generated, but also in educational institutions where Shakespeare is taught. Conservative and radical appropriations alike, she argues, have been instrumental in constructing 'the colonial subject'. All quotations from *The Tempest* are taken from the Arden edition, edited Frank Kermode (London 1954). Ed.]

1. Kate McLuskie, 'Feminist deconstruction: the example of Shakespeare's *The Taming of the Shrew*', *Red Letters*, 12 (1981), 33.

2. Alan Sinfield, 'Reproductions, interventions', in *Political Shakespeare: New Essays in Cultural Materialism* (Manchester, 1985), pp. 130–3, 132.

3. I am indebted to the work on *The Tempest* by Francis Barker and Peter Hulme, Paul Brown and Rob Nixon, all of which has made this chapter possible.

4. Trevor R. Griffiths, '"This island's mine": Caliban and colonialism', *YES*, 13 (1983), 163–9.

5. Barker and Hulme, '"Nymphs and Reapers heavily vanish": the discursive con-texts of *The Tempest*', in John Drakakis (ed.), *Alternative Shakespeares* (London, 1985), p. 195 [see essay 2 – Ed.].

6. Griffiths, 'This island's mine', p. 178.

7. Rob Nixon, 'Caribbean and African appropriations of *The Tempest*', *Critical Inquiry*, 13 (1987), 557–8.

8. Griffiths, 'This island's mine', p. 176.

9. Barker and Hulme, 'Nymphs', p. 194.

10. Thomas Cartelli, 'Prospero in Africa', in *Shakespeare Reproduced*, ed. Jean Howard and Marion O'Connor (New York, 1987), pp. 99–115 [see essay 7 – Ed.].

11. Paul Brown, '"This thing of darkness I acknowledge mine": *The Tempest* and the discourse of colonialism', in Jonathan Dollimore and Alan Sinfield (eds), *Political Shakespeare* (Manchester, 1985), p. 68; Barker and Hulme, 'Nymphs and Reapers', p. 119; Cartelli, 'Prospero in Africa' pp. 100–1.

12. Cartelli, 'Prospero in Africa', p. 107.

13. P. B. Acharya, *Tragicomedies: Shakespeare, Kalidasa and Bhavabhuti* (New Delhi, 1978), pp. xii–xiii.

14. C. D. Narasimhaiah (ed.), *Shakespeare Came to India* (Bombay, 1964), p. v.

15. Nixon, 'Caribbean and African appropriations', p. 577.

16. Brown, 'This thing of darkness', p. 62.

17. Griffiths, 'This island's mine', p. 166, emphasis added.

18. Nixon, 'Caribbean and African appropriations', pp. 562–5.

19. Ibid., pp. 564–5.

20. See Errol Lawrence, 'Just plain common-sense: the "roots" of racism', CCS (Centre for Contemporary Cultural Studies) (1982), pp. 47–94.

21. Ibid., p. 71.

22. Angela Davis, *Women, Race and Class* (London: Women's Press, 1982), p. 197.

23. Ibid., p. 174.

24. See Brown, 'This thing of darkness', p. 67, and Leslie A. Fiedler, *The Stranger in Shakespeare* (Hertfordshire, 1974), p. 206.

25. Nixon, 'Caribbean and African appropriations', pp. 561–2.

26. George Lamming, *The Pleasures of Exile* (1960; New York, 1984), p. 111.

27. Errol Lawrence, 'In abundance of water the fool is thirsty: sociology and black "pathology"' in CCCS (1982), pp. 95–142, 113–14.

28. Maria Mies, *Patriarchy and Accumulation on a World Scale: Women in the International Division of Labour* (London and New Jersey, 1986), quoted by Pratap Rughani, 'Kipling, India and Imperialism' (unpublished paper), p. 19.

29. Brown, 'This thing of darkness', p. 51.

30. See Kermode, Arden edition, p. 32; and Anne Barton, 'Leontes and the spider: language and speaker in Shakespeare's last plays', in P. Edwards, I. S. Ewbank and G. K. Hunter (eds), *Shakespeare's Styles: Essays in Honour of Kenneth Muir* (Cambridge, 1980), pp. 131–50, 137.

31. The English Department of Miranda House has been instrumental in initiating (in Delhi) the critical examination of English studies in India; it has also provided a forum for regular discussion of critical theory and its applicability in the Indian classroom and published feminist criticism by university lecturers in Delhi. This perhaps bears out my contention that, given the increasing feminisation of English studies, and women's alienation from the dominant concerns of the discipline, a third world feminist criticism will play a central role in overhauling English studies in India.

32. See also Karen Newman, '"And wash the Ethiop white" – femininity and the monstrous in *Othello*', in Jean E. Howard and Marion F. O'Connor (eds), *Shakespeare Reproduced: the Text in History and Ideology* (New York and London, 1987), p. 142. Femininity and race are picked up in the references to other women, as in the apparently trivial banter about Dido 'which has never properly been explained' (Kermode, Arden edition, p. 46). This exchange both differentiates between African Tunis and Carthage, centre of the Old World, and introduces the idea of identification between the two worlds: 'Tunis, sir, was Carthage' (II.i.78).

33. Homi Bhabha, Introduction to Frantz Fanon, *Black Skins, White Masks*, trans. Charles Lam Markmann (London and Sydney, 1986), p. xv.

34. Benita Parry, 'Problems in current theories of colonial discourse', *Oxford Literary Review*, 9 (1987), 27–58, 43

35. Ibid., p. 43.

8

'Miranda, Where's Your Sister?': Reading Shakespeare's *The Tempest*

ANN THOMPSON

These are Prospero's first words in *The Tempest, or The Enchanted Island*, the adaptation of Shakespeare's play created for the most part by William Davenant, with some input from John Dryden, in 1667. They act as a clear signal to a knowing audience or reader that this is not the original. Davenant's Miranda does indeed have a younger sister, Dorinda, and the two are described in the *Dramatis Personae* as 'Daughters to Prospero, that never saw Man'. Dorinda is balanced, and ultimately partnered, by another new character, Hippolito, heir to the dukedom of Mantua, 'one that never saw Woman'. In the insistent pattern of parallels and repetitions which characterises Davenant's version, Ariel has a female consort, Milcha, and even Caliban has a twin sister named after their mother, Sycorax, whom he proposes as a bride for Trinculo.[1] This proliferation of female roles can presumably be attributed in part to the need to provide employment for actresses on the Restoration stage.

In contrast, women are notably absent from Shakespeare's *Tempest*. Miranda at one point stresses her isolation and lack of female companionship by saying 'I do not know / One of my sex, no woman's face remember, / Save from my glass, mine own' (III.i.48–50),[2] though at the beginning of the play she had claimed at least a vague recollection: 'Had I not / Four or five women once that tended me?' (I.ii.46–7). Apart from Miranda herself, the only females mentioned in the First Folio's list of the 'Names of the Actors' are Iris, Ceres, Juno and the Nymphs, all of whom are 'spirits' explicitly impersonated by Ariel and his 'fellows'. While Ariel is clearly a male spirit, he is also required to impersonate a 'nymph of the sea' (I.ii.301) and a half-female harpy (stage direction at III.ii.52), indicating a degree of ambiguity about his gender. The part has often been performed by women or by androgynous youths. Conversely, the part of Miranda would in actuality have been performed by a boy actor on Shakespeare's stage.

Miranda, in Shakespeare's play, has no sister and apparently no mother. It is odd that she does not even inquire about the fate of the latter, though she might have been prompted to do so by Prospero's reply to her question 'Sir, are not you my father?' In his only reference to his wife Prospero says 'Thy mother was a piece of virtue, and / She said thou wast my daughter' (I.ii.56–7). This is apparently all that needs to be said about her. Some fifty lines later, Miranda demonstrates that she has fully internalised the patriarchal assumption that a woman's main function is to provide a legitimate succession when asked to comment on the wickedness of Prospero's brother: 'I should sin / To think but nobly of my grandmother: / Good wombs have borne bad sons' (I.ii.117–19).

The worldly cynicism of such standard jokes was formerly thought inappropriate to the innocent Miranda, and they were often omitted from performances from the late eighteenth century to the early twentieth century; Davenant's Miranda more explicitly denies that she had a mother when she remarks with a coy naïvety to Dorinda that she thinks Prospero 'found us when we both were little, and grew within the ground' (I.ii.332–3). In Shakespeare's version, Miranda's destined spouse, Ferdinand, is also motherless, and *his* sister's absence is curiously stressed: although the distance from Naples to North Africa is not enormous, Alonso insists that Claribel is 'so far from Italy removed / I ne'er again shall see her' (II.i.108–9), and Antonio expresses her remoteness even more extravagantly:

> She that is Queen of Tunis; she that dwells
> Ten leagues beyond man's life; she that from Naples
> Can have no note unless the sun were post –
> The man 'i' th' moon's too slow – till newborn chins
> Be rough and razorable;
> (II.i.244–8)

Claribel had to wait until 1949 for the female poet H. D. to make her visible and give her a voice.[3] Shakespeare's Caliban has no sister and his mother, Sycroax, is long dead by the time the play's events take place. Sycorax also has a North African connection, having been banished by the Algerians, who apparently spared her life because she was pregnant. Her power is at least recognised by Prospero, Ariel and Caliban, though she is vilified by the two former characters as a 'hag' and a 'foul witch'. Oddly, Shakespeare draws on the lines Ovid gave another notorious female enchantress, Medea, for Prospero's big 'conjuring' speech, 'Ye elves of hills, brooks, standing lakes, and groves' (V.i.33 ff.), but Medea herself is not mentioned.

The fact that I have chosen nevertheless to discuss *The Tempest* in the context of this book [*Feminist Criticism: Theory and Practice*, ed. Susan Sellers] may seem perverse, but my choice is a deliberate one and relates precisely to the *absence* of female characters. I want to ask what feminist criticism can do in the face of a male-authored canonical text which seems to exclude women to this extent. Much early feminist criticism consisted merely in privileging female characters and identifying with their viewpoints, especially if they could be claimed to be in any way subversive or protofeminist. This is clearly impossible in *The Tempest*: even nineteenth-century female critics, who on the whole participated enthusiastically in the trend of aggrandising and romanticising Shakespeare's heroines, could not find a great deal to say for Miranda. Anna Jameson wrote in *Shakespeare's Heroines* (first published in 1833) that in Ophelia and Miranda Shakespeare had created two beings in whom 'the feminine character appears resolved into its very elementary principles – as modesty, grace, tenderness', but added that by the same token Miranda 'resembles nothing on earth',[4] and Mrs M. L. Elliott remarked in *Shakespeare's Garden of Girls* (1885) that Miranda was too ethereal and thus tended to be more popular with male than with female readers.[5] Anyone who has taught the play recently will know that these seem very moderate views compared to the opinions of twentieth-century female students, who find Miranda an extremely feeble heroine and scorn to identify with her. Perhaps, then, *The Tempest* can be used as something of a test case for discovering what else a feminist approach may offer beyond this character-based level.

Faced with a comparable problem in relation to *King Lear*, where modern readers hesitate to identify with either the stereotype of the bad woman represented by Goneril and Regan or with the stereotype of the good woman represented by Cordelia, Kathleen McLuskie writes:

> Feminist criticism need not restrict itself to privileging the woman's part or to special pleading on behalf of female characters. It can be equally well served by making a text reveal the conditions in which a particular ideology of femininity functions and by both revealing and subverting the hold which such an ideology has for readers both female and male.[6]

I shall attempt in the remainder of this essay to explore the 'ideology of femininity' at work in *The Tempest*, both through a reading of the play and through a survey of some of the most influential ways in which it is currently being reproduced in literary criticism.

Despite her small and comparatively passive role, the text claims that Miranda is nevertheless crucial to the play. Explaining the storm, Prospero tells her: 'I have done nothing but in care of thee' (I.ii.16). A feminist critic might ask in what sense this is true, and whether Miranda's gender is significant: would the play have worked in the same way if Prospero had had a son? How does sexuality, and especially female sexuality, function in this narrative? Reading the play with an explicit focus on issues of gender, one is immediately struck by its obsession with themes of chastity and fertility, which occur in its figurative language as well as in its literal events. These themes are often specifically associated with female sexuality. In the first, rather startling metaphor of this kind, Gonzalo imagines the very ship which seems to founder in the opening scene as being 'as leaky as an unstanched wench' (I.i.47–8), a phrase interpreted as alluding either to a sexually aroused (insatiable) woman or to one menstruating 'without the use of absorbent padding', as the Oxford editor puts it. In his long narrative speech to Miranda in the second scene, Prospero uses a metaphor of birth to describe Antonio's treachery – 'my trust, / Like a good parent, did beget of him / A falsehood' (I.ii.93–5), and seems almost to claim that he gave a kind of second birth to Miranda in his sufferings on the voyage to the island:

> When I have decked the sea with drops full salt,
> Under my burden groaned, which raised in me
> An undergoing stomach to bear up
> Against what should ensue.
>
> (I.ii.155–8)

This scene also introduces the literal contrast between the chaste Miranda and the 'earthy and abhorred' Sycorax who arrived on the island pregnant (by the devil himself, according to Prospero at I.ii.319) and there 'littered' or 'whelped' her subhuman son. It is notable that the acknowledged, if evil, power of Sycorax is effectively undermined by the bestial stupidity of her son, rather as the power of Tamora is defused in *Titus Andronicus* and that of the Queen in *Cymbeline*. As in the earlier plays, the son of the witch-like woman is a rapist (or would-be rapist); Caliban is accused of attempting to rape Miranda, and he does not deny the charge:

> O ho, O ho! Would't had been done!
> Thou didst prevent me – I had peopled else
> This isle with Calibans.
> (I.ii.348–50)

He later promises Stephano that Miranda, seen as one of the spoils of victory, will 'bring thee forth brave brood' (III.ii.103). It is perhaps not surprising, therefore, that Ferdinand's 'prime request' to Miranda on first seeing her is 'If you be maid or no' (I.ii.428), a topic to which he returns twenty lines later, ignoring Prospero's intervention in the dialogue.

Miranda's chastity apparently has a quasi-mystical power. She herself swears 'by my modesty, / The jewel in my dower' (III.i.53–4), and tells Ferdinand: 'I am your wife if you will marry me; / If not, I'll die your maid' (III.i.83–4). Prospero warns Ferdinand in what seem to be unnecessarily harsh terms against breaking her 'virgin-knot before / All sanctimonious ceremonies' (IV.i.15–16), threatening dire consequences:

> No sweet aspersion shall the heavens let fall
> To make this contract grow; but barren hate,
> Sour-eyed disdain, and discords shall bestrew
> The union of your bed with weeds so loathly
> That you shall hate it both. Therefore take heed,
> As Hymen's lamps shall light you.
> (IV.i.18–23)

Ferdinand's reply is comparably graphic:

> As I hope
> For quiet days, fair issue, and long life,
> With such love as 'tis now, the murkiest den,

The most opportune place, the strong'st suggestion
Our worser genius can, shall never melt
Mine honour into lust, to take away
The edge of that day's celebration
When I shall think or Phoebus' steeds are foundered,
Or night kept chained below.

(IV.i.23–31)

Ostensibly reassuring, such language seems to suggest that the minds
of both men are dwelling in morbid detail on the possibilities of completing Caliban's attempted violation: the image of Miranda as a rape
victim interferes disturbingly with the image of Miranda as a chaste
and fertile wife. The masque which Prospero organises for the entertainment of the young couple in this scene explicitly banishes lust in
the form of Venus and Cupid, and emphasises the blessed fertility of
honourable marriage. and yet, reading as a woman, I continue to get
the feeling that the play protests too much on this score.

The speakers in the masque promise rewards for premarital
chastity. As Ceres sings:

Earth's increase, foison plenty,
Barns and garners never empty,
Vines with clust'ring bunches growing,
Plants with goodly burden bowing,
Spring come to you at the farthest,
In the very end of harvest!

(IV.i.110–15)

This language echoes that of the earlier scene in which Gonzalo specu-
lates on what he would do, 'Had I plantation of this isle' (II.i.141), to
make nature bring forth 'all foison, all abundance' (II.i.161), in a
utopian vision which is at the same time colonialist in so far as the
'commonwealth' is subject to his royal command. Sebastian jokes that
he will 'carry this island home in his pocket and give it his son for an
apple', to which Antonio replies: 'And sowing the kernels of it in the
sea, bring forth more islands' (II.i.88–91), similarly invoking a picture
of benign exploitation and a fantasy of magical male fecundity.

The play at times takes the power of the sea to give birth, or
rebirth, quite seriously: later in II.i.249 Antonio refers to all the
courtiers as 'sea-swallowed, though some cast again', a metaphor repeated by Ariel when, disguised as a harpy, he tells the 'men of sin'
that Destiny 'the never-surfeited sea / Hath caused to belch up you'
(III.iii.55–6). These are both parodies of birth: birth from the mouth

rather than from the uterus. A cruder version of what the body can throw forth arises at II.ii.101–2, when Stephano sees Trinculo, hiding under Caliban's cloak, as the 'seige' or excrement of the 'mooncalf'. More seriously, in his Medea-inspired speech, Prospero claims the power to resurrect the dead: 'Graves at my command / Have waked their sleepers, oped, and let 'em forth (V.i.48–9), though Ferdinand asserts elsewhere that it is Miranda who 'quickens what's dead' (III.i.6). At the end of the play, after Ferdinand's apparent death 'mudded in that oozy bed' of the sea (V.i.151), he rhetorically attributes his 'second life' to Prospero (V.i.195), although it is Miranda's literal fertility which will, as Gonzalo explains, permit Prospero's 'issue' to become kings of Naples (V.i.205–6).

How, then, can a feminist interpret this pattern of references? What is going on in this text which seems, on the one hand, to deny the importance – and even in some cases the presence – of female characters, but which simultaneously attributes enormous power to female chastity and fertility? One noticeable feature of the handling of these themes is the insistence on male control: Prospero must control Miranda's sexuality before he hands her over to Ferdinand. Alonso, her father, formerly controlled Claribel's sexuality, but the play is ambivalent about his decision (a willing version of Desdemona's father Brabantio?) to 'lose' or 'loose' her to an African rather than to a European suitor (II.i.123),[7] and she herself is said to have been 'Weighed between loathness and obedience' in the matter (II.i.128). Men are seen as capable of controlling the fertility of nature, and Prospero even controls Ceres, the goddess of harvests, in so far as the play makes it clear that she is represented in the masque by his servant Ariel (IV.i.167). Recent criticism of *The Tempest* suggests two theoretical frameworks for discussing this question of control, the psychoanalytical and the political, both of which can be utilised in a feminist approach.

The traditional reading of *The Tempest* prevalent in the nineteenth century and earlier twentieth century interpreted Prospero's control of its events and characters as entirely benign; he was often seen as the representative of Art itself, or even identified with Shakespeare as author. Freudian and post-Freudian psychoanalytic studies of the play have undermined this view, exposing the darker side of the 'family romance' by suggesting that Prospero's control might be more problematic and that his concern with his daughter's sexuality might indicate an incestuous desire for her. In David Sundelson's essay '"So rare a wonder'd father": Prospero's *Tempest*', the play is fraught with anxieties and uncertainties on this level which are only partially resolved by its endorsement of what he calls both Prospero's and the play's 'paternal narcissism: the prevailing sense that there is no worthiness like a father's, no accomplishment or power, and that Prospero is the father *par excellence*'.[8] Coppélia Kahn, writing on 'The Providential Tempest and the Shakespearean Family', agrees in seeing the play as a 'fantasy of omnipotence' in which Prospero, coming from Milan to the island, 'went from child-like, self-absorbed dependency to paternal omnipotence, skipping the steps of maturation in between'. Miranda, like Marina in *Pericles* and Perdita in *The Winter's Tale*, doubles the roles of mother and daughter, uniting chastity and fertility in a non-threatening way. Yet, in so far as Kahn claims that 'Prospero's identity is based entirely on his role as father, and his family is never united or complete' – indeed he is left at the end in a state of social and sexual isolation – the 'romance' is still a narrative of imperfect wish fulfilment representing the universally ambivalent desire we all have both to escape from our families and to continue to be nurtured by them.[9] Both these readings lay stress on the tensions that arise in the play and the sheer struggle involved in asserting the supposedly natural harmony of patriarchal control: it appears that an 'unstanched wench' constitutes a serious threat to this order.

Stephen Orgel has pointed out a danger in the tendency of psychoanalytic readings to treat the play as a case-history, either of the author or of the characters, overlooking the extent to which the reader, playing the role of analyst, is a collaborator in the resultant fantasy. He further notices that while psychoanalysis evokes an unchanging, essential human nature, the theoretical framework does change:

> Recent psychoanalytic theory has replaced Freud's central Oedipal myth with a drama in which the loss of the seducing mother is the crucial trauma. As men, we used to want reassurance that we could successfully compete with or replace or supersede our fathers; now we want to know that our lost mothers will return.
>
> (p.52)[10]

In consequence, his essay, called 'Prospero's Wife', transfers the centre of interest from the present, dominant father to the absent mother, a strategy comparable to the one employed by Coppélia Kahn in her essay on 'The Absent Mother in *King Lear*'.[11] It is, as Orgel acknowledges, a problematic strategy in so far as it deals not with the text itself but with the gaps and blanks that Shakespeare has chosen not to fill in. Indeed, he begins his study with the defensive statement 'This essay is not a reading of *The Tempest*', and worries about the possible parallels with such currently unfasionable texts as Mary Cowden Clarke's *The Girlhood of Shakespeare's Heroines*. Nevertheless, his work is highly suggestive for feminist critics in its willingness to explore a whole network of feminine allusions and absences, ranging from the obvious one of his title to more obscure issues such as the puzzling references to 'widow Dido' at II.i.70–90, Dido being a 'model at once of heroic fidelity to a murdered husband and [of] the destructive potential of erotic passion' (p. 51). He also challenges the traditional view of *The Tempest* as a happy courtship comedy, remarking that while the play does move towards marriage, the relationships are 'ignorant at best, characteristically tense, and potentially tragic'. He sees this as typical of the author:

> relationships between men and women interest Shakespeare intensely, but not, on the whole, as husbands and wives. The wooing process tends to be what it is here: not so much a prelude to marriage and a family as a process of self-definition.
>
> (p.56)

Current political approaches to *The Tempest* often have links with psychoanalytic approaches. Orgel exemplifies one such link as he moves from his discussion of the missing wife, by way of speculations about Shakespeare's own family experiences, to an analysis of power and authority in the play in terms of the ways these issues were conceived in Jacobean England. He points out that in setting up the contest for the island between Caliban, who claims his inheritance from his mother, and Prospero, whose authority is self-created, Shakespeare is representing positions which were available – indeed, normative – at the time. Further, in his edition of *The Tempest*, Orgel goes on to consider the real-life significance of political marriages like the one in the play where Prospero goes to considerable trouble to marry his daughter to the son of his chief enemy, thereby staging a counter-usurpation of Naples by Milan.

The fact that *The Tempest* was performed at court in 1613 during the wedding festivities of King James's daughter Elizabeth and Frederick the Elector Palatine gives a further resonance to such speculations. This historical circumstance is the starting point for Lorie Jerrell Leininger's feminist reading. 'The Miranda Trap: Sexism and Racism in Shakespeare's *Tempest*'.[12] She imagines the sixteen-year-old princess as the real-life equivalent of Miranda: beautiful, loving, chaste and above all obedient to her all-powerful

father. Miranda's role as the dependent female is crucial to the
play's dynamics of power in so far as Caliban's enslavement is
justified by his attempt to rape her: 'Prospero needs Miranda as
sexual bait, and then needs to protect her from the threat which is
inescapable given his hierarchical world' (p. 289). Shakespeare's
play allows Miranda no way out of this situation, but Leininger
invents an epilogue for a modern Miranda who refuses to participate in the play's assumptions that Prospero is infallible, that
Caliban is a 'natural' slave, and that a daughter is a 'foot' in a family
organism of which the father is the head.

Most political readings of *The Tempest*, however, centre on the
issue of colonialism. This is the focus of Francis Barker and Peter
Hulme's essay '"Nymphs and Reapers heavily vanish": The Discursive
Con-texts of *The Tempest*',[13] and of Paul Brown's essay '"This thing
of darkness I acknowledge mine": *The Tempest* and the Discourse of
Colonialism'.[14] Both employ the technique of intertextuality to relate
the play to nascent seventeenth-century European colonialism, re-
assessing the 'sources' in the context of New World voyage materials
and arguing that anxiety and ambivalence result from the struggle to
create a self-justifying, colonialist discourse. We are encouraged in
these readings to be deeply suspicious of Prospero and to sympathise
with Caliban as the representative of an exploited Third World.
Brown draws on Freudian theory to point out an analogy between the
political operations of colonialism and the modes of psychic repression, and he uses the Freudian concept of 'dreamwork' to discuss
the way in which Prospero's discourse subordinates that of the other
inhabitants of the island, as, for example, when he imposes his
memory of earlier events on both Caliban and Ariel in Act I, scene ii.

An explicitly feminist version of this kind of reading, and one which
is moreover undertaken from a Third World viewpoint, is performed
by the Indian critic Ania Loomba as the final chapter of her book
Gender, Race, Renaissance Drama.[15] Loomba is critical of the tendency
of 'alternative' readings of *The Tempest* to seize upon Caliban as a
symbol of exploitation and potential rebellion, and points out that
some anti-colonialist or anti-racist readings have been unthinkingly
sexist: the specific repression of Miranda has been neglected. Setting
out to delineate the limits of the text's supposed 'radical ambivalence',
she discusses the myth of the black rapist, the significance of Sycorax
as 'Prospero's other', and the contradictory position of Miranda as
typical of that of all white women in the colonial adventure: the
nature of her participation confirms her subordination to white men.

Both psychoanalytic and political theoretical approaches nevertheless deny some of the pleasures experienced by earlier generations of audiences and readers who were apparently able to identify more readily with the viewpoint of Prospero as white male patriarch and coloniser. Today, white male critics in Britain and the United States understandably feel uncomfortable and guilty about participating in these attitudes. Reading the play as a woman and as a feminist, it is possible to feel good about delineating and rejecting its idealisation of patriarchy, and one can go beyond the play to consider the conscious and unconscious sexism of its critical and stage history. Reading as a white British person, my conscience is less clear: women as well as men benefited (and still benefit) from the kind of colonialism idealised in *The Tempest*.

The current situation as I have sketched it above seems to leave two major questions unanswered (and unanswerable within the scope of this essay): first, is it possible for a staging of *The Tempest* to convey anything approaching a feminist reading of the text (without rewriting it or adding something like Leininger's epilogue); and secondly, what kind of pleasure can a woman and a feminist take in this text beyond the rather grim one of mapping its various patterns of exploitation? Must a feminist reading necessarily be a negative one?

From *Feminist Criticism: Theory and Practice*, ed. Susan Sellers (Hemel Hempstead, 1991), pp. 45–55.

NOTES

[Ann Thompson sketches the lines along which a feminist interpretation might run. Noting the isolation of Miranda, the shadowiness of other women referred to but not appearing in the play, and the apparent fear of female sexuality demonstrated by men, she finds a disturbing connection between images of woman as rape victim and woman as dutiful wife. Thompson rejects the delineation of partriarchy in *The Tempest*, but at the end poses the challenging question: 'Must a feminist reading necessarily be a negative one?' References are taken from *The Tempest*, ed. Stephen Orgel (Oxford and New York, 1987). Ed.]

1. Maximilian E. Novak and George Robert Guffey (eds), *The Works of John Dryden* (vol. X, Berkeley, CA, and London, 1970). I would like to thank Andrew Gurr for drawing my attention to the line which forms my title.

2. References and quotations from *The Tempest* are from the Oxford Shakespeare text, ed. Stephen Orgel (Oxford and New York, 1987).

3. See *By Avon River* (New York, 1949). For a discussion of H. D.'s transformation of *The Tempest* in this experimental work, see Susan Stanford Friedman. 'Remembering Shakespeare Differently: H. D.'s *By Avon River*', in Marianne Novy (ed.), *Women's Revisions of Shakespeare* (Urbana and Chicago, 1990), pp. 143–64.

4. *Shakespeare's Heroines*, 1897 reprint (London), pp. 134,149.

5. *Shakespeare's Garden of Girls*, published anonymously (London, 1885), p. 265.

6. 'The Patriarchal Bard: Feminist Criticism and Shakespeare: *King Lear* and *Measure for Measure*', in Jonathan Dollimore and Alan Sinfield (eds), *Political Shakespeare* (Manchester, 1985), pp. 88–108.

7. The First Folio's spelling, 'loose', was the normal spelling of 'lose', but most modern editors, with the exception of Stephen Orgel, print 'loose', presumably because it carries an undertone of greater sensuality.

8. In Murray M. Schwartz and Coppélia Kahn (eds), *Representing Shakespeare: New Psychoanalytic Essays* (Baltimore, MD and London, 1980), pp. 33–53.

9. In Schwartz and Kahn, *Representing Shakespeare*, pp. 217–43. Passages cited are on p. 238 and p. 240.

10. 'Prospero's Wife', in Margaret W. Ferguson, Maureen Quilligan and Nancy J. Vickers (eds), *Rewriting the Renaissance: The Discourses of Sexual Difference in Early Modern Europe* (Chicago and London, 1986), pp. 50–64. This essay was first published in *Representations*, 8 (1984), 1–13. [See essay 1 above. Subsequent references in parentheses in the text – Ed.]

11. In Ferguson, Quilligan and Vickers, *Rewriting the Renaissance*, pp. 33–49.

12. In Carolyn Ruth Swift Lenz, Gayle Greene and Carol Thomas Neely (eds), *The Woman's Part* (Urbana and Chicago, 1980), pp. 285–94.

13. In John Drakakis (ed), *Alternative Shakespeares* (London and New York, 1985), pp. 191–205 [see essay 2 above – Ed.].

14. In Dollimore and Sinfield, *Political Shakespeare,* pp. 48–71.

15. Manchester (1989), pp. 142–58 [see essay 7 above – Ed.].

9

'What cares these roarers for the name of king?': Language and Utopia in *The Tempest*

DAVID NORBROOK

I

'Where's the Master?'[1] That is the question that comes instinctively to King Alonso's lips as his ship is buffeted by the tempest. But the master has left the stage: the work on this ship is impersonally structured and does not need the direct presence of a figure of authority. So little respect does the boatswain have for traditional hierarchies that he refuses to answer. When Antonio repeats the question, the boatswain dismisses the king and all the courtiers with a summary 'You mar our labour ... What cares these roarers for the name of king?' 'Roaring' connotes misrule and rebellion, roaring boys or girls. In a remarkably defiant gesture, the boundless voice of the elements and of social transgression is pitted against the name of king, the arbitrary language of power. *The Tempest* is structured around such oppositions between courtly discourse and wider linguistic contexts. Throughout the play there is a tension in Ariel between the subordination of his[2] highly wrought fusion of music and poetry to Prospero and the desire to become 'free / As mountain winds', to liberate a purified poetry from the constraints of domination (I.ii.499–500).[3] Utopian discourse pervades the play, most notably in Gonzalo's vision of a world where nature would produce all in common and '[l]etters should not be known' (II.i.148). But every figure on the island has some kind of vision of a society that would transcend existing codes and signs: 'Thought is free,' sing Stephano and Trinculo (III.ii.121).

That libertarian impulse in the play is doubtless why it appealed so strongly to Milton, who rewrote it in *Comus*, transferring Caliban's less attractive qualities to the aristocratic Comus, giving a more rigorous utopian discourse to the lady, and assigning the agency of the resolution not to the aristocrats but to the Ariel-figure and a nature goddess.[4] Continuing that utopian tradition, Shelley found in *The Tempest* a central instance of the utopian power in poetry which 'makes familiar objects be as if they were not familiar'.[5] Ariel had for him the same utopian implications as the egalitarian spirit Queen Mab. Shelley was also alert to the claims of Caliban, as we can see from the significant parallel he draws in his preface to *Frankenstein* between Mary Wollstonecraft Shelley's novel and Shakespeare's pioneering science fiction.[6]

Walter Cohen has recently noted Shelley's perceptive reading of the political implications of romance and has proposed a revised utopian reading of *The Tempest*.[7] But twentieth-century criticism has tended on the whole towards the dystopian, assuming that Gonzalo's ideals are held up for ridicule. Mid-century 'neo-Christians', to use Empson's term, made a sharp distinction between modern political ideas with their sentimental utopianism and the traditional orthodoxy which held that man was a fallen Caliban and therefore needed strict hierarchical order to keep him in line.[8] Coleridge has been a dominant influence in twentieth-century readings of Shakespeare, and Coleridge's interpretations were marked by a revulsion against the radicalism of his age. Hence while Coleridge claims, with reference to *The Tempest*, that Shakespeare 'is always the philosopher and the moralist', without political partisanship, he goes on to present him as a 'philosophical aristocrat' for whom the mob is 'an irrational animal'.[9] With this frame of reference established, accounts of Shakespeare's impartiality had a heavy weighting. Again in the Coleridge tradition, this political conservatism was linked with a turn towards language: Shakespeare's plays were valued for their concreteness as opposed to the etiolated abstractions of Enlightenment egalitarianism. These conservative readings have been strengthened by more recent historical work linking the masque scene with court entertainments; Shakespeare's late turn

to romance can be seen as marking a rejection of popular taste for
an elite aristocratic genre.[10] So dominant have courtly readings
become that radical and anti-colonialist critics have tended to accept
their historical premises even while contesting their political
outlook.[11] The best recent readings have indeed drawn attention to
contradictions and complexities in the play which open themselves
to a radical interpretation.[12] But the general assumption is that these
openings would have been unconscious effects of discourse, while
Shakespeare and his audiences would have belonged to Prospero's
party and seen the play as celebrating the restoration of monarchical
legitimacy as a return to a transcendent natural order.[13] Terry
Eagleton sees Shakespeare as subordinating language, as signified by
Ariel, to a conservative discourse of the body: the plays 'value social
order and stability', and in seeking an organic unity of body and
language *The Tempest* propagates a 'ridiculously sanguine ideology
of Nature'.[14]

Some recent developments in literary theory have tended to reinforce these dystopian readings. Contemporary deconstructionists,
like the neo-Christians, oppose the abstract utopianism of the
Enlightenment to the need for a turn towards language (there are
important linking factors, as in the continuing influence of
Heidegger). Language and utopia still go together for Jürgen
Habermas and other theorists of universal pragmatics, for whom the
'utopian perspective of reconciliation and freedom ... is built into
the linguistic mechanism of the reproduction of the species'.[15] But
poststructuralists have argued that this quest for undistorted communication implies an ultimately fixed and essentialist notion of
human nature, which can become repressive and mystifying, prematurely suppressing the particularities of gender and class in the name
of a false universality of a subject that is held to be free of the constraints of discourse.[16] Utopia, it can be argued, is utopia, it sup-
presses rhetoric and hence must fail to recognise its ineluctable basis
in the materiality of language and power.[17] In a celebrated essay,
Derrida attacked Lévi-Strauss for idealising the Brazilian Indians as a
people blessed in the absence of writing. Such idealisation can be
seen as belonging to a humanist tradition that goes back to
Rousseau's – and, one might add, Montaigne's and Gonzalo's – idealisation of letterless primitives. The logocentric analysis, Derrida
argues, in repressing writing represses also the materiality of discourse.[18] A simple opposition between language and nature would
in effect reinforce the ideology of the western colonisation. And it

could then be argued that *The Tempest's* utopianism is complicit in the ideology. Prospero's ideal spirits dance 'with printless foot' (V.i.34), and Ariel may represent a vision of pure thought breaking free from the material embodiment of language and time, operating between two pulsebeats (V.i.102). Ariel's utopian vision seems pathetically illusory by the standards of Lacanian psychoanalysis, a dream of return to an androgynous state before the name of the father or king, an unmediated sucking at the place of the bee's being (V.i.88); thus Eagleton can see him as a 'closet aesthete'.[19]

The more it is insisted that the individual subject cannot escape the specificities of language or discourse, the more the subject may seem to be inexorably determined by existing power structures from which it cannot escape. Foucault has reminded us of all kinds of ways in which thought is not free. While the classic utopian impulse to a transcendent critique is branded as totalitarian and essentialist, immanent critiques are often seen as inexorably contained. And indeed the play itself may seem to undermine idealist bids for an emancipated poetry. The roarers that the boatswain evokes turn out to have been controlled by Prospero with his power to work up the elements to 'roaring war' (V.i.44, cf. I.i.2, 204), and the rebellion of those seditious roarers Stephano, Trinculo, and Caliban will be evoked by the very power that then contains it. The roars that pervade the play are those of the tormented bodies of Prospero's enemies: 'I will plague them all, / Even to roaring' (IV.i.192–3, cf. I.ii.369); and Ariel's triumphant cry of 'Hark, they roar!' (IV.i.262) is underscored by Prospero's threat to return his servant to the howling agony of captivity in the tree. Music in the play may seem not so much emancipatory as deceitful and manipulative, plunging Ferdinand and Alonso into mourning and guilt which the facts do not quite merit, making the wind sing legitimism.[20] The whimsical refrain of barking dogs to Ariel's first song turns nasty when the dog Tyrant bears down on the conspirators. Prospero commends Ariel's performance as the harpy in terms that sinisterly conflate aesthetics and violence: 'a grace it had, devouring' (III.iii.84).

These newer anti-humanisms, then, may tend to confirm the dystopian perspectives of the neo-Christian anti-humanists. There is room, however, for a reading that would remain open to utopian perspectives in a way that poststructuralist methodologies cannot allow, taking account of the cogent criticisms of blandly transcendental views of the subject which recent theory has been able to make, but without surrendering some notion of the possibility of the subject as rational agent. Such a reading could lay no more claim than its adversaries to being final and exhaustive, but it would, I believe, be more genuinely historical than those which offer the play as absolutist propaganda, for it would take fuller account of the discursive and social contexts. There is no need for twentieth-century readings to be more royalist than the King's Men. A theoretical interest in language was part of the social and intellectual context of Shakespeare and his company – provided that the context is not narrowed down too specifically to courtly discourse but takes account of the immense linguistic curiosity stimulated by Renaissance humanism.

If the term 'humanism' in current discourse tends to connote an abstract resistance to the materiality of language, then Renaissance humanism was a very different phenomenon. It had made its own sharp linguistic turn, an exaltation of rhetoric against scholastic metaphysics, and thus can be seen as paralleling contemporary anti-humanisms in refusing to take for granted a fixed human essence; the attack on abstract generality gave the drama a heightened epistemological status.[21] But Renaissance humanism also had a generalising, philosophical impulse, an advanced sociological and historical consciousness which looked forward to the Enlightenment.[22] While old arguments about monarchy's being part of the order of nature came to look increasingly feeble, more rationalistic theories of natural law could have a strong critical element. More's *Utopia* plays the transcendent social blueprint of the second book against the immanent critique of courtly language in the first book; More says that it would be pointless for a humanist at court to start reciting the speech in the pseudo-Senecan play *Octavia* which prophesies an egalitarian society.[23] As Erica Sheen has shown, Seneca's plays were very much in Shakespeare's mind when he wrote the last plays.[24] Seneca's prose writings opened up an egalitarian discourse of natural law. His plays, however, made him the very type of the compromised court intellectual, writing for a small elite, and More could still feel an affinity with this status. But by Shakespeare's time the possibilities for a politically critical drama had been transformed by the emergence of professional repertory companies which despite their residual status as royal servants derived their economic strength from a far wider public. Shakespeare's career reflects not just individual genius but the excitement of a whole collective institution at the possibilities of what amounted to a cultural revolution: the emergence of a literary public sphere which prepared the way for the formation of a political public sphere. That excitement, however, was certainly manifested in individuals, and recent radically anti-intentionalist readings have given too little credit to the possibility that the writer as agent could achieve a degree of independence from the prevailing structures of power and discourse.

On this account of the context, it is not surprising that *The Tempest* manifests an acute and sophisticated awareness of the relations between language and power. The play is not overtly oppositional or sensationally 'subversive'; but it subjects traditional institutions to a systematic, critical questioning. The play does not consider language and power as timeless absolutes; rather than counterposing an unmediated, presocial nature to a deterministically conceived language, it is concerned with language in specific social contexts, with the effect of political structures on linguistic possibilities. All of the play's utopian ideals, not excepting Ariel's, come up for ironic scrutiny in the course of the play, precisely because they tend to an idealism that refuses to recognise the material constraints of existing structures of power and discourse. But that awareness need not imply a pessimistic determinism. A sceptical relativism about claims to an unproblematic 'human nature' is played against a searching, universalising quest for a more general notion of humanity. The play gives the effect at once of tremendous constriction and specificity, manifested in its rigorously classical form, and of the immense expansion through time and space characteristic of the romance mode. Critics have often counterposed romance to realism as the mode of aristocratic escapism. But *The Tempest* is a hard-headed play, rigorous in following through its own logic once the initial supernatural postulates are granted. As several critics have noted, it is not so much that the play is a romance as that it stages, and in the process distances itself from, the romance scenario of dynastic redemption that Prospero is staging.[25] And yet the play also recognises a certain congruence between a narrowly aristocratic romantic impulse and a broader utopian project. As Shelley, Fredric Jameson, and Raymond Williams have argued in their very different idioms, such imagination of alternatives may be an essential mode of a radical politics in resistance to a world-weary empiricism.[26]

The magic island of Shakespeare's play is at once an instance and an allegory of the players' project of opening up new spaces for discourse. It is a place where no name, no discourse, is entirely natural; language and nature are neither simply conflated nor simply opposed to each other. Prospero abandons the island without leaving behind a colonial force, nor does he refute Caliban's claim that 'this island's mine'. But if Caliban's matrilineal claim may seem to subvert patriarchal authority,[27] it is itself called in question by his own recent arrival. The only figures who can be said to have some natural claim to priority, Ariel and his fellow-spirits, are, precisely, not natural but supernatural, and they do not seem to think of land as something to be possessed; the spirits' history too is left open, and it is possible that Ariel has accompanied Sycorax to the island. At two points in the play the exchanges between Prospero and Ariel focus on uncertainty about what that word 'human' really means, implying that it is an open rather than a fixed category (I.ii.284; V.i.20). Arriving on the island makes all conventional codes unfamiliar. Prospero sets up a dizzying relativisation of the human by claiming that Ferdinand is a Caliban to most men and they are angels to him (I.ii.481–2). Similarly, Caliban will say that Miranda surpasses Sycorax as greatest does less; in each case, the hyperbolical comparison is at the same time undercut by the awareness that there is nothing else to compare them with – as long as she is on the island Miranda has no rival to prevent her being Prospero's 'nonpareil' (III.ii.98). Having asked Miranda a question, Ferdinand is none the less astonished when she answers it in his own language (I.ii.429). Miranda cannot believe that Ferdinand is 'natural' (l.419), and describes him as 'it' (l.412). In a parallel episode Stephano is astonished that Caliban speaks his language (II.ii.65), though this is not surprising to us as the play has explained that Miranda taught it to him. The Italian Trinculo scornfully observes that in England the monster would be taken for a man (II.ii.29–30).[28] When the courtiers finally wake out of their trance, they 'scarce think ... their words / Are natural breath' (V.ii.155–7). In a remarkable alienation effect at the end, Miranda turns to the newly-arrived courtiers – and implicitly the audience – and hails them as a 'brave new world' (V.i.183). A world which seems to Gonzalo itself a utopia looks out at the old world and finds in it a utopia, only to be greeted with Prospero's weary ''Tis new to thee'. This repeated defamiliarisation makes it very hard to see the end of the play as no more than the restoration of a natural social order. At the same time, it reminds us that when characters project an image of a new world they cannot escape the conceptual apparatus they have brought from the old.

II

This is certainly true of Gonzalo's utopian discourse, his vision of a world where all things will be in abundance:

> Had I plantation of this isle, my lord ...
> I'th' commonwealth I would by contraries
> Execute all things, for no kind of traffic
> Would I admit; no name of magistrate;
> Letters should not be known; riches, poverty,
> And use of service, none; contract, succession.
> Bourn, bound of land, tilth, vineyard, none;
> No use of metal, corn, or wine, or oil;
> No occupation, all men idle, all,
> And women, too, but innocent and pure;
> No sovereignty ...
> All things in common nature should produce
> Without sweat or endeavour. Treason, felony,
> Sword, pike, knife, gun, or need of any engine
> Would I not have, but nature should bring forth
> Of it own kind all foison, all abundance
> To feed my innocent people ...
> I would with such perfection govern, sir,
> T'excel the golden age.
>
> (II.i.141–66)

Gonzalo's speech contains many stock topoi, but most scholars agree that it derives particularly from Montaigne's 'Of Cannibals' – with the interesting additional specificity of the reference to women.[29] Montaigne's highly primitivistic essay with its vision of an ideal community may seem to be innocent of More's sophisticated analysis of discourse, an epitome of the idealist repression of writing which poststructuralism has condemned.[30] Gonzalo's speech is often seen as reducing that primitivism to absurdity. But a closer reading of Montaigne's essay suggests a more complex intertextuality. [...]

Montaigne's essay had a powerful influence in England. The Leveller William Walwyn was to declare it as one of his favourite texts. This does not prove that Shakespeare was a proto-Leveller – the political conditions of the 1640s were very different from those of the 1610s, and Walwyn was only about ten when *The Tempest* was first performed. But the sources of Leveller ideas were available much earlier, and we need to allow more generous intellectual horizons for Shakespeare and his audience than some critics have been prepared to grant.[31] The scene in which Gonzalo outlines his utopia

parallels Montaigne in illustrating the process of ideological forgetting: 'The latter end of his commonwealth', Antonio points out,
'forgets the beginning' (II.i.155). He is so used to commanding that
his own social status is simply invisible to him, and he can see
himself as king of an egalitarian society. The scene builds up a very
complex interaction between a generalising aspiration and a reminder of the limits of specific social contexts, and in particular of
courtly discourse. The context of Gonzalo's utopian speech resembles the situation imagined by More, where a Senecan prophecy of a
golden age is recited at court. Gonzalo imagines a world with no
letters, 'no name of magistrate': unmediated nature is pitted against
the name of the king. And as Lowenthal has argued, he has a somewhat more rationalistic cast of mind than the more conservative
courtiers.[32] But the speech-act he is performing in evoking this
utopia is strongly hierarchical, its aim is to console the king, and
Gonzalo's soft primitivism bears the stamp of someone used to euphemising awkward social realities. The immediately preceding
scene has ended with an image of a ruler commanding silence:
Prospero says to Miranda 'speak not for him' – an injunction which
in later scenes she consistently disobeys, but at this point we are left
with courtly discourse as repression. The new scene opens with
courtly discourse as euphemism.

Gonzalo immediately sets up his discourse in class terms:

> Our hint of woe
> Is common: every day some sailor's wife,
> The masters of some merchant, and the merchant
> Have just our theme of woe; but for the miracle –
> I mean our preservation – few in millions
> Can speak like us.
>
> (II.i.3–8)

If Alonso grieves too much for the loss of his son he will be debas-
ing himself to the level of common people like the master of a merchant vessel – Gonzalo had of course been anxious enough for the
master's help during the storm.[33] Instead, he should enjoy a sense
of social superiority which will come from the exclusiveness of his
delivery. There emerges a careful counterpoint between two linguistic groups. The discourse of Gonzalo, Adrian, and Francisco is
idealising: Francisco is brought into the scene only to give a hyper-
bolising set-piece invoking the pathetic fallacy to express his
confidence in Ferdinand's safety (ll.111–20). To use Montaigne's

phrase, they 'hyperbolise the matter': 'What impossible matter will he make easy next?' asks Antonio, whose discourse by contrast seems radically materialist. Sebastian and Antonio stress the bodily origins of the spirit: 'He receives comfort like cold porridge' (l.10); 'he's winding up the watch of his wit' (l.13); 'what a spend-thrift is he of his tongue!' (l.25); they compare Adrian and Gonzalo to cocks crowing out their words; they are confident that the others will 'take suggestion as a cat laps milk' (l.286). Gonzalo's '[t]he air breathes upon us here most sweetly' meets a materialistic retort: 'As if it had lungs, and rotten ones' (ll.48–9). By defamiliarising words into things Sebastian and Antonio draw attention to the speech-acts themselves and their social context, rather than passing through to their content; and when Ariel has put the others into a trance they satirically represent their rebel-lion as an eruption of the political unconscious, if not a roaring then at least a snoring: 'It is a sleepy language ...', says Sebastian, '[t]there's meaning in thy snores' (ll.209, 216). The prevailing scepticism about discourse extends even to Alonso: 'You cram these words into mine ears against / The stomach of my sense' (ll.104–5). In reproaching Antonio, Gonzalo himself comes to see his own discourse in material terms:

> The truth you speak doth lack some gentleness,
> And time to speak it in – you rub the sore
> When you should bring the plaster.
>   (ll.135–7)

Gonzalo's utopia is thus marked as another plaster for the king. But Alonso has no interest in such speculations: 'Prithee no more. Thou dost talk nothing to me.' Utopia is of course nowhere, nothing; and there may be a further sly pun in 'no More'.[34] Gonzalo ruefully re-treats and says that he was only talking in order to give mirth to Antonio and Sebastian – his utopian vision was no more than the fantasy of a court jester.

Gonzalo's facile idealism, then, is undercut by a materialist cri-tique. One might even see Antonio as anticipating certain kinds of Foucauldianism, seeing all attempts to change society as the installa-tions of ever greater apparatuses of surveillance and domination. It is Antonio who first introduces the utopian theme at line 85, when Gonzalo is speaking; of the parallels between ancient Carthage and modern Tunis:

> **Antonio**   His word is more than the miraculous harp.
> **Sebastian**   He hath raised the wall, and houses too.

The story of Amphion whose music raised the walls of Thebes had become a familiar commonplace, signifying that poetry had a central part to play in politics by instilling civil order and harmony. In their reductive reading, the myth becomes a rather ridiculous example of the way court poets use hyperbole to blow up their own achievements.

Antonio's own viewpoint, however, is hardly beyond criticism; the play does not endorse his cynicism. But its criticism of courtly discourse remains sharp. One point that Gonzalo adds to Montaigne is that his utopia would have no treason, felony, sword, pike, knife, gun, or need of any engine – that is, instrument of warfare or political violence. This is a characteristic emphasis, for behind his euphemising discourse he is shown to be acutely conscious of the need for violence to maintain monarchical power, and a chain of allusions links the utopian speech with his relations with the sailors at the beginning and end of the play. Gonzalo's sample of a decorous compliment is:

> It is foul weather in us all, good sir,
> When you are cloudy.
> (ll.139–40)

This is a direct inversion of the boatswain's comment to Alonso at the beginning: for Gonzalo the king's very name will of course control the roaring elements. During the storm, however, he was less confident; the boatswain acidly commented that the courtiers' howls of fear were 'louder than the weather or our office' (I.i.36–7). If Gonzalo's authority could command the roaring elements to silence, he would not handle a rope more (I.i.21–3). Gonzalo had then taken up the reference to a rope, not as a means of work but as an instrument of punishment – and a socially indecorous one at that, as opposed to the aristocratic beheading: 'Stand fast, good Fate, to his hanging, make the rope of his destiny our cable … If he be not born to be hanged, our case is miserable' (I.i.30–3). Antonio simply makes this reference to hanging more brutally literal: 'hang, cur, hang' (l.43).

Such a situation had a strong sociopolitical charge. The figure of the ship of state had a greater appeal for seventeenth-century radicals than the traditional figure of the body politic because it viewed the state as an artificial construct rather than part of the order of nature, and implied progress towards a new destination. The figure of the pilot daringly wresting control of the ship of state from its commander was to be used to justify the Puritan Revolution.[35] In this scene, the artisanal connotations are pushed further in that tenor and vehicle have become detached: the aristocrats stand around ineffectually while the real business goes on without them. But they still want overall control. Gonzalo has not forgotten the rope at the end of the play. Even so acute a critic of sentimental readings as Harry Berger describes that much-cited passage where Gonzalo says that they have all found themselves as his 'closing speech',[36] but in fact Gonzalo's 'all of us' (V.i.212–13) turns out to exclude the sailors who had tried to save his life. In his actual last speech he returns to the storm scene:

> I prophesied if a gallows were on land
> This fellow could not drown. (*To Boatswain*) Now, blasphemy,
> That swear'st grace o'erboard, not an oath on shore?
> Hast thou no mouth by land? What is the news?
>
> (V.i.217–20)

This is a striking piece of forgetting: it was the courtiers who were swearing, the boatswain gave orders to the courtiers but did not abuse them directly; and his response now is to ignore Gonzalo's taunts and give a precise account of recent events. In fact Gonzalo swears, however mildly, more than anyone in the play except Sebastian.[37] This is not to deny that he is a genial man, who has been very kind to Prospero. The trouble is that such genial goodness may itself become complacent at court; moral qualities need to be seen in a political context.

III

The same applies to Prospero himself. It has been tempting to allegorise him as a figure of Shakespeare or James I. But these readings too easily assume that the play identifies with Prospero as a natural source of authority; and that Shakespeare engages with politics only at the level of direct topical allegories. While the original audience might well have picked up some resonance with the contemporary hopes over the Palatine marriage, there is also a more generalising sociological consciousness at work in the plays, which means that we need to pay some attention to the discourse in which Shakespeare situates Prospero. The later Shakespeare, and Jacobeans in general, were tending to give more and more sociological specificity to Italian settings by drawing on the discourses by which Italians represented their own history. Particularly influential were Machiavelli and Guicciardini, who offered a radically sceptical analysis of political power which undercut any claim by monarchy to be natural.[38] In the later Renaissance many republican city-states had been taken over by *signori*, rulers with little sense of communal responsibility and sought legitimacy in noble connections, in a kind of refeudalisation (or what Sebastian terms '[h]ereditary sloth') (II.i.221), rather than in popular consent. Guicciardini opens his history with a lament for the monarchical harmony of late fifteenth-century Italy before the foreign invasions in the 1490s, which led eventually to Spanish absolutist hegemony. But even though Guicciardini himself favoured the Medici dynasty, he presented at length the constitutional debates about differing forms of democratic rule; and what gradually emerges is that beneath that superficial harmony there were deep-rooted republican resistances, which meant that the people were often glad to welcome foreign armies against their ruling houses. The unpopular King Alphonso of Naples, who 'knew not (with most Princes now a dayes) how to resist the furie of dominion and rule', abdicated in favour of his son Ferdinand but the people refused to allow him into the city; the precedent was to be used by supporters of the execution of Charles I.[39] Guicciardini places the immediate blame for the foreign invasions on the ambition of Giovan Galeazzo Sforza, the *de facto* ruler of Milan who was anxious to gain legitimacy for his line, but ended up by sacrificing Milan's political autonomy altogether to his personal dynastic vanity.

What sign is there in *The Tempest* of a possible republican subtext? It may seem unduly literal-minded to imagine Shakespeare as considering the precise political status of his Italian states; but there is clear evidence that this was done by his collaborator in his last plays, John Fletcher. About 1621 Fletcher wrote with Philip Massinger a tragicomedy, *The Double Marriage*, which echoed *The Tempest*, with an exiled duke and his daughter as central characters. The play glorifies 'the noble stile of Tyrant-killers'; at the climax the hero brings in the head of the tyrannical king of Naples 'to cries of 'Liberty'.[40] The political climate in 1621 had become more sharply polarised, and Shakespeare certainly does not undercut monarchical legitimacy in the same way. Nevertheless, it is worth remembering that his audience would have contained people who were far from taking an absolutist dynastic perspective for granted, and the play does permit a certain detachment from the courtly viewpoint. Prospero assures us that his people loved him (I.ii.141); but he does belong to this political world. He speaks of 'signories' (I.ii.71) and he sees his power purely in personal terms, as a matter of safeguarding his dynasty: he talks familiarly of 'my Milan' (V.i.310), while for Ferdinand 'myself am Naples' (I.ii.435). Though Prospero condemns Antonio for allowing Milan to stoop to Naples (I.ii.112–16), by the end of the play he has handed the dukedom over to Naples in order to secure his line. His words as he reveals Ferdinand and Miranda to the courtiers at the end scarcely escape banality: 'a wonder to content ye / As much as me my dukedom' (V.i.170–1). His tone is echoed by Gonzalo's breathless 'Was Milan thrust from Milan that his issue / Should become kings of Naples?' (V.i.205–6). The union between Milan and and Naples is a strikingly representative instance of the social processes by which the *signorie* sought legitimacy; the upstart Milanese has definitely made good.

The characteristic genre of such dynastic triumphs was the romance, whose aristocratic closure predominates in Prospero's world over utopian openings; Miranda and Ferdinand are stranded within a very narrow courtly discourse. For Prospero, making Ferdinand do manual work is a punishment degrading him to the level of his slave. He lost his dukedom because the element of work in the public life, as valorised in the republican ethos, seemed to him too degrading, he preferred a private retreat into Neoplatonic contemplation which 'but by being so retired, / O'er-prized all popular rate' (I.ii.91–2).[41] His language and that of the courtiers generally reflects the growing class-bound stratification urged by Castiglione and courtly theorists: the rhetoric of courtly praise and dispraise rather than republican persuasion.[42] Ferdinand observes rather clumsily that on his father's death 'I am the best of them that speak this speech': language is the king's (I.ii.430). Idealising compliments are directed to the noble, though always with an underlying political pragmatism – Miranda is learning to let Ferdinand wrangle for a score of kingdoms and call it fair play (V.i.174–5). The base are abused – Caliban is given plenty of opportunity to learn how to curse. Martines has noted that sixteenth-century political discourse in Italy reveals a growing polarity between an abstract aristocractic utopianism and a dark view of the populace as irredeemably base; as Berger has shown, such polarities are characteristic of Prospero's discourse.[43] He reminds Caliban six times in less than seventy lines that he is a slave (I.ii.308–73) and Caliban fears that his art could make Setebos a vassal (I.ii.373): Prospero extends feudal relations of service and bondage. Prospero's irascibility has come to the fore in recent productions; idealisations of Prospero require a certain suppression of the play's language. Miranda has to protest that 'My father's of a better nature, sir, / Than he appears by speech' (I.ii.497–8). These points remain relatively inconspicuous in the play, which certainly is not a satire of Prospero; nor are the elements of romance cynically dismissed as mere aristocratic fantasy. Shelley's sense of the play as utopian would have involved a recognition of the political importance of a sense of wonder, of defamiliarisation, which even a narrowly class-based romance could project. As with Gonzalo, the point is not that Prospero is an evil man but that his political position entails a limited perspective.

Shakespeare's questioning of legitimacy extends even to the genre *par excellence* of the naturalisation of authority, the court masque.[44] Prospero's betrothal masque is the richest expression of his ideal society; and whereas in Gonzalo's utopia all things are in common, in Prospero's golden age there is a hierarchical structure in which the labour of the reapers is ultimately motivated by the transcendent gods and goddesses who are figures of the leisured aristocracy. As Berger has noted, however, there are signs of tension even within the masquing speeches, reflecting Prospero's tendency to oscillate between idealistic and radically pessimistic views of man. This tension in the end cannot be sustained and the masque collapses; recent criticism has rightly drawn attention to the ways in which the resolution is very different from the Stuart norm – forming an interesting parallel with *Cymbeline*, as Erica Sheen shows in her essay.[45] The aim of the masque was to naturalise the king's name, to turn courtiers into gods and goddesses; Prospero dissolves his masque and its courtly language melts into air, leaving (according to a perhaps non-authorial stage direction) 'a strange hollow and confused noise', an undifferentiated roaring that undercuts the confident marks of social difference. The pageants are 'insubstantial'.

Prospero's 'revels' speech has given rise to a great deal of critical banality, but it is as well to be wary about taking it as a statement of Shakespeare's view of life in general; it needs to be read rather less transcendentally. The two other most celebrated comparisons of life to a play are those of Jacques in *As You Like It* and Macbeth's 'poor player' speech, and neither is unequivocally endorsed: Shakespeare seems to have been wary about generalisations about Life. Prospero is in fact in no mood to say farewell to the world, he wants his dukedom back and in a previous scene he has had Ariel disguised as a religious spirit tell lies about Ferdinand's death in order to facilitate his ends. In a political context, the specificities of the 'revels' speech become more evident. At the climax of the Jacobean masque, these alleged gods and goddesses would come down into the dancing area and mingle with the audience. Court masques were in many ways very substantial things, giving the necessary concrete presence to the royal name by elaborate scenery; their fabric was definitely not baseless. There were clear sacramental overtones: the substance, the body, of the king became divinely transformed. Jonson's preface to *Hymenaei* highlights this physicality with characteristic ambivalence. On the one hand the '*bodies*' are transitory and inferior in comparison to their conceptual souls; on the other hand, Jonson as a firm defender of religious and secular ceremony fiercely disputes the 'fastidious *stomachs*' of rivals like Daniel whose 'ayrie tasts' lay too little emphasis on the external body.[46] As Jonson noted, it was the custom at the end of masques to 'deface their *carkasses*': in the spirit of *potlatch*, courtiers would tear down the scenery, the whole point being the physical concreteness of the manifestation of honour so that its destruction was all the more potent a sign of the donor's greatness.

Prospero's speech, and the whole episode, then highlight the ways in which his spectacle is unlike a court masque. His masque really is insubstantial, because as prince in exile he does not have any actors, musicians, and set-designers. There is something almost ludicrous in the contrival of this spectacle for an audience of just three, even if Ferdinand dutifully declares that there are enough of them for paradise (IV.i.123–4). Prospero's situation on the island parodies the top-heavy social structure of late Renaissance despotisms, with the aristocracy syphoning off more and more wealth to expend in conspicuous courtly consumption, while representing the people as a mere grumbling margin to the transcendent centre of the court. But in Prospero's case the situation is pushed to the point of absurdity by the absence of any subjects at all apart from Caliban; and in an ideological forgetting directly parallel to Gonzalo's, Prospero's masque can last only as long as Caliban is forgotten. The political point is rubbed home when we learn that Ariel, though intending to remind Prospero about the conspiracy when he was playing the part of Ceres, had 'feared / Lest I might anger thee' (IV.i.168–9). The masque cannot reach a climax with the performers mingling with the audience, as was the rule at court, for the performers are spirits. Precisely because they really are what the courtiers pretended to be, supernatural beings, bodiless air, they cannot be taken back with Prospero to Milan. There is an ironic parallel to Stephano's exclamation: 'This will be a brave kingdom to me, where I shall have my music for nothing' (III.ii.142–3). [...]

Prospero's masque dissolves because its actors were not natural aristocrats but spirits; but 'spirit' was a familiar term for 'actor', reminding us that the real agency involved was that of a professional repertory company.[47] Despite their royal label, the King's Men owed most of their revenue to public performances; Shakespeare's plays were thus able to pit different discourses against each other with far greater freedom than courtly literature.[48] Prospero may have staged the storm, but the common players staged Prospero. Greenblatt notes that as a joint-stock company the King's Men had the same kind of autonomy as the Virginia Company, whose members, as we have seen, did distance themselves from the royal viewpoint.[49] As Erica Sheen has pointed out, the play frequently alludes to the company's own repertorial self-consciousness: Prospero may dismiss his spirits as a 'rabble' of 'meaner fellows' (IV.i.37, 35), but he depends on their work.[50] The link between language and work recurs throughout the play. Even Ariel's more visionary language is the product of work, of careful crafting, and has a material, bodily aspect: the spirits' feet may be printless, but they still '[f]oot it featly' (I.i.378). Prospero's feet may indeed be his tutor (I.ii.470). To return for a moment to the opening scene, the boatswain complains that the courtiers' panicking howls and curses are 'louder than the weather or our office' (I.i.36–7): courtly discourse is contrasted not only with natural sounds but with the sailors' practically oriented work-language under the absent master's directing whistle.[51] To Sebastian's 'A pox o' your throat,' the boatswain bluntly replies: 'Work you, then.' Shakespeare researched the sailors' language with great sociolinguistic precision.[52] The master's whistle may seem to be merely a figure for the playwright's authority, the sovereign author displacing the sovereign prince in a valorisation of an individualistic bourgeois work-ethic. But there is a parallel between the master's disappearance at the beginning of the play and Prospero's renunciation at the end: in each case authority is transferred to the process of dramatic production in which the company collaborates with the audience – or the reader. Prospero's epilogue thus gives a final twist to the confrontation between the king's name and the public air:

> Gentle breath of yours my sails
> Must fill, or else my project fails.
>   (V.i.329–30)

From *The Politics of Tragicomedy: Shakespeare and After,* ed. Gordon McMullan and Jonathan Hope (London and New York, 1992), pp. 21–54.

NOTES

[David Norbrook argues Patterson's case (essay 6) at greater length, that we can find in *The Tempest* 'a possible republican subtext', and that the language of radical utopianism permeates the play. Challenging many postcolonial critics, he notes that, although Shakespeare was directly patronised by royalty in the company of the King's Men, he need not have constructed his plays as supportive of the ruling political power or as reflecting the royal viewpoint, since the company's greatest source of revenue came from public performances attended by the entire social spectrum. This enables Shakespeare to 'pit different discourses against each other with far greater freedom than courtly literature', a factor which complicates moral and political issues in *The Tempest*, and in particular gives a voice to alternative political systems. Quotations are from *The Tempest*, ed. Stephen Orgel (Oxford and New York, 1987). Ed.]

1. For comments on earlier drafts I am grateful to W. R. Elton, Margot Heinemann, Frank Romany, and Erica Sheen.
    The edition used for quotations is the New Oxford, edited by Stephen Orgel (Oxford and New York, 1987). This edition is sharper politically than Kermode's New Arden edition, which has, despite its great merits, tended to fix authoritarian readings of the play.

2. Ariel's gender is not specified in any of the play's speeches, and from the eighteenth century through to the early twentieth century the part was regularly played by a woman (see Orgel's edition, p. 70). The indeterminacy arises in the first instance from the fact that Prospero shields his relationship with Ariel from the other characters, so that there are no third-person references in the dialogue. A stage direction in Act III scene iii does define Ariel as male, however, and the part was a male one in the Davenant–Dryden version. Nevertheless, the text itself is open to a large degree of indeterminacy in the question of a spirit's sexuality.

3. On Ariel as language, see Terry Eagleton, *William Shakespeare* (Oxford, 1986), pp. 94–5. Some recent critics have been drawing attention to utopian elements in the play: see Annabel Patterson, *Shakespeare and the Popular Voice* (Oxford, 1989), p. 154ff; Kiernan Ryan, *Shakespeare* (Hemel Hempstead, 1989), p. 97ff; and Graham Holderness in a forthcoming piece which he kindly showed me.

4. On language and utopia in *Comus* see David Norbrook, *Poetry and Politics in the English Renaissance* (London, 1984), p. 259ff. The relations between *The Tempest* and *Comus* have recently been studied by

Mary Loeffelholz, 'Two masques of Ceres and Proserpine: *Comus* and *The Tempest*', in Mary Nyquist and Margaret W. Ferguson (eds), *Remembering Milton: Essays on the Texts and Traditions* (New York and London, 1987) pp. 25–42, and Christopher Kendrick, 'Milton and sexuality: A symptomatic reading of *Comus*', Ibid., pp. 43–73.

5. 'A defence of poetry', in *Shelley's Prose or The Trumpet of a Prophecy*, ed. David Lee Clark, with a preface by Harold Bloom (London, 1988), p. 282. On the Shelleys and *The Tempest* see Christopher Small, *Ariel Like a Harpy: Shelley, Mary and 'Frankenstein'* (London, 1972), p. 123ff.

6. *The Letters of Mary Wollstonecraft Shelley, vol. 1: 'A Part of the Elect'*, ed. Betty T. Bennett (Baltimore and London, 1980), pp. 263 n. 9, 292, 334.

7. Walter Cohen, *Drama of a Nation: Public Theater in Renaissance England and Spain* (Ithaca and London: Cornell University Press, 1985), p. 384ff, notes Shelley's readings of Calderón; Shelley was interested in parallels between Shakespeare and Calderón.

8. William Empson, 'Hunt the symbol', *Essays on Shakespeare*, ed. David B. Pirie (Cambridge, 1986), pp. 231–43 (first published in *The Times Literary Supplement*, 23 April 1964).

9. *Coleridge's Shakespearean Criticism*, ed. Thomas Middleton Raysor, 2 vols (London, 1960), vol. I, 122.

10. Gary Schmidgall, *Shakespeare and the Courtly Aesthetic* (Berkeley, Los Angeles, and London, 1981), continues the authoritarian tradition and sees the play as defending 'the Tudor theory of obedience' against 'an increasingly obstinate Parliament' (p.171 n.13). See David Norbrook's review in *English*, 31 (1982), 247–52. More directly topical readings have been offered by Glynne Wickham, 'Masque and anti-masque in *The Tempest*', *Essays and Studies*, 28 (1975), 1–14; Frances A. Yates, *Shakespeare's Last Plays: A New Approach* (London, 1975); David M. Bergeron, *Shakespeare's Romances and the Royal Family* (Lawrence, KS, 1985), p. 111; and, most fully documented, Michael Srigley, *Images of Regeneration: A Study of Shakespeare's 'The Tempest' and its Cultural Background* (Acta Universitatis Upsaliensis. Studia Anglistica Upsaliensia 58, Uppsala, 1985). As Orgel points out (Orgel [ed.], p. 1ff), the evidence scarcely warrants calling *The Tempest* a 'court play', but I would not rule out the possibility of the play's having some connection with enthusiasm for the Palatine match of 1613. That would not, however, make the play absolutist given that the strongest supporters of the Palatine match were those most anxious about the growing hegemony of counter-Reformation absolutism both abroad and potentially in England.

11. Readings of the play as treating colonialism go back at least as far as Jack Lindsay and Edgell Rickword (eds), *A Handbook of Freedom* (London, 1939), p. 103; see also Bruce Erlich, 'Shakespeare's colonial

metaphor: on the social function of theatre in *The Tempest'*, *Science and Society*, 41 (1977), 43–65; Thomas Cartelli, 'Prospero in Africa: *The Tempest* as colonialist text and pretext', Jean E. Howard and Marion F. O'Connor (eds), *Shakespeare Reproduced: The Text in History and Ideology* (New York and London, 1987), pp. 99–115; Rob Nixon, 'Caribbean and African appropriations of *The Tempest'*, *Critical Inquiry*, 13 (1986–7), 557–78; Ania Loomba, *Gender, Race, Renaissance Drama* (Manchester, 1989), ch. 6.

12. For readings that align the play with colonial discourse but are in differing degrees alert to unconscious complexities and contradictions, see Paul Brown, '"This Thing of Darkness I Acknowledge Mine": *The Tempest* and the discourse of colonialism', in Jonathan Dollimore and Alan Sinfield (eds), *Political Shakespeare: New Essays in Cultural Materialism* (Manchester, 1985), pp. 48–71; Francis Barker and Peter Hulme, 'Nymphs and Reapers Heavily Vanish: the discursive con-texts of *The Tempest'*, in John Drakakis (ed.), *Alternative Shakespeares* (London and New York, 1985), pp. 191–205; Peter Hulme, 'Prospero and Caliban', in *Colonial Encounters: Europe and the Native Caribbean, 1492–1797* (London and New York: Methuen, 1986), pp. 89–134; Stephen Greenblatt, 'Martial law in the land of Cockaigne', in *Shakespearean Negotiations: The Circulation of Social Energy in Renaissance England* (Oxford, 1988), pp. 129–63. Deborah Willis, 'Shakespeare's *Tempest* and the discourse of colonialism', *Studies in English Literature 1500–1900*, 29 (1989), 277–89, questions monolithic accounts of colonial discourse.

13. E.g. Leonard Tennenhouse, *Power on Display: The Politics of Shakespeare's Genres* (New York and London, 1986), pp. 177–8.

14. Terry Eagleton, *William Shakespeare* (Oxford: Blackwell, 1986), pp. 1, 93, 99. In support of Eagleton's claim that Shakespeare seems to have read Derrida, it can be pointed out that Caliban's ' 'Ban, 'Ban, Ca-Caliban' seems to echo the old refrain 'Da, da, da–Deridan': *A New Variorum Edition of Shakespeare, The Tempest*, ed. Horace Howard Furness (Philadelphia and London: J. B. Lippincott, 1892), p. 141.

15. Jürgen Habermas, *The Theory of Communicative Action*, trans. Thomas McCarthy (Boston, 1984), vol. 1, 598.

16. Mary Louise Pratt, 'Linguistic utopias', in Nigel Fabb et al. (eds), *The Linguistics of Writing: Arguments Between Language and Literature* (Manchester, 1987), pp. 48–66. Pratt identifies the ideal speech situation with ideals of homogeneous patriarchal nationhood; she is acute on the blindness to gender and other inequalities often found in pragmatics, but the overall identification of Habermasian rationalism with organicist nationalism may be questioned.

17. But for a rhetorical analysis of utopian discourse see Louis Marin, *Utopics: Spatial Play*, trans. Robert A. Vollrath (New Jersey, 1984).

18. Jacques Derrida, 'The violence of the letter: from Lévis-Strauss to Rousseau', in *Of Grammatology*, trans. Gayatri Chakravorty Spivak (Baltimore and London, 1976), p. 101ff. For extensive discussion of this issue, often with reference to *The Tempest*, see the special issue of *Critical Inquiry*, 12 (Autumn 1985), on '"Race", writing and difference', and responses in vol. 13.

19. Eagleton, *William Shakespeare*, p. 95.

20. David Lindley, 'Music, masque, and meaning in *The Tempest*', in David Lindley (ed.) *The Court Masque* (Manchester, 1984), pp. 47–59, sees the music of the masque as pragmatically rhetorical rather than unproblematically retaining older symbolic values.

21. Victoria Kahn, 'Humanism and the resistance to theory', in Patricia Parker and David Quint (eds), *Literary Theory/Renaissance Texts* (Baltimore and London, 1986), pp. 373–96; cf. Jonathan Dollimore, *Radical Tragedy: Religion, Ideology and Power in the Drama of Shakespeare and his Contemporaries* (Brighton, 1984), p. 10ff.

22. The best discussion of this topic is Graham Holderness, *Shakespeare's History* (Dublin and New York, 1985). For an instance see David Norbrook, '*Macbeth* and the politics of historiography', in Kevin Sharpe and Steven N. Zwicker (eds), *Politics of Discourse* (Berkeley, Los Angeles, and London, 1987), pp. 78–116. I now think that I overstressed the degree of Shakespeare's reaction against this politically rationalistic vein in humanism.

23. Cf. David Norbrook *Poetry and Politics in the English Renaissance*, p. 26.

24. See Erica Sheen, '"The Agent for his Master": Political Service and Professional Liberty in *Cymbeline*', *The Politics of Tragicomedy: Shakespeare and After*, ed. Gordon McMullan and Jonathan Hope (London and New York, 1992), pp. 55–76. In his adaptation of *The Tempest* Aimé Césaire has Prospero banished by the Inquisition, among other crimes, for reading Seneca's tragedies: *Une Tempête* (Paris, p. 1960), p. 21.

25. On the unusual generic complexities of *The Tempest* see Cohen, *Drama of a Nation*, p. 390ff; R. S. White, '*Let Wonder Seem Familiar*': *Endings in Shakespeare's Romance Vision* (New Jersey and London, 1985), p. 159ff; Brown, '"This thing of Darkness I Acknowledge Mine"', p. 61ff; Hulme, 'Prospero and Caliban', p. 115ff.

26. Fredric Jameson, *The Political Unconscious: Narrative as a Socially Symbolic Act* (Ithaca, NY, 1981), p. 103ff; cf. Raymond Williams, 'The tenses of writing', in *Writing in Society* (London, 1983), pp. 267–8.

27. See Orgel's edition, pp. 37–8.

28. In a stimulating analysis of such twists Terence Hawkes none the less flattens out one complexity by assuming that all the characters are

imagined as speaking English: *That Shakespeharian Rag: Essays on a Critical Process* (London and New York, 1986), p. 54 [essay 3 above – Ed.].

29. Margaret Hodgen, 'Montaigne and Shakespeare again', *Huntington Library Quarterly*, 16 (1952–3), 23–42 argues that some details of the speech may have been taken from other writers on the New World; if he did consult further sources the hypothesis that he read Montaigne's essay closely and critically would be strengthened. See also Valentina P. Komarova, 'Das Problem der Gesellschaftsform in Montaignes *Essays* und Shakespeares *Sturm*', *Shakespeare Jahrbuch*, 122 (1986), 75–90.

30. Michel de Certeau, 'Montaigne's "Of Cannibals"', in *Heterologies: Discourse on the Other*, trans. Brian Massumi, foreword by Wlad Godzich (Manchester, 1986), pp. 67–79.

31. See 'Walwyns just defence', in *The Writings of William Walwyn*, ed. Jack R. McMichael and Barbara Taft (Athens and London, 1989), pp. 399–400: 'Go ... to these innocent Cannibals, ye Independent Churches, to learn civility.'

32. Leo Lowenthal, *Literature and the Image of Man: Sociological Studies of the European Drama and Novel, 1600–1900* (Boston, 1957), pp. 71, 75. Lowenthal, however, sees the courtiers as relics of feudalism, whereas the sociological situation is more complex.

33. The word 'masters' was socially equivocal and appears in the sense of 'servants' in Prospero's later 'Weak masters' (V.i.41); the multiple usages are part of a process of problematising power relations.

34. John X. Evans, '*Utopia* on Prospero's island', *Moreana*, 18 (1981), 81–3.

35. Michael Walzer, *The Revolution of the Saints: A Study in the Origins of Radical Politics* (Cambridge, 1965), pp. 179–82; John M. Wallace, *Destiny His Choice: The Loyalism of Andrew Marvell* (Cambridge, 1968), pp. 131–2.

36. Harry Berger Jr, 'Miraculous harp: a reading of Shakespeare's *Tempest*', *Shakespeare Studies*, 5 (1969), 253–83 (264).

37. Frances A. Shirley, *Swearing and Perjury in Shakespeare's Plays* (London, 1979), p. 148. Bergeron, in his highly courtly reading, finds it necessary to transfer the 'gallows-style humour' from Gonzalo to the boatswain: *Shakespeare's Romances and the Royal Family*, p. 111. Lowenthal, *Literature and the Image of man*, pp. 226–7, finds parallels between Gonzalo and the boatswain, both of them being more directed to rational goals than the courtiers and both cursing in a nominalist, self-expressive vein in contrast to the almost realist cursing of the courtiers (on cursing see also p. 73ff); Lowenthal even argues that the boatswain 'speaks as if he had read Montaigne, and Gonzalo answers as if he were Montaigne' (p. 227).

38. On Guicciardini and Machiavelli respectively see G. K. Hunter, 'English folly and Italian vice: the moral landscape of John Marston', in *Dramatic Identities and Cultural Tradition: Studies in Shakespeare and his Contemporaries* (Liverpool, 1978), pp. 103–32, and William W. E. Slights, 'A source for *The Tempest* and the context of the *Discorsi*', *Shakespeare Quarterly*, 36 (1985), 68–70. On Italian cultural history see Lauro Martines, *Power and Imagination: City-States in Renaissance Italy* (London, 1979); on Guicciardini's discourse see J. G. A. Pocock, *The Machiavellian Moment: Florentine Political Thought and the Atlantic Republican Tradition* (Princeton, NJ, 1975), pp. 114–56, 29–71 (and on Milan, 55, 150). Shakespeare would probably have known the essay 'of books' (II, x) in which Montaigne praised Guicciardini's accuracy, though he censured him as too cynical. Guicciardini's history was translated into English in 1579 by Geoffrey Fenton, and became a source for political theory: see e.g. Robert Dallington's *Aphorismes Civill and Militarye* (London, 1613).

39. *The Historie of Guicciardin*, trans. G. Fenton (London, 1579), pp. 28, 64ff; Wallace, *Destiny His Choice*, p. 83. Speaking in support of the Virginia Company in the 1614 Parliament, Richard Martin, a friend of Christopher Brooke and other Jacobean poets with an interest in Virginia, said that the colony would become a bridle for the Neapolitan courser if the youth of England were able to sit him (*Commons Journals*, I, 488).

40. *The Double Marriage*, I.i, V.i in *The Works of Francis Beaumont and John Fletcher*, ed. A. R. Waller, 10 vols (Cambridge, 1908), vol. VI, 325, 405. For parallels with *The Tempest* see especially II.i. The play notes that the rulers of Naples in fact came from Spain, hence the Spanish names of Shakespeare's dynasty. The major source was Comines: see E. M. Waith, 'The sources of *The Double Marriage* by Fletcher and Massinger', *Modern Language Notes*, 64 (1949), 505–10; the English translation had frequent cross-references to Guicciardini. Montaigne praises Comines in 'Of books'.

41. On work in *The Tempest* see Lowenthal, *Literature and the Image of Man*, p. 62ff, and Hulme, *Colonial Encounters*, p. 131ff. Hawkes, *That Shakespeharian Rag*, p. 3ff, offers a more critical view of the play's work-ethic than Lowenthal; but it is worth remembering that in its context the play's valorisation of work criticises the neo-feudal ethos (cf. Berger, 'Miraculous harp', 257).

42. Cf. Peter Burke, 'Language and anti-language in early modern Italy', *History Workshop*, 11 (Spring 1981), 24–32.

43. Martines, *Power and Imagination*, p. 452ff, 'The lure of utopia'; Berger, 'Miraculous harp', 262, notes the parallel with More's itself rather than academic utopianism which had its roots in Florentine Neoplatonism.

44. I cannot here do justice to the text of Prospero's masque, which has been discussed by Lindley, 'Music, masque and meaning in *The Tempest*', p. 51ff, and Ernest B. Gilman, '"All eyes": Prospero's inverted masque', *Renaissance Quarterly, 33 (1980)*, 214–30; Glynne Wickham, 'Masque and anti-masque in *The Tempest*', *Essays and Studies*, 28 (1975), 1–14; Irwin Smith, 'Ariel and the masque in *The Tempest*', *Shakespeare Quarterly*, 21 (1970), 213–22; Berger, 'Miraculous harp', 270ff; and Hawkes, *That Shakespeharian Rag*, pp. 5–7 [essay 3 above – Ed.]. John Gillies, 'Shakespeare's Virginian masque', *English Literary History*, 53 (1986), 673–707, argues that the masque in *The Tempest*, far from glorifying the ideology of colonisation, goes directly against the court masques on that theme.

45. Sheen, 'The Agent for his Master'.

46. *Ben Jonson*, ed. C. H. Herford and Percy and Evelyn Simpson, 11 vols (Oxford, 1925–52), vol. VII, 209–10. Catherine M. Shaw, '*The Tempest* and *Hymenaei*', *Cahiers Elisabethains*, 26 (October 1984), 29–40, notes similarities but not differences between these works. Bergeron, *Shakespeare's Romances and the Royal Family*, pp. 197–8, notes possible similarities with Daniel's *Vision of the Twelve Goddesses*, which lays more emphasis on the masque's insubstantiality. It is possible that Shakespeare was indeed aligning himself more with Daniel than with Jonson: the two poets were contesting the political implications of the masque (see David Norbrook, *Poetry and Politics in the English Renaissance*, p. 201).

47. Emrys Jones, *The Origins of Shakespeare* (Oxford, 1977), p. 146 n.

48. The social basis of the drama has of course been much debated. Cohen, *Drama of a Nation*, p. 388, speaks of the 'subversive contradiction between artisanal base and absolutist superstructure'; I would question whether even the ideological 'superstructure' needs to be considered unequivocally absolutist.

49. Greenblatt, 'Martial law in the land of Cockaigne', 148, 160.

50. I owe this point to an unpublished paper by Erica Sheen.

51. For a detailed sociological analysis of the storm scene, see Lowenthal, *Literature and the Image of Man*, pp. 221–9.

52. There was a politics in the degree of Shakespeare's sociolinguistic specificity. A. F. Falconer points out in *Shakespeare and the Sea* that he 'has not only worked out a series of manoeuvres, but has made exact use of the professional language of seamanship ... He could not have come by this knowledge from books, for there were no works on seamanship in his day, nor were there any nautical word lists or glossaries' (quoted by Orgel, p. 208).

10

'The open worlde': the Exotic in Shakespeare

JOHN GILLIES

To the extent of actually being set in 'a wonderland of discovery and romance, where monsters dwelt and miracles were common', *The Tempest* creates a more conventionally geographic impression of 'the exotic' than other plays. However, since the setting of *The Tempest* is – like its characters, plot and themes – notoriously elusive, the task of defining 'the exotic' in this play is less than straightforward. For all this, Prospero's island seems the obvious place to start.

Rather as in the 'Bermuda Pamphlets', the story of the island is set within a voyage narrative: framed by an initial moment of shipwreck and a final moment of deliverance. The importance Shakespeare attaches to this framing device – and to the idea of voyaging which it mediates – is suggested by the unique construction of the opening scene. The shipwreck is at once plausibly 'real' and an emblem of the contingency, boundedness and fragility of human order.[1] The writing, moreover, conveys dramatic immediacy and nautical understanding at levels unprecedented in Shakespeare, and – one suspects – in voyage literature too (the various accounts of the storm in the Bermuda pamphlets are woodenly rhetorical by comparison).[2] Both as immediate fact and as governing idea, voyaging establishes a commanding perspective on the island. Soon after the opening scene, we hear that the wrecked 'ship' represents the last of three ill-starred voyages to the island: each occasioned by varieties of hubris through which first Sycorax, then Prospero and now

Alonso, are cast out from the world of men. The exorbitance of these and other castaways is mirrored in the 'terminal' geography of the island. A desert 'where man doth not inhabit', the island befits those ''mongst men ... most unfit to live' (III.iii.57–8). Storm-infested (like 'the still-vexed Bermudas' [I.ii.230]), the island mirrors the disordered passions of the castaways in its own weather. To have ventured so far is not merely to have spanned a gulf of sea, distance and time, but in some way to have overstepped the limits of the properly human. The traditional debate about the island's exact geographic whereabouts is beside the point. Like More's 'Utopia' – or *Meta Incognita* ('Unknown bound', Martin Frobisher's name for Greenland) – the island is a seamless compound of geography and poetry. It is a Renaissance version of what Seneca the Elder called 'the bounds of things, the remotest shores of the world' (*rerum metas extremaque litora mundi*).

In the second scene, Prospero rehearses what a Renaissance geographer might have recognised as the island's 'natural and moral history'.[3] This unfolds in three poetic geographic 'moments' corresponding respectively to the 'voyages' of Sycorax, Prospero and Alonso; each moment (effectively, a generation) having its own identity and tropology. The original moment of the island's 'natural and moral history' is a species of dispersal myth, governed by the trope of 'confusion'. The second moment is a species of 'plantation' myth, governed by the trope of separation. The third is a species of 'renewal' or 'regeneration' myth, governed by the figure of *discordia concors* (and the emotion of 'wonder'). While I use the word 'myth' loosely to describe the narrative character of all three moments, each does in fact have a subtly distinct discursive character. The original moment (performed as a ritualised narrative of remote or first things) has a properly 'mythological' character. The 'colonial' moment has a more 'historical' (or dialogical or 'controversialised') character. The moment of 'renewal' has a prophetic or visionary character.

The ritual or mythic character of Sycorax's story emerges in the manner of its telling. The narrative is rehearsed by Prospero to Ariel in an urgent, quasi-liturgical monologue. Responses are invited, but as in a liturgy, their purpose seems only to confirm. No room is allowed for disagreement or even minor variations in detail. There is also a suggestion of ritual repetition. Prospero assures Ariel that he 'must / Once in a month recount what thou hast been, / Which thou forget'st' (I.ii.263–65). Like origin myths generally, the purpose of this monthly performance is to create identity and confirm subjection. In what we might think of as a performance-within-a-performance (*The Reign of Sycorax*, perhaps), the island is remembered as entering narrative or 'history', and thereby becoming a geographical entity: a land (*geos*) capable of description (*graphos*). What it 'becomes' is a new version of Scythia, the eternal *eschatia*. The name 'Sycorax' is glossed by Stephen Orgel as 'an epithet for Medea, the Scythian raven', largely on the basis of the roots *Sy* ('Scythia') and *korax* ('raven').[4] *Corax*, however, resonates with Scythia in a more direct way. In John Speed's 1626 map of Europe, the Caucasus Mountains are labelled 'Ye Montaine Corax'.[5] Not only are these at the Colchian end of the Black Sea, but they are inscribed within the Medea myth by George Sandys in his edition of the *Metamorphoses*, when he explains the golden fleece as a poeticism for gold originating from mines in the Caucasus.[6]

Sycorax does not so much *find* 'a howling wilderness', as *make* one (literally). Thus she imprisons Ariel ('a spirit too delicate / To act her earthy and abhorred commands') within 'a cloven pine', where Ariel's groans 'Did make wolves howl' (I.ii.274–5, 279, 290). The very existence of Ariel (a combination of 'airy' spirit and *genius loci*) on the island suggests an inherent capacity for nurture. While Ariel could hardly be said to possess a moral nature, he/she is clearly associated with a motif of 'temperance', which figures the island as 'temperate' in both a climatic sense and a moral sense.[7] In the first instance (as I have argued elsewhere), this motif derives from a topos of Virginian propaganda.[8] Ultimately, however, the motif of 'temperance' derives from the ancient moral-geographic discourse of *temperies* which explained the moral qualities of particular races by reference to the temperateness of their native climates.[9] The suggestion of the motif of 'temperance' in *The Tempest* is that, for all its remoteness and apparent inhospitability, the island is potentially 'temperate' and 'fruitful'. Under Sycorax, however, such potential (*meliora natura*) is stifled and perverted or 'confused'. Thus Sycorax tries to force an 'airy' spirit to perform 'earthy' commands. Thus, too, she adopts a New World 'devil' (another kind of *genius loci*) as a god.[10] The name 'Setebos' is more than just a random echo of the voyage narratives. By worshipping the god which Antonio Pigafetta describes as being worshipped by the Patagonian Indians of the storm-beaten wilderness of Tierra del Fuego, Sycorax is identified with the most remote, God-forsaken and degenerate of sixteenth-century Amerindian types.[11] The 'infamous promiscuity' of such worship is recapitulated at a sexual level. If Prospero is to be believed, Sycorax has had intercourse with 'the devil himself', resulting in Caliban, 'the son that she did litter here' (I.ii.284). The word 'litter' suggests her complete abandonment of the maternal role. Caliban is born and reared 'in the bestial state', without nurture, culture or 'language'. While an entirely original piece of myth-making, *The Coming of Sycorax* is recognisably a species of dispersal myth. Like Ham, progenitor of the Canaanite, the Negro and other supposedly bestial and slavish races, Sycorax is an outcast from the world of men, a wanderer beyond bounds and an active promoter of the degeneracy of her 'vile race'. Renaissance geographers would have recognised a telling consonance between the ideas of dispersal, isolation, sorcery, matriarchy and degeneration.

While Sycorax reduces nature on the island to the state of wilderness and abomination, Prospero and Miranda attempt to reclaim it (both in the sense of improving it, and in the sense of taking possession of it). The second moment in the island's history is patently colonial: the island is nurtured, worked, territorialised, troped, 'translated', idealised and commodified. All these themes are present in Caliban's memory of his 'first encounter' with Prospero. Caliban's name (an anagram of 'cannibal') and his education permanently implicate him within the full colonial discourse of reclamation, demarcation and territory-formation. Prospero and Miranda are inveterate line-drawers, dichotomising between: good and bad, pure and impure, useful and useless, fertile and barren, cultivated and uncultivated, bestial and human, languaged and languageless. Having learned their 'language', Caliban has no choice but to dichotomise too. Even in the act of cursing the time he showed Prospero 'all the qualities o' th' isle', Caliban automatically distinguishes between 'fresh springs' and 'brine-pits', 'barren place and fertile' (I.ii.340–1); which is to say between the useful or commodifiable and the useless or uncommodifiable. There is also a distinction here between different types of commodities. 'Brine-pits' might seem useless by comparison with 'fresh springs' but they were mined for salt in the New World and seem privileged by comparison with the unreclaimable nature associated with Sycorax: an 'unwholesome' fenland possessed by the creeping or hybrid abominations of Leviticus ('toads, beetles, bats' [I.ii.340]). The fact that the first-encounter phase of the colonial experience is bitterly remembered from a post-encounter perspective, discourages any temptation to idealise it. It is significant, too, that there are two narratives to contend with here

and not just one. Unlike *The Coming of Sycorax*, the early relationship of Prospero and Caliban is a matter of dispute. Caliban sees his
education as a pretext for dispossession. Prospero and Miranda
regret the over-optimism of their early attempt to educate Caliban,
as well as the incaution of lodging him in their 'own cell' (I.ii.340).
Neither party is entirely right or entirely wrong. Colonialism, it
seems, is inherently controversial. But Caliban is right to see his education as a strategy of subjection and a step in the direction of his
present 'abjection': his excommunication from the clean, the human
and the natural. Like the Hebrews in Canaan, or like Conrad's
Kurtz (with his 'society for the suppression of savage customs'),
Prospero and Miranda identify the impure (in the form of what
Julia Kristeva calls 'the abject' or outcast) as a way of defining the
pure. As colonisers, they correspond to what Kristeva calls the
'deject' (one who defines himself by excluding another), a 'deviser
of territories, languages, works'.[12]
    The third moment in the 'natural and moral history' of the island
is intimated rather than lived. Though renewal is experienced by
various characters after the second scene – most notably by
Ferdinand, in the fourth-act masque of Ceres – the idea is already
present in Ariel's song and Ferdinand's 'wonder'. As in the masque
of Ceres, discord becomes concord, opposites are harmonised
and bereavement is translated into 'something rich and strange'
(I.ii.405).
    Each of the three moments of the island outlined in the second
scene – origin myth, colonial history and prophecy of renewal – recur
throughout the play. Echoes of the dispersal/degeneration myth represented by *The Reign of Sycorax* can be detected in the curious reference to Alonso's daughter, Claribel, and in the apparition of 'several
strange shapes' with a banquet. The function of the Claribel 'story' is
obscure unless we understand it as a dispersal myth. Alonso has recently sailed from the African city of Tunis, having married his daughter – very much against her own inclination and the advice of his
court – to 'an Ethiope'. The combination of geographical and moral
'extravagance' figures him as a voyager in the ancient mould: a con-
fuser of categories like Seneca's Jason, or an impious overreacher like
Paterculus's Crassus – recognising 'no limits' (*modum*) and accepting
'no bounds' (*terminum*). Appropriately, Alonso's exorbitance results
in utter 'confusion'. Insofar as both his children are abandoned or
castaway (in both a geographical and a moral sense), Alonso also reca-
pitulates the example of Ham. Such contexts may help to explain the

severity of Prospero's view of Ferdinand, and the brutality of his corrective regime:

> I'll manacle thy neck and feet together.
> Sea-water shalt thou drink; thy food shall be
> The fresh-brook mussels, withered roots, and husks
> Wherein the acorn cradled.
>
> (I.ii.465–8)

Though Ferdinand's re-education turns out to be rather more genteel in practice, the harsh primitivism of this symbolic diet identifies him as a version of unreclaimed 'natural' man; hence a symbolic relative of Caliban.[13] The connection is underlined by the symbolic identity of their corrective ordeals: Caliban entering *'with a burden of wood'* at the opening of Act II scene ii, and Ferdinand entering *'bearing a log'* at the opening of the very next scene, Act III, scene i. Both are treated as slaves, the generic occupation of the outcast and naturally degenerate.

The mythology of dispersal and degeneration is echoed again in the masque of 'shapes'. While the stage direction (*Enter several spirits, in strange shapes bringing in a table and a banquet, and dance about it with gentle actions of salutations, and inviting the King and his companions to eat, they depart* [III.iii.19–20]) implies a scene of pure fantasy, it is significant that the shapes should 'depart' rather than vanish, and that the stage audience should take them as real rather than imaginary. Thus Sebastian thinks he sees 'a *living* drollery' (III.iii.21, my italics), and Antonio and Gonzalo believe they have just been presented with living proof of travellers' tales. Realism is again underlined when Prospero – having just complimented Ariel on his performance as the harpy – compliments his 'meaner ministers' for having performed 'their several kinds' with 'good *life* and observation strange' (III.iii.86–7, my italics). If, then, the performance seems real to the stage audience and realistic to the stage-manager, what is it supposed to be imitating? Gonzalo takes the 'shapes' for 'islanders':

> For certes these are people of the island,
> Who though they are of monstrous shape, yet note
> Their manners are more gentle-kind than of
> Our human generation you shall find
> Many, nay almost any.
>
> (III.iii.30–4)

Beneath the compliment lurks a commonplace anthropological distinction based on the dispersal theory. The 'islanders' are 'people' but not 'of / Our human generation'; they are 'gentle-kind' but not humankind (hence, 'of monstrous shape'). They are 'people' in the sense of having descended from Adam, but they are not 'of our human generation' in the sense that their cultural and biological evolution has become side-tracked through geographic dispersal and isolation. If the logic seems biblical or Mandevillian ('earthly beings are more discrepant from one another, because they are in a remote place, and for that reason are more diverse'), it is also scientific by the most advanced sixteenth-century criteria. Thus, in a typical rationalisation of dispersal mythology, Francis Bacon explained the cultural backwardness of the Amerindians as a product of the 'oblivion' wrought in that part of the world by vast inundations. All Amerindians would, supposed Bacon, be descended from mountain-dwelling peoples, 'the remnants of generation ... [who] ... were, in such particular deluge, saved'.[14] The descendants would be correspondingly degenerate because 'the remnant of people which hap to be reserved are commonly ignorant and mountainous people, that can give no account of the time past, so that the oblivion is all one as if none had been left' (p. 228). In moral-geographic terms, mountains are like islands: both are isolated and correspondingly likely to produce oblivious 'generations' of *semi-hommes*. This may be why Gonzalo detects 'mountaineers' among his 'islanders':

> When we were boys,
> Who would believe that there were mountaineers
> Dewlapped like bulls, whose throats had hanging at 'em
> Wallets of flesh? Or that there were such men
> Whose heads stood in their breasts? Which now we find
> Each putter-out of five for one will bring us
> Good warrant of.
>
> (III.iii.43–9)

An educated man, Gonzalo sees what Renaissance 'anthropology' would have led him to see on a remote island: a selection from the traditional gallery of monstrous types – 'people' who are not just culturally or racially different from 'our human generation', but absolutely different: the products of what Bacon (following Pliny) called a 'pretergeneration', an errant or unnatural birth of a type commonly recorded in popular 'Mirabilaries'.[15] The simultaneously 'mythological' and yet 'scientific' character of Gonzalo's construction

of the 'islanders' suggests much about Prospero's mythological construction of the island's prehistory. Specifically, it reinforces the
point that Prospero's prehistorical myth (*The Reign of Sycorax*) is
indeed a species of dispersal myth, and as such closely related to the
speculations of Renaissance anthropologists and geographers concerning 'the natural and moral history' of remote and newly discovered regions of the world. By the same token, it provides us with a
'scientific' context for Caliban.

The second moment in the island's 'natural and moral history',
that of 'discovery' and colonisation, is re-enacted at greater length.
The 'discovery' phase of this moment, represented by the original
encounter of Prospero and Caliban, is echoed in the encounter of
Caliban with Trinculo and Stephano. Just as before, Caliban falls at
the feet of a seemingly god-like European (Stephano) who confers
the gift of 'language' upon him – though this time in a bottle of
sack. The allusiveness of this discovery-episode makes it more explicitly colonial than the first. Thus, confronted by Caliban's pros-
trate body, Trinculo is not reminded of Mandevillian monsters so
much as of 'a dead Indian' (II.ii.33). While Trinculo is at a loss how
to identify Caliban – who, like Antony's crocodile, conspicuously
frustrates the categorising rhetoric of 'comparison and analogy' – he
is full of ideas for making money out of him. Virtually all the jokes
of his first speech ('What have we here, a man or a fish?' [II.ii.24ff.])
are about turning Caliban into a sideshow exhibit. Cashing in on
Caliban is also Stephano's first reaction: 'If I can recover him and
keep him tame and get to Naples with him, he's a present for any
emperor that ever trod on neat's leather' (II.ii.68–70). Most other
jokes at Caliban's expense also turn on the idea of commodification.
In the last of his 'first encounters' with Europeans, Caliban is
identified by Antonio as 'a plain fish, and no doubt marketable'
(V.i.269). Another phase of the colonial moment is echoed in the
progress of Trinculo, Stephano and Caliban. The comic insurrection
plot is a replay of Caliban's original insurrection. Just as before, the
goals are sovereignty of the island, sexual possession of Miranda
and the begetting of a dynasty.

The third moment, that of renewal, is also developed at some
length. Though renewal is experienced by most characters – even
Caliban in the course of his encounter with Stephano ("Ban, 'Ban,
Cacaliban / Has a new master – Get a new man!' [II.ii.183–4]) – it is
epitomised by Ferdinand and some members of the courtier group.
This is because, in order to be renewed, a character must be capable

of recognising past errors and enduring whatever penitential ordeal Prospero thinks fit to impose. For Ferdinand, this means undergoing a ritual of humility and restraining his sexual feelings for Miranda. His reward is the betrothal masque of the fourth act, a prophetic vision of harmony in which spring is reconciled with summer, earth with air, air with water, and temperance ('temperate nymphs' [IV.i.132]) with sexual appetite ('sunburned sicklemen' [IV.i.134]).[16]

The tripartite structure of the 'natural and moral history' of Prospero's island has an obvious resonance with the discourse of the New World in general and that of Virginia in particular. Within a year or so of the play's first performance, a pamphlet entitled *The New Life of Virginea* was published. In the dedication, the author, Robert Johnson, explains his intention of dividing the story of Virginia into three parts: 'The first is nothing else but a briefe relating of things alreadie done and past: The second, of the present estate of the businesse: And the third doth tend as a premonition to the planters and adventurers for the time to come'.[17] Though primarily a short history of the colony's progress up to the time of writing (1612), the first part includes an account of the pre-colonial settlement of the country, which Johnson sees as originating in the dispersal of Babel. The presumption of 'the race and progenie of *Noah*' in building the infamous tower:

> ... so highly provoked the Maiestie of God, that ... he subverted their devices and proud attempt, infatuating their understanding by confounding their tongues, and leaving each one to his severall waies, to follow the pronesse and follie of his owne heart, so that from this scattering and casting them out like unprofitable seed upon the dust of the earth, did spring up (as weeds in solitarie places) such a barbarous and unfruitfull race of mankinde, that even to this day (as is very probable) many huge and spatious Countries and corners of the world unknowne, doe still swarme and abound with the innumerable languages of this dispersed crue, with their inhumane behaviour and brutish conditions.
>
> (pp. B–B1)

'The sundrie nations of *America*: which as they consist of infinite confused tongues and people' represent a conspicuous case in point; as does the aboriginal region corresponding to Virginia, where God 'did never vouchsafe the hand of the weeder, to clense and give redresse to so desolate and outgrowne wildernesse of humaine nature' (pp. B1–B2). Having thus accounted for the physical existence and the moral condition of the natives, Johnson procedes to describe the discovery and naming of Virginia and the ultimate goal of the colonial enterprise: 'to replant this unnatural vine to make it fruitfull' (p. B3). The initial attempt at settlement, however, does not effectively alter Virginia's moral status:

> the common sort (of colonists) ... grew factious and disordered out of measure ... in which distemper that envious man stept in, sowing plentifull tares in the hearts of all, which grew to such speedie confusion, that in a few moneths Ambition, sloth and idlenes had devoured the fruits of former labours, planting and sowing were cleane given over ... and so that Virgine voyage ... which went out smiling on her lovers with pleasant lookes, after her wearie travailes, did thus returne with a rent and disfigured face.
>
> (pp. C–C1)

The early 'plantation' is thus represented as having reverted to the wilderness which it is supposed to be reclaiming. Mutiny is described in the language of the aboriginal dispersal myth. Suggestively, in view of the rebelliousness of the younger male generation (Ferdinand and Caliban) in *The Tempest*, a clear sense of a generation gap emerges between the mutineers and the colonial government. Thus Johnson blames 'those wicked Impes ... or those ungratious sons that dailie vexed their fathers hearts at home, and were therefore thrust upon the voyage', for fomenting rebellion and then returning 'with false reports of their miserable and perilous life in *Virginea*' (p. C2). The first phase of Johnson's narrative ends with the arrival of Sir Thomas Dale and Sir Thomas Gates at the colony, and with the restoration of order and the establishment of a 'temperance' among the colonists, befitting the 'temperateness' of the climate. As 'their first and chiefest care was shewed in setling Lawes divine and morall', Dale and Gates finally succeed in bringing 'the hand of the weeder' to Virginia (pp. D, B2).

The second part of Johnson's narrative – a brief account of the present state of the colony and the commodities of the country – effectively serves as a prologue to 'the third and last division' of his discourse: that concerning 'The New Life of Virginea' (p. D4). The project of renewal is divided into a three-fold labour: 'upon yourselves, upon your English, and upon the poore Indians' (p. E2). In the spirit (and to some extent in the hierarchising idiom) of Prospero, Johnson insists that government is impossible without austere self-discipline. Thus: 'you shall lay the foundation in your owne steps ... When thus your light shall guide their feete, sweete will that harmonie be betweene the head and members of the bodie, then may sleepe the rigour of your lawes' (pp. E2, E3). With self-discipline established, colonial government (the second labour) becomes not only possible but easy. Martial law (Dale's 'Lawes divine and moral') may be dispensed with, and the colonists can be allowed to 'live as free English men, under the government of iust and equall lawes, and not as slaves' (p. E3). The third labour of renewal concerns 'the poore Indians' (p. E4). These 'however they may seeme unto you so intollerable wicked and rooted in mischiefe' are to be considered as 'no worse then the nature of Gentiles' and thus redeemable in principle (p. E4). The strategy which Johnson suggests bears an extraordinary resemblance to Prospero's initial treatment of Caliban:

> Take their children and traine them up with gentlenesse, teach them our English tongue, and the principles of religion ... make them equal with your English in case of protection wealth and habitation ... Insteed of Iron and steele you must have patience and humanitie to manage their crooked nature to your forme of civilitie: for as our proverbe is, Looke how you winne them, so you must weare them.
>
> (p. F)

From John Gillies, *Shakespeare and the Geography of Difference* (Cambridge, 1994), pp. 140–55.

NOTES

John Gillies discusses the 'colonial politics' of *The Tempest* in the historical perspective of Elizabethan 'poetic geography' adduced from contemporary maps and writing about voyages. The notion of 'the exotic' refers to lands and peoples beyond the known world of the time belonging, literally, to the margins of Elizabethan maps. In this context, colonial consciousness was a very different phenomenon from the one assumed in our postcolonial world, and knowledge of this informs *The Tempest*. Quotations from *The Tempest*, ed. Stephen Orgel (Oxford and New York, 1987). Ed.]

1. For some traditional examples of 'the shipwreck' as an emblem of tragic hubris see Guy de Tervarent, *Attributs et Symboles dans l'Art Profane 1450–1600* (Genève, 1958), especially 'Naufrage', p. 282, and 'Tronc Brisé dont une Branche Reverdit', p. 389. The polemical attitude of the 'Bermuda Pamphlets' – with their shrill celebration of God's mercy in preserving the company of the *Sea Venture*, which was

earlier supposed to have sunk with all hands in a storm off the Bermudas – indicates that the wreck had been represented by the opponents of the Virginia Company as a divine judgement on the hubris of its activities.

2. In addition to its specifically dramatic effects – confused outcries, sounds – and its emblematic point (the argument between Gonzalo and the boatswain), the wreck has precise technical logic. As the ship is driven towards a lee shore, the sailors strike the topsail and set the foresail in an attempt to increase the ship's stiffness in the water and improve its ability to point into the wind. (See *The Tempest*, Stephen Orgel [ed.], The Oxford Shakespeare [Oxford and New York, 1987], Appendix A.)

3. The phrase would have been familiar from what was perhaps the most famous late-sixteenth-century account of the New World, *The Natural and Moral History of the Indies* by Joseph de Acosta. It was translated by Edward Grimston in 1604.

4. Orgel (ed.), *The Tempest*, Oxford, pp. 19–20; also p. 115, note to line 258. Orgel notes Kermode's theory that Sycorax 'is strongly influenced by the Circe legend' because of a suggestion in Conti's *Mythologiae* that Circe 'was born in Colchis, in the district of the Coraxi tribe' (p. 19). But he points out that no mention of the Coraxi is found in Conti.

5. Speed, 'The Description of Europe' in *A Prospect of the Most Famous Parts of the World*, between pp. 7 and 8. Speed's map provides the missing documentary link between Sycorax and Scythia.

6. Sandys, *Ovid's Metamorphoses Englished*, p. 253. On the Herodotean assumption that the 'marvelous' (in the sense of the precious or rare) would always be associated with the 'monstrous', Sandys supposes that the mythological monsters which guard the golden fleece must have been real animals such as the 'Alergatoes' which threaten the 'Divers for Pearle in the inland Lakes' of America.

7. For the motif of 'Temperance' in the play, see John Gillies, 'Shakespeare's Virginian Masque', *English Literary History* (1986), 673–707.

8. Ibid., 678–82.

9. See John Gillies, *Shakespeare and the Geography of Difference* (Cambridge, 1994), ch. 1, section 2 and note 37.

10. Setebos is described as a 'great deuyll' in Antonio Pigafetta's *A Briefe Declaration of the Voyage or Navigation Made Abowte the Worlde*, in Edward Arber (ed.), *The First Three English books on America*, [?1511] –1555 A.D., p. 252. Caliban's description of Setebos as 'my dam's god' (I.ii.376) is fully consistent with Pigafetta's account of Setebos as a devil, in view of Prospero's repeated references to Caliban as a devil.

11. Antonello Gerbi ('The Earliest Accounts on the New World', in Fredi Chiapelli (ed.), *First Images of America: The Impact of the New World on the Old* (2 vols [Berkeley, Los Angeles and London, 1976] vol. 1, 37–43), points out that Pigafetta's grotesquely primitive portrait of giant-like Patagonians, 'remained a legend for several centuries – a cliché and a stimulus for the inquisitive European mind. No less a philosopher than Vico made the *Patacones* the prototypes of a barbaric and heroic humanity' (p. 42). Well before Vico, however, the Patagonian is routinely depicted as the most primitive Amerindian type on the early seventeenth-century *carte à figures*.

12. Julia Kristeva, *Powers of Horror: an Essay on Abjection*, trs. Leon S. Roudiez (New York, 1982), p. 8. The passage is particularly suggestive of Prospero and Caliban: 'The one by whom the abject exists is thus a *deject* who places (himself), *separates* (himself), situates (himself) … Situationist in a sense, and not without laughter – since laughing is a way of placing or displacing abjection. Necessarily dichotomous, somewhat Manichaean, he divides, excludes, and without, properly speaking, wishing to know his abjections is not at all unaware of them.'

13. 'Husks wherein the acorn cradled' would represent a dystopian version of human diet in the golden age – a diet of acorns.

14. Francis Bacon, 'Of Vicissitude of Things' in *The Essays*, ed. John Pitcher (Harmondsworth, 1985), p. 229. Further references to this essay appear in the text.

15. Francis Bacon, *The Advancement of Learning*, ed. G. W. Kitchin (London, 1976), pp. 70–1. The fact that Gonzalo makes detailed reference to two types of Mandevillian monster – bull-headed men and 'such men / Whose heads stood in their breasts' – strongly suggests that each one of the 'shapes' originally represented *a specific type* of Mandevillian monster. This would exactly account for the wording of Prospero's compliment to his spirit-actors. These 'meaner ministers' perform '*their several kinds*' with 'good life'.

16. Gillies, 'Shakespeare's Virginian Masque'.

17. Robert Johnson, *The New Life of Virginea* (London, 1612), The English Experience, no. 332 (Amsterdam and New York, 1971), 'The Epistle Dedicatorie'. Further citations from this work are given in the text.

Further Reading

Recent, theory-based criticism of *The Tempest* is very difficult to arrange under discrete categories, since the issues of power, gender, colonialism and race are intertwined. Therefore, I have presented the items in a single list, hoping the titles will guide readers to issues that interest them, adding occasional comments where the approach is not self-evident. For earlier criticism reference can be made to the Macmillan Casebook on *The Tempest*, edited by D. J. Palmer, or the chapter on 'The Late Comedies' by Michael Taylor in *Shakespeare: A Bibliographical Guide*, New Edition, ed. Stanley Wells (Oxford: Clarendon Press, 1990), pp. 159–80.

Jonathan Bate, 'The Humanist *Tempest*', *Shakespeare: La Tempête: Etudes Critiques* (Actes du Colloque de Besançon, Université de Franche-Comté, 1993), pp. 5–20. [An antidote to recent theory, historicising the play as a product of Renaissance humanism and educational theory]

Paul Brown, '"This thing of darkness I acknowledge mine": *The Tempest* and the discourse of colonialism', in *Political Shakespeare: New Essays in Cultural Materialism*, ed. Jonathan Dollimore and Alan Sinfield (Ithaca NY: Cornell University Press, 1985), pp. 48–71. [Postcolonialism and cultural materialism]

Thomas Cartelli, 'Prospero in Africa: *The Tempest* as colonialist text and pretext' from *Shakespeare Reproduced: The Text in History and Ideology*, ed. Jean E. Howard and Marion F. O'Connor (New York and London: Methuen, 1987), pp. 99–115. [Postcolonial and Althusserian]

Kate Chedgzoy, *Shakespeare's Queer Children: Sexual Politics and Contemporary Culture* (Manchester: Manchester University Press, 1995). [Gender politics, Jarman's film]

Walter Cohen, *Drama of a Nation: Public Theater in Renaissance England and Spain* (Ithaca and London: Cornell University Press, 1985).

Terry Eagleton, *William Shakespeare* (Oxford: Blackwell, 1986). [Marxist]

Bruce Ehrlich, 'Shakespeare's colonial metaphor: on the social function of theatre in *The Tempest*', *Science and Society*, 41 (1977), 43–65.

Malcolm Evans, *Signifying Nothing: Truth's True Contents in Shakespeare's Text* (Brighton: Harvester Press, 1986).

Howard Felperin, *Shakespearean Romance* (Princeton NJ: Princeton University Press, 1972), pp. 246–83. [Self-reflexivity]

Leslie Fiedler, *The Stranger in Shakespeare* (New York: Stein & Day, 1972). [Caliban as 'outsider']

John Gillies, 'Shakespeare's Virginian Masque', *English Literary History*, 53 (1986), 673–707.

Stephen J. Greenblatt, 'Learning to Curse: Aspects of Linguistic Colonialism in the 16th Century', in Fredi Chiapelli (ed.), *First Images of America: The Impact of the New World on the Old* (Berkeley: University of California Press, 1970), pp. 561–80. [New historicist]

Trevor R. Griffiths, '"This Island's Mine": Caliban and Colonialism', *Yearbook of English Studies*, 13 (1983), 159–180.

Donna B. Hamilton, *Virgil and 'The Tempest': The Politics of Imitation* (Columbus: Ohio State University, 1990).

Peter Hulme, 'Prospero and Caliban', in *Colonial Encounters: Europe and the Native Caribbean, 1492–1797* (London and New York: Methuen, 1986), pp. 89–134.

Coppélia Kahn, 'The Providential Tempest and the Shakespearean Family', in *Representing Shakespeare*, ed. Murray M. Schwartz and Coppélia Kahn (Baltimore: Johns Hopkins University Press, 1980). [Feminist]

Lorie Jerrell Leininger, 'The Miranda Trap: Sexism and Racism in Shakespeare's *Tempest*', in Carolyn Ruth Swift Lenz, Gayle Greene and Carol Thomas Neely (eds), *The Woman's Part: Feminist Criticism of Shakespeare* (Urbana and Chicago: University of Illionois Press, 1980), pp. 285–94. [Feminist]

Mary Loeffelholz, 'Miranda in the New World: *The Tempest* and Charlotte Barnes's *The Forest Princess*', in *Women's Re-Visions of Shakespeare: On the Responses of Dickinson, Woolf, Rich, H. D., George Eliot, and Others* (Urbana and Chicago: University of Illinois Press, 1990), pp. 58–75.

Dominique Mannoni, *Prospero and Caliban: The Psychology of Colonization* (New York: Praeger, 1964).

Leah S. Marcus, 'The blue-eyed witch', in *Unediting the Renaissance: Shakespeare, Marlowe, Milton* (London and New York: Routledge, 1996), pp. 1–37. [Shows that criticism can inform textual decisions, and vice versa; contribution to 'New Philology']

Katharine Eisaman Maus, 'Arcadia lost: politics and revision in the Restoration *Tempest*', *Renaissance Drama*, N.S. 13 (1982), 189–209.

Rob Nixon, 'Caribbean and African appropriations of *The Tempest*', *Critical Inquiry*, 13 (1986–7), 577–8.

Bernard J. Paris, '*The Tempest*: Shakespeare's Ideal Solution', in Norman N. Holland, Sidney Homan, and Bernard J. Paris (eds), *Shakespeare's Personality* (Berkeley, Los Angeles and London: University of California Press, 1989), pp. 206–25. [Psychoanalytical reading]

Kiernan Ryan, *Shakespeare* (Hemel Hempstead: Harvester Wheatsheaf, 1989). [Marxist]

Meredith Anne Skura, 'Discourse and the Individual: The Case of Colonialism in *The Tempest*', *Shakespeare Quarterly*, 40 (1989) 42–69.

David Sundelson, 'So Rare a Wonder'd Father: Prospero's *Tempest*', in Murray M. Schwartz and Coppélia Kahn (eds), *Representing Shakespeare* (Baltimore: Johns Hopkins University Press, 1980).

Alden T. Vaughan, 'Shakespeare's Indian: The Americanization of Caliban', *Shakespeare Quarterly*, 39 (1988), 137–53.

Alden T. Vaughan and Virginia Mason Vaughan, *Shakespeare's Caliban: A Cultural History* (Cambridge: Cambridge University Press, 1991).

R. S. White, *'Let Wonder Seem Familiar': Endings in Shakespeare's Romance Vision* (London: Athlone, 1985).

Deborah Willis, 'Shakespeare's *The Tempest* and the Discourse of Colonialism', *Studies in English Literature*, 29 (1989), 277–89. [*Riposte* to postcolonial readings]

Richard Wilson, 'Voyage to Tunis: New History and the Old World of *The Tempest*', *English Literary History*, 64 (1997), 333–57.

Chantal Zabus, 'A Calibanic Tempest in Anglophone and Francophone New World Writing', *Canadian Literature, Litterature Canadienne*, No. 104 (1985), 35–51. [On creative appropriations of *The Tempest*]

Notes on Contributors

Francis Barker is Professor of Literature at the University of Essex. He is the author of *The Tremulous Private Body* (1984, 1995) and of *The Culture of Violence* (1994), and joint editor of a number of volumes, most recently *Colonial Discourse/Postcolonial Theory* (1994). He is writing a book on artificiality, with the working title *Breathing Simulacra*.

John Gillies teaches Theatre and Drama at La Trobe University, Melbourne, and has been awarded an Australian Research Council Fellowship to work on a study of Shakespeare in Australia and Asia. His book *Shakespeare and the Geography of Difference* (1994) was published by Cambridge University Press.

Stephen Greenblatt teaches English at Berkeley and at Harvard Universities, and he is general editor of the Norton Shakespeare. He is the author of *Renaissance Self-Fashioning: From More to Shakespeare* (1980), *Shakespearean Negotiations: The Circulation of Social Energy in Renaissance England* (1988) and *Learning to Curse: Essays in Early Modern Culture* (1994).

Terence Hawkes is a Professor of English at the University of Wales, Cardiff. His books include *Shakespeare and the Reason* (1964), *Metaphor* (1972), *Shakespeare's Talking Animals*(1973), *Structuralism and Semiotics* (1977), *That Shakespeharian Rag* (1986) and *Meaning by Shakespeare* (1992). He is also General Editor of the *New Accents* series and editor of *Alternative Shakespeares Volume 2* (1996) which appears within the series.

Peter Hulme is Professor of Literature at the University of Essex. He is the author of *Colonial Encounters: Europe and the Native Caribbean, 1492–1797* (1986), and editor of *Wild Majesty: Encounters with Caribs from Columbus to the Present Day* (1992), and joint editor of a number of volumes, most recently *Colonial Discourse/Postcolonial Theory* (1994). He is currently completing a book entitled *Visiting the Caribs: Travellers to Dominica, 1877–1992*.

Ania Loomba is Associate Professor at the Centre for Linguistics and English at the Jawaharlal Nehru University, New Delhi. She has published *Gender, Race, Renaissance Drama* and various essays on Renaissance theatre as well as Postcolonial Theory. Her forthcoming publications include a book on Shakespeare and race, and a project on Renaissance Drama and travels to the East.

Ruth Nevo was born in South Africa and in 1950 settled in Israel, where she taught at the Hebrew University until retirement. She has published *The Dial of Virtue* (1963), *Tragic Form in Shakespeare* (1972), *Comic Transformations* (1980), *Shakespeare's Other Language* (1987), and translations of Hebrew poetry. Since retirement she has taken up an old preoccupation and has become a full-time painter. She is a member of the Israel Association of Painters and Sculptors and of the Israeli Academy of Science and Humanities.

David Norbrook is Professor of English at Maryland University after being Fellow at Magdalen College, Oxford. His publications include *Poetry and Politics in the English Renaissance* (1984) and *The Penguin Book of Renaissance Verse* (with H. R. Woudhuysen, 1992). He has published *Writing the English Republic: Poetry, Rhetoric and Politics 1627–1660* (Cambridge, 1999).

Stephen Orgel is the Jackson Eli Reynolds Professor of Humanities at Stanford University. His most recent book is *Impersonations: The Performance of Gender in Shakespeare's England* (Cambridge, 1996), and he is the author of *The Illusion of Power* (Berkeley, CA, 1975), *Inigo Jones* (London and Berkeley, 1973, in collaboration with Sir Roy Strong), and *The Jonsonian Masque* (Cambridge, MA, 1965). His editions include *Ben Jonson's Masques, Marlowe's Poems and Translations*, and *The Tempest* and *The Winter's Tale* in The Oxford Shakespeare series.

Annabel Patterson is the Karl Young Professor of English at Yale University. She has written several books on early modern literature. The most recent is *Early Modern Liberalism* (Cambridge: Cambridge University Press, 1997).

Ann Thompson is Professor of English and Head of Department at Roehampton Institute, London (University of London). Among her many publications are *Shakespeare's Chaucer* (1978), *The Taming of the Shrew* (ed. 1984), *Shakespeare, Meaning and Metaphor* (with John O. Thompson, 1987), *'King Lear': The Critics' Debate* (1988), *Teaching Women: Feminism and English Studies* (ed. with Helen Wilcox), and *Which Shakespeare?* (1992). Her current research includes a new edition of *Hamlet* for Arden 3, for which she is also the General Editor. She holds the General Editorship of *Feminist Readings of Shakespeare* (a series from Routledge). Together with Sasha Roberts, she is working on an anthology entitled *Women Readers of Shakespeare, 1600–1900*.

Index